Other Success Studybooks

Book-keeping for the Small Business
Chemistry
Economics
Investment
Mathematics
Principles of Accounting
Principles of Accounting: Answer Book
Twentieth Century World Affairs
Biology
Commerce
Geography: Human and Regional
Geography: Physical and Mapwork

Success in
NUTRITION

Magnus Pyke, Ph.D.,
F.R.I.C., F.Inst.Biol., F.R.S.E.

John Murray

© Magnus Pyke 1975

Printed in Great Britain by
Richard Clay (The Chaucer Press) Ltd.,
Bungay, Suffolk

Cased 0 7195 3186 1
Paperback 0 7195 3198 5

Foreword

In a world where, in some places there are people dying of starvation, while in other places they are dying of diseases brought about by over-eating, understanding of the science of nutrition is vital to anyone who wants to see changes for the better. Today, as never before, people are increasingly aware of the fact that the world's food resources are limited, and that the problems of human wellbeing far outreach those which are the daily concern of, say, economists and politicians. It is not merely the quantities of food available in a given place at a given time that concern us; our concern is the food itself. What is in it? Does it contain components, in the right amounts, necessary to a particular community to keep it healthy? Is it the food that the community has long been eating by tradition, and has this traditional diet been nutritionally adequate? What is the *real* value of all those attractively packaged foods on the supermarket shelf? These, and countless other questions, are constantly being asked by scientists and lay public alike, with daily newspapers keeping the problems ever-fresh in our minds.

The challenges faced by nutritionists have never been greater than they are today, and the science of nutrition has itself changed radically during the last decade or so. Significant advances in knowledge have taken place in three main directions.

First, we now know more about the chemical composition of the diet. Second, we have greater understanding of the physiological processes by which components of the diet are digested and absorbed into the body, and that the use the body can make of these components is limited by its own balance. So the precise dietetic needs of one individual are not the same as another's. Third, we have come to realize the importance of social factors in eating habits. Wealth or poverty will govern diet, so will religion, tradition, custom and many other things.

Anyone studying nutrition today is making a valuable contribution to the understanding of one of the world's greatest problems, and if the understanding can be turned to practical account, the student will have taken an important step towards a solution of the problem.

Success in Nutrition is a self-contained course in basic nutritional science. You may be concerned only with your own nutrition, or with the nutritional needs of your family or a larger community. You may, however, intend to follow a trade or profession where a knowledge of nutrition is essential. The book provides all the early material you will need, and gives a solid foundation to further study.

If you are studying nutrition as part of a formal course, you will find that this book covers syllabus material for a large number of examinations. These include: O level and A/O level (Food and Nutrition); A level (Home Economics); OND and HND (especially Hotel and Catering Operations or Institutional Housekeeping and Catering); membership examinations of the Hotel Catering and Institutional Management Association; the nutrition papers set by the Royal Society of Health. It is also suitable for first-year university students.

M.P.

Acknowledgments

In acknowledging the help which he has received in producing a book, an author must certainly thank those who have made immediate practical contributions. I am grateful to all who read and commented on the text, but I am especially indebted to Dr. Jean Macqueen who edited it so knowledgeably, and handled every detail with expert care. I am indebted, too, to Michael Colleer for his criticisms as the book evolved, and for his material contributions to a number of the Units. In the later stages Mrs. Frankie Cable very kindly read the text and made useful comments. Particular acknowledgment must be made to the drive and enthusiasm of Irene Slade, whose stimulus played a significant part in bringing the book into existence.

The illustrations have been given considerable distinction by the inclusion of line drawings by Don Mackean to whom I should like to express my gratitude. (These appear on pages 12, 17, 18, 20, 22, 125, 142, 163, 166 and 168.)

The Table of Food Composition on page 203 is a modified version of that published in the *Manual of Nutrition*, 1970, and is reproduced by permission of the Controller of Her Majesty's Stationery Office.

But besides these, I want to express gratitude to my one-time teacher, Professor Sir Jack Drummond, FRS. If anything I have written sparks the enthusiasm of just one student (although, of course, I hope for more) as his writing did for me when I was one, part of my debt to all those named will be repaid.

M.P.

Contents

Unit One
The Science of Nutrition

1.1 Introduction

The science of nutrition is concerned with the various useful ingredients—or *nutrients*—of which foods are composed. It is concerned with the amounts of these nutrients which are required for the proper growth and functioning of the body, the way in which each one is useful to the body, and what happens when there is too little or too much of one or other component in a person's diet. Nutrition is thus a quantitative science; that is to say it is a study of the *amount* of each nutrient required by an individual. It is not sufficient to know that protein, for example, is a necessary constituent of the diet; we must know the amount required as well, for sometimes it is as harmful to eat too much of a nutrient as too little. Nutritional science therefore deals both with the amounts of each nutrient necessary for the functioning of the body and also with the amounts contributed by different kinds of food.

Although the function and the required amount of each nutrient must be taken into account, it is also important to recognize that there may be quite wide variations between the quantities needed by different individuals. The human species is uniform to some degree and the nutritional requirements of men or women, old people or children can be assessed within certain limits of precision. Nevertheless, general statements concerning needs—for example, that 'children require a daily pint of milk' or that 'a glass of orange juice each day is necessary for health'—are not expressions of scientific truth, even if the contents of protein and calcium in the milk and vitamin C in the orange juice are expressed and interpreted in scientific terms.

Two further points must also be remembered in studying nutrition. The first is that all science is merely the minimizing of doubt. Our knowledge of nutrition has justified itself by the degree of command which it has enabled us to achieve over events by which, indeed, the correctness of our scientific knowledge has been verified. Understanding of the chemical structure of vitamin D, first elucidated in 1932, soon led to the prevention of rickets, the bone disease of children. Nevertheless, our understanding of the chemistry of vitamin D-active substances in diet and as they occur in the body is still developing. Our nutritional knowledge is now considerable but, as always in science, there is certainly more to know.

Finally, it must always be remembered that success in nutrition can only be recognized in *health*, and the concept of health is a complicated one. Not for nothing is it often bracketed with happiness. Nutrition is in some respects a branch of chemical science or, more exactly, of *biochemistry*—that is, the chemistry of life: but it is more than this. Children cannot grow properly unless they are given the right food to eat: this is part of the science of nutrition. But there is also now good scientific evidence to show that children and young animals grow better if they are given attention and love as well as vitamins and proteins. An expert committee of the World Health Organization has defined health, towards which good nutrition is intended to contribute, as 'complete physical, mental and social well-being and not the mere absence of ill-health and infirmity'. This definition comprises a great deal. Its lesson to the student of nutrition is, however, that although nutritional science is an important and rewarding area of study, the nutritionist must always remember that man does not live by bread alone.

1.2   Life as a Chemical Process

It was Antoine Lavoisier, the gifted French chemist, who in 1785 first presented quantitative evidence to support his flash of fundamental insight that *'la vie est une fonction chimique'*—life is a chemical process. Before his time the nature of life, as also the nature of fire, had not been properly understood in scientific terms, although Leonardo da Vinci had suspected a possible link between the two nearly 300 years before. Lavoisier correctly deduced that fire and combustion were due to the chemical reaction of the newly discovered element, oxygen, with another element such as carbon, with the consequent violent release of energy in the form of heat and light. It is a testimonial to his remarkable insight that he soon after deduced that life involved a similar chemical reaction.

Lavoisier studied the basic process by which energy was released by the combustion—that is, the combination with oxygen—of fuel derived from food, and the relation of the whole reaction to the amount of muscular work done. Even though he had to design much of his own apparatus, he measured with remarkable accuracy the amount of oxygen absorbed by a living body and related it to the amount of the main combustion product, carbon dioxide gas, given off in the breath. Many of these experiments were carried out with the active help of Mme Lavoisier and were performed on his two assistants, Seguin and Du Pont. Lavoisier trained these men so well in exact observation that when, after his own execution as an aristocrat in the French Revolution— his father had purchased a minor title of nobility—they emigrated to America, they still retained their training. Du Pont, for example, was once invited to go shooting with a party of his American hosts and noticed how seldom they hit the game they aimed at. He decided therefore to take advantage of his chemical skill and found backers to set him up in business to provide gunpowder of a quality superior to anything then available in the colony. From these beginnings arose the great chemical firm of Du Pont de Nemours.

More important than this, however, was the sequence of productive and stimulating discoveries which followed Lavoisier's precise and convincing studies of the chemical nature of life processes. Chemical analysis showed that food consisted of several different kinds of substance. In the main it was found to be made up of *carbohydrates*, comprising sugars, starches, fibrous materials and related compounds, *proteins*, nitrogen-containing compounds present in all living cells and the major component (apart from water) of muscular tissue in live animals and the meat of dead ones, and *fats*, found in both animals and plants. In addition to these, food was found to contain mineral substances like phosphorus, iron, sulphur, calcium and many more.

The science of nutrition which has grown from Lavoisier's understanding of its chemical basis is made up of three interwoven threads. The first is concerned with the fundamental process of 'combustion' by which life goes on or, more precisely, with the *energy* which distinguishes a living creature from a non-living one. We know now that this energy is a product of the chemical combination of biological fuel of some sort or other—that is, food—usually with oxygen. It can be measured as heat, just as can the available energy of coal, even though part of it is in fact realized as movement. This first aspect of nutritional science includes the establishment of the amounts of energy to be derived from different foods and the way in which the cells and tissues of the body enable this energy to be released, as well as the efficiency with which the energy input can be converted into work output. In addition, it is concerned with the way in which the body of an animal or a man operates in equilibrium with its fuel supply, either drawing on 'banked' fuel stocks in times of hardship, or, on the other hand, laying down fat and becoming obese.

The second theme has been the study of the way in which food not only provides the fuel to keep the biological machine going, but also contributes the chemical compounds which build up the body structure. During the last two or three decades, that part of biochemistry which has been called *molecular biology* has developed into one of mankind's most remarkable intellectual achievements. Molecular biology has led to an understanding of the way in which the great 'guidance' molecules, DNA and RNA (deoxyribonucleic acid and ribonucleic acid), operate so that an infant child, let us say, grows and develops into an adult man whereas an infant pig or an infant baboon—remarkably similar to an infant child though it may be—grows and develops with every detail perfect into the adult animal we expect to see. The characteristic 'brickwork' of each individual structure is made up from the protein components of the food each creature eats, and its pattern is controlled by the DNA, the architect, as it were, of the structure, with the help of the RNA as foreman. This second aspect of nutritional chemistry is primarily concerned with the nitrogen metabolism by which the proteins constituting much of the muscular structure and the other tissues of the body are formed; but it can also be taken to include the mobilizing of mineral elements to make bones and teeth, and the elaboration of certain biologically specialized molecules incorporating, say, iron or iodine.

The third strand of nutritional science has been the discovery, mainly within the present century, of the vitamins and other so-called *accessory food factors*. It is interesting that in 1898, a date within the memory of people still living today, C. F. Langworthy of the United States Department of Agriculture summed up the scientific knowledge of nutrition of his day thus: 'Foods have a dual purpose: building and repair, and energy for heat and work. Foods consist of the nutrients protein, fat and carbohydrate and various mineral salts.' We now know that this is much less than the truth. Yet it remained the basis of what was taught as nutritional science even up to the time of the First World War. As late as 1918, the British Ministry of Food publicly condemned the use of fruit, tomatoes and vegetables as wasteful and unnecessary. Because these foods contribute negligible energy they were dismissed as being little better than coloured water in solid form. At the same period, young children in Copenhagen were being treated for an eye disease, xerophthalmia, and becoming blind or even dying from a lack of vitamin A which today is incorporated routinely in margarine. In the principal hospital in Vienna, other children suffering from the bone disease called rickets were for the first time being treated with vitamin D, the chemistry of which was just beginning to be understood. In 1916, a British army surrendered to the Turks at Kut-el-Amara, not because the troops were starving but because in the mixed garrison the English soldiers were sick with beri-beri and the Indian soldiers with scurvy. Beri-beri occurs when the diet is lacking in vitamin B_1 (thiamine) and scurvy is due to a deficiency of vitamin C (ascorbic acid). Sufficient of these compounds could even then have been dropped to the men from a single aeroplane to keep the defence going had the necessary nutritional knowledge been available.

1.3   Life as a Physiological Process

Life is indeed a chemical process, as Lavoisier deduced nearly two centuries ago. Later units of this book will describe the relationship between the chemical energy produced when various nutrients are burnt in the laboratory and that given out when the same substances are used as biological fuels by the body. The chemical transformations of the different types of nutrient, of carbohydrates, proteins and fats, are also understood in considerable detail. The chemistry of twenty or more vitamins has been worked out, and for many of these we understand the ways in which they contribute to the smooth mechanism of the life process and the nature of the different types of breakdown which appear as the various deficiency diseases. But in spite of all this, in spite of the fact that a living organism is indeed a chemical engine, it is an engine which can only operate within the quite narrow limits of physiological possibility.

The great French physiologist Claude Bernard, who died in 1878, first drew attention to the importance of the stability of the internal medium in which living cells exist. For higher animals such as ourselves, the temperature of our bodies must remain steady within 1 °C or little more, or we are brought to a standstill by fever. The body temperature of birds is maintained at a temperature 4 °C higher than ours, but it too must be kept constant. Other animals lack the ability to keep their own living substances at a constant temperature, and frogs and other amphibia, fish and the numerous kinds of invertebrates and micro-organisms, even though they depend on the temperature of their environment, can also only function within relatively narrow physiological limits. This is why we can control the growth and activity of micro-organisms either by cooling them to a temperature below that at which they can function, as we do when food is deep-frozen, or, alternatively, by killing them by heating food beyond the upper limits at which they can survive.

The human body is, to be sure, a chemical engine but it can only operate properly when the balance of acidity and alkalinity in the blood is maintained at one exact point; this is a precise concentration just on the alkaline side of neutrality. Similarly, specific levels of mineral substances like calcium or magnesium and an exact concentration of glucose must be steadily maintained in the body's fluids and tissues.

The complex and delicate mechanism which maintains the stability of the internal environment of the body constitutes the main scope of the science of *physiology*. While it is reasonable for a nutritionist to appreciate the degree to which life is a chemical process, he must also bear in mind that it is equally a physiological one. The individual person whom he sets out to nourish is, it is true, an individual. At the same time he is a community of living cells of many different types, each one of which needs to be fed. Yet each cell can only function while the exact conditions of physiological well-being are maintained. Each cell requires protein, for example, yet if the cells of a human body were to receive unchanged the protein of a beefsteak or the white of an egg, their life would be brought to a stop. It is fair to describe the beefsteak as a valuable protein food, yet when we do so we are making a number of assumptions. Before its value can be realized, the cells which may eventually benefit from it must be protected by the complicated physiological barrier of the digestive system which takes the steak to pieces, rejects the part of it that would otherwise be harmful and allows only the useful components to pass into the tissues of the body. Even when such nutrient components of food reach these tissues, their concentration is kept within acceptable limits by physiological balance mechanisms. There are biochemical systems at work by which the more complex nutrients are broken down into simpler substances, some of which may be used and some flushed out of the system by way of the kidneys and discarded in urine.

The demands made on the body are always changing. The chemical components of food entering the system, which themselves are different every day, have to be used, stored or discarded. The body's energy requirements vary widely: with the temperature around it, for example, or with its physical activity. But throughout the stress of these demands, the physiological mechanism must maintain the fluids within the body in the chemically constant state within which alone it is possible for its cells to function.

1.4   Life as a Social Process

Much that is commonly understood as nutritional science, comprising the main part of this book, is concerned with the chemical knowledge which represents a triumph of modern research from which great human benefit has accrued. The discoveries upon which it is based have been derived from observations not necessarily made on people. Rats, chickens and guinea pigs have been used, although experimental organisms other than man may not always provide information which is relevant to man. For some work, the most convenient experimental animals were blackbeetles, while certain tests relevant to man have been carried out using yeasts and bacteria. Lavoisier expressed a greater truth than he knew when he said that life is a chemical process. In fact, one of the most profound discoveries of our century has been that of the underlying uniformity of the chemical process of all life on earth. Certainly there are differences between creatures lying higher or lower in the phylogenetic scale—between a worm and an elephant, for example. But the similarities are more striking than the differences.

Next, there are the physiological imperatives described in Section 1.3, which govern the possibilities of life as rigidly as do the chemical ones. These are comparatively simple for lower creatures like moulds and yeasts, but more elaborate for multicellular organisms such as higher animals possessing a variety of organs, all of which must function in harmony.

But these higher animals are something more than chemical engines and physiological systems. For these, and especially for man, life is also a social process. A man is not only a colony of living cells; he is himself a unit of a larger social colony. Chemical understanding of nutrition is today complete enough for us to mix together in a laboratory all the ingredients required to supply the needs of the body. Sugars and protein, fat, twenty-odd minerals and as many vitamins can be dispensed in appropriate amounts and artificially fed through a tube passed into the stomach to keep an unconscious victim of a road accident alive indefinitely. Eventually he may be restored to his senses, discharged from the clinical environment of the hospital, and returned to his home, family and work. When this happens, although his chemical requirements of nutrients may remain the same, what he actually eats and his consequent nutritional well-being will be affected by the kind of society in which he lives.

Only in the most extreme circumstances do people become so dehumanized that they will eat anything that is edible. The unconscious patient already mentioned, reduced by injury to a state less than human, takes into his system whatever is administered to him. In an equally inhuman state is the starving victim of a concentration camp reduced to such straits that he is prepared to push aside anyone attempting to share with him such scraps of food as may be available. But the rarity of cannibalism even under the most drastic conditions of want is an indication of the degree to which social restraints control man's dietary behaviour. Taboo and custom are potent factors in people's nutrition and they affect primitive communities and technological societies alike. Beliefs governing which edible materials are considered to be acceptable and which disgusting are entirely irrational. For example, the British are as affronted at the idea of not merely eating horses and ponies but even exporting them to be eaten by Belgians as any Hindu is at the idea of eating beef. And they are as horrified at the idea of killing a dog, whether or not the possibility of eating it crosses their mind, as is a religious Hindu at killing a cow.

These taboos are manifestations of social behaviour which affect diet and which consequently affect nutrition. When Captain Cook was exploring Polynesia and was thus released from the constraints of his own tribal group he accepted cooked dog without demur and commented favourably on its flavour.

There are accepted beliefs in all societies about which foods are suitable for men and which for women, and these may have little relation to nutritional needs. In societies in which money is not important—such as among the Eskimos, and in parts of South East Asia—there are always social customs and habits affecting what people eat. In our own society, the relation between income, food intake and nutritional well-being has been emphasized by many writers. Whether money is used at all in a community, and if so, the way in which it is distributed (under a capitalist or communist system, for example) are clearly expressions of social behaviour which affect nutrition by affecting the gradation of prosperity within the group.

The most extreme example of the influence of social factors on nutrition is apparent when the society goes to war. Sometimes this social action may cause general undernutrition and hardship to all the individuals of the society; sometimes only certain categories of people are affected. These may be the women and children, perhaps, while the fighting men remain amply fed. Alternatively, in modern societies special arrangements may be made to ensure that the mothers and children are properly nourished and it is the adult members of the social group whose nutritional status deteriorates. Recently considerable attention has been paid to the deficiency disease of young children called *kwashiorkor*, or perhaps more exactly *protein–calorie malnutrition* which has been found in a number of developing countries (see also Section 5.7(b)). Primarily, kwashiorkor is a social phenomenon. Although, as its alternative name implies, it is due to a serious lack of enough to eat (that is, of calories) and especially to a shortage of protein, it is brought about by the *social* custom by which a nursing infant, who may be growing and thriving on his mother's milk, is abruptly weaned when his mother begins another pregnancy. Not only is he suddenly deprived of milk and given a starch gruel instead, but he is also sent away from home to be looked after by an aunt or some other female relative.

The cause of another disease, *rickets* (see Section 10.1), is also quite well understood. The amounts of vitamin D, calcium, and phosphorus in the diet, the quality of the flour selected and whether such flour is used to make bread or some other product, the amount of sunlight, the kind of dress favoured by the people concerned—all these are factors influencing the likelihood of rickets occurring, and this knowledge allowed the medical authorities virtually to wipe out rickets in Great Britain. In the 1970s, however, nutritional rickets in children again began to appear. It was however essentially confined to children of Indian and Pakistani origin. The reason for this was primarily social. The public-health authorities were making provision for a supply of vitamin D considered adequate for everyone, but they overlooked the fact that because the social customs of the Asians were different—for example, they ate chapattis rather than bread and butter—their needs were different.

These examples illustrate how dietary habits, which are very much a product of the social influences by which an individual is surrounded, exert a powerful effect on nutrition. Custom and ritual may appear to us to exert a stronger influence in non-industrialized societies than they do in the West. People in such societies are often poor, which itself affects the composition of their diet, usually for the worse. The members of western societies, however, find themselves influenced by powerful forces of fashion and accepted behaviour, reinforced by the pervasive pressures of the commercial system characteristic of capitalist communities or by other equally powerful forces of social persuasion in industrialized communist societies. For example, social forces have within little more than two generations led to the almost universal acceptance of so-called 'breakfast cereals' for the first meal of the day. These articles are comparatively recent inventions and can only be produced by industrialized communities. Less recently, the introduction of refined sugar has brought about a social change in the composition of the diet in many lands, which has had a detrimental effect on people's health.

1.5   A Definition of Food

In our introduction to the science of nutrition we have so far seen that the purpose of nutrition is to support *health* by means of the food each individual eats. Now we can attempt to define *food*.

When life is considered as a *chemical* process, food can be defined thus:

> *Food is anything, either solid or liquid, possessing a chemical composition which enables it, when swallowed, to do one or more of three things:*

(a) to provide the body with material from which it can produce work, heat or other forms of energy;

(b) provide material for growth, maintenance, repair or reproduction;

(c) supply substances which normally regulate the production of energy or the processes of growth, repair or reproduction.

Water is not included in this definition of food. Rather, we should think of water as the environment within which, and only within which, the biochemical processes of life can proceed. Although man, and the other terrestrial creatures like him, lives on dry land, he evolved like the rest of creation from ancestors who originally came from the sea. It is interesting that the relative concentrations of the various mineral salts present in plasma (the liquid part of blood in which the corpuscles are suspended) are the same as those which existed in sea water in Mesozoic times.

This definition of food includes all those substances which form part of recognized foodstuffs from which the nutrients, carbohydrates, fats, proteins, vitamins and minerals, are derived, and certain other groups of substances as well. These include alcohols and some, but not all, of the intermediate substances present in plants, such as organic acids and certain hemicellulose compounds midway between carbohydrate and structural materials like the cellulose and lignin present in wood. Similarly, there are corresponding intermediate substances in animal foods midway between protein and the structural components of tendons or bones.

But while our definition will include these if they provide at least some nourishment, it excludes other materials which, although they may be eaten do not contribute to the body's nutrition. Salt, for example, is a food whereas pepper is not, for although it may be considered to have an agreeable taste, it has no nutritional value at all. On the other hand, gelatin, although it is used in cooking for technical rather than nutritional reasons, is a protein although not a particularly valuable one, and must consequently be classified as a food. Pectin, however, which is also useful as a technical adjunct to make jam set, appears to contribute nothing to nutrition and cannot therefore be considered as a food.

The definition of food we have given may be considered to cover all the topics included in the science of human nutrition. This only applies, however, when life is accepted as a purely chemical process. As soon as human life is seen as something more than this, such a definition becomes insufficient. In the main this book necessarily deals with the chemical understanding of nutrition. If, however, it is to be true to its title and to serve as a text for those who wish to succeed in the practice of good nutrition, the definition of food must be extended in at least two respects. Food must not only perform the three chemical functions set out above but must also:

(d) conform to the prejudices, beliefs and taboos of the people to whom it is presented so that they will be prepared to eat it;

(e) be available without restriction by social or community barriers which might prevent people from eating it.

Obviously, articles of food cannot have any nutritional function if they are not eaten. If they do not exercise a nutritional effect they cannot, in that sense, any longer be defined as food. Throughout history social factors have prevented otherwise edible material from being eaten—factors by which, for example, women or children may be forbidden to eat certain foods or by which groups may be prevented by economic barriers from consuming food which can easily be seen to be physically available. The nutritional state of a hungry man is in no way ameliorated by the fact that there are ample supplies in the grill room of the Savoy Hotel. Such factors as these, in addition to those of biochemistry and physiology, must therefore be included within the ambit of nutritional science.

Unit Two

Digestion and Absorption

2.1 Introduction

Most of the foods taken into the mouth require some kind of alteration before they can be absorbed into the blood and carried to the cells of the body where their constituent nutrients exercise their function. The initial breakdown of food into a form in which it can be taken in is *digestion*; the process of assimilation through the permeable lining of the digestive tract is *absorption*.

We can think of the human body as a complex tube of which the upper opening is the mouth and the lower opening the anus. The tissues of the body surround this tube. Substances taken into the tube through the mouth cannot be considered to be within the body itself until they have been broken down and absorbed through the permeable membranes of its lining. If a swallowed object is resistant to digestion, it does not become a part of the living system but passes out of the body again unchanged.

Only a few food components are soluble and of sufficiently small molecular size to pass directly through the lining of the digestive system into the blood. Among these are salt, glucose and other monosaccharide sugars (see Section 3.2) and alcohol. The main components of food, including polysaccharides like starch, fats and proteins, have large complex molecules and are insoluble in water. Furthermore, they are sometimes combined with the indigestible structural scaffolding of the food. Before they can be absorbed, the food must be reduced in size by the grinding and chewing action of the teeth and the kneading and pressing action of the muscles surrounding the digestive tract down which it passes. Digestion is, however, mainly a chemical process brought about by *enzyme activity*.

Enzymes are biological catalysts—that is, they are substances which speed up chemical reactions. A catalyst for laboratory use may be a metal like copper, iron or manganese, or it may be a more complex substance. Enzymes are always proteins, with large and intricate molecular structures, and usually have to be associated with supplementary compounds called *co-enzymes* before they can function. There are many kinds of enzyme, and the action of each is *specific*, that is, it speeds up one particular reaction and has no effect on any other. Enzyme action can be compared with that of the slide of a zip-fastener. The two pieces of fabric held together by a zip-fastener can be torn apart by main force; but when a slide exactly designed to fit the fastener is used, they separate smoothly and easily. Similarly, a protein molecule, for example, *can* be broken down by prolonged boiling with a strong acid—a process clearly impossible within the digestive tract—but in the presence of the appropriate enzyme its components are separated rapidly at body temperature

The Nomenclature of Enzymes

In naming an enzyme, we usually attach the suffix -*ase* either to the name of the compound affected by the enzyme, or to the name of the kind of chemical action with which the enzyme is associated.

Examples of enzymes named from the substances with which they interact are:

amylases: enzymes concerned with *amylose* (a particular carbohydrate);
lipases: enzymes concerned with *lipids* (the chemical term for common fats);
proteases: enzymes concerned with *proteins.*

Examples of enzymes named after the reactions they promote are:

oxidases: enzymes which bring about oxidation, that is reaction with oxygen;
phosphatases: enzymes which bring about phosphorylation, that is reaction with phosphate;
hydrogenases: enzymes which bring about hydrogenation, that is in effect reaction with hydrogen (although, of course, no free hydrogen is present in the body).

In addition to these nomenclature systems, a number of enzymes still retain the trivial names they were given when they were first described. Among these are the following:

ptyalin: an amylase secreted by the salivary glands in the mouth;
pepsin: a protease secreted by the stomach;
trypsin: an enzyme concerned with the breakdown of protein and protein components in the small intestine.

In the following sections the actions of enzymes concerned with digestion are described. Enzymes, however, are required for *all* the many interdependent biochemical reactions of which the living process consists: that is to say, they are an essential part of the machinery of life itself.

2.2 The Digestive Tract

The digestive tract (see Fig. 2.1) comprises four main parts:

(*a*) It begins at the *mouth* where the food is broken down mechanically by the process of mastication.

(*b*) From the mouth food passes down the *oesophagus* into the *stomach.*

(*c*) The partially digested food is expelled from the stomach largely in liquid form, in a series of discrete squirts through the *pylorus* into the *small intestine.* This is a long, narrow, convoluted tube made up of three sections, the *duodenum* (named from the Latin *duodecem,* meaning twelve, because it is roughly 12 inches long), the *jejunum* (from the Latin *jejunus* meaning hungry, because it is usually found to be empty at *post mortem* examination) and the *ileum*, the name of which is derived from the Latin for colic.

(*d*) The ileum of the small intestine leads into the *large intestine* which is made up of four parts, the *caecum*, the *ascending colon*, on the right side of the abdomen, the *transverse colon* extending from right to left, and the *descending colon* on the left side of the abdomen. The large intestine terminates at the *rectum*.

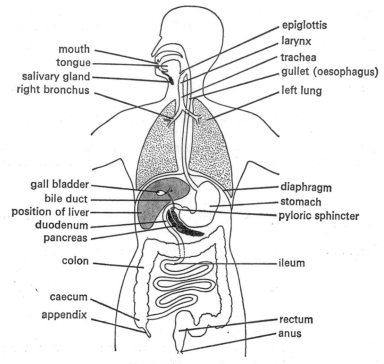

Fig. 2.1 The digestive tract

2.3   The Processes of Digestion

(*a*) The Mouth

A nutritionist must always bear in mind that the crushing and grinding of food by *mastication* is a matter of real importance. Old people in particular may easily suffer from malnutrition because of lack of teeth or through badly fitting dentures which prevent food from being chewed satisfactorily.

The mouth also contributes to the digestive process by the secretion of saliva by the three pairs of *salivary glands* (see Fig. 2.1). Usually saliva is secreted by these glands by a process of reflex action. That is to say, a nerve impulse aroused by the sense of taste or smell activates the glands to produce saliva; but the sight or even the thought of food can also 'make the mouth water'.

Saliva has two functions in digestion:

(*i*) It contains *mucin* which lubricates dry food, and consequently assists with its mixing and makes it easier to swallow.

(*ii*) It contains an amylase (Section 2.1), *ptyalin*, which is concerned with the break-up of the very large molecules of starch. Ptyalin splits starch into dextrins, which still have quite large molecules, and will also break down dextrins into the soluble sugar *maltose* (see Section 3.2(*b*)).

(*b*) The Stomach

The stomach has two functions in the digestive process. Firstly, it acts as a container for food undergoing digestion, so that people can obtain their food in the form of meals, rather than having to eat continuously or at least take their daily food supply in a series of small portions. Secondly, it allows salivary digestion of starch begun in the mouth to continue until it is stopped by the acid present, and the digestion of protein and of a small amount of fat to begin.

(*i*) **Gastric enzymes.** Three digestive enzymes are secreted in the stomach:

pepsin: which breaks down protein;

rennin: which converts the soluble protein in milk, *caseinogen*, into a form in which it can combine with calcium to produce *calcium caseinate* which can be digested by pepsin;

lipase: (present only in low concentration) which plays some part in breaking down fat.

(*ii*) **Hydrochloric acid** is secreted in the stomach at a rate of approximately 200 ml an hour, and its concentration can reach about 0.5 per cent. The effectiveness of pepsin in breaking down protein is largely due to the presence of this acid.

The hydrochloric acid, together with the pepsin, digests and destroys bacteria and consequently acts as an antiseptic. A healthy person whose stomach is secreting a normal concentration of hydrochloric acid is therefore in some measure protected against food-poisoning bacteria. The degree of antisepsis is limited however: if such bacteria are present in excessive numbers some of them may escape destruction and cause infection and disease.

(*iii*) **Mucus**, a slimy, viscid substance secreted by the stomach in addition to enzymes and hydrochloric acid, serves in some degree to protect the stomach itself against its own acidity. The amount secreted increases markedly when irritant substances are eaten.

(*iv*) **Stomach movement.** Waves of muscular contractions of the stomach occur in groups at intervals of 20 seconds or so, and help digestion by moving the stomach contents about, mixing them with the gastric secretions. Gradually the digested food is forced into the lower part, the *pylorus*, which as the pressure increases, opens to allow spurts of the liquefied mass or *chyme* to pass into the small intestine until the stomach is entirely emptied.

(c) The Small Intestine

The long, convoluted tube of the small intestine is a highly effective digestive organ. Digestion in the stomach takes place under quite strongly acid conditions, but the contents of the small intestine are slightly alkaline. Further digestion there is brought about by a series of enzymes, some of which are produced by glands outside the intestine, just as the salivary glands are situated outside the mouth.

(*i*) **Pancreatic enzymes.** The *pancreas* is made up of a group of specialized cells which lie in the loop of the duodenum (see Fig. 2.1), constituting what the butchers call sweetbread. Its function in digestion is to supply protein-, carbohydrate- and fat-splitting enzymes to the small intestine. These are:

Protein-splitting enzymes: Trypsin, a powerful enzyme acting more rapidly than the pepsin in the stomach, breaks down protein more completely. It also splits some proteins unaffected by pepsin, including some associated with 'gristle' and meat fibres. *Chymotrypsin* supplements the action of trypsin in breaking down partially degraded protein.

Carbohydrate-splitting enzymes: Pancreatic diastase or *amylase* splits starch much more efficiently than the ptyalin present in saliva, so much so that it can bring about digestion even of uncooked starch in raw potato or flour. It is interesting that while this enzyme plays an important part in the digestive system of adults, very little of it is produced by the pancreas of infants. This is one reason why pap or gruel made from starchy flour is so unsatisfactory a diet for babies.

Fat-splitting enzymes: Lipase, secreted by the pancreas, passes into the small intestine and splits fats into fatty acids and glycerol (see Unit 4). Fat itself is insoluble in water (although it can form emulsions like the cream in milk) but both fatty acids and glycerol are water-soluble. Furthermore, the alkali present in the small intestine changes part of the fatty acids into their alkali-metal salts, or *soaps*, which greatly facilitate the absorption of fat through the intestinal wall, whence it eventually reaches the bloodstream. But while pancreatic lipase brings about a significant proportion of the digestion of fat, its activity must also be related to that of *bile* (see paragraph (*iii*) below), produced not by the pancreas but by the liver.

(*ii*) **Intestinal enzymes.** These are secreted by the cells lining the small intestine. They can be divided into groups in the same way as the pancreatic enzymes.

Protein-splitting enzymes: Peptidases are a group of enzymes which complete the breakdown of protein fragments into their constituent amino acids (see Section 5.2). *Nuclease* can split nucleic acids, which although they are not proteins are concerned with protein synthesis, and are present in the nuclei of the cells of both animal and plant foods.

Carbohydrate-splitting enzymes: Maltase, sucrase (also called *invertase*) and *lactase* are supplementary carbohydrate-splitting enzymes. Maltase splits the sugar maltose into the simpler sugar glucose, and sucrase splits 'ordinary' sugar (sucrose) into glucose and fructose. Lactase splits lactose, the sugar present in milk, into its simpler constituent sugars, glucose and galactose. In contrast to pancreatic diastase, which is present in active concentration in the digestive juices of adults but which is largely lacking in those of infants, lactase is normally (although not invariably) present in the digestive tracts of infants and children but is lacking in certain adults, particularly if they are not accustomed to drinking milk. People with this deficiency develop diarrhoea and certain other symptoms if they drink milk: the condition is called *lactose intolerance* (see also Section 3.7).

Fat-splitting enzymes: Intestinal lipase supplements the action of the lipases secreted in the stomach and by the pancreas (*gastric lipase* and *pancreatic lipase* respectively).

(*iii*) **Bile** is an alkaline liquid with a colour which varies from reddish-brown to yellow or even green. It has a musky smell and tastes bittersweet. In healthy people, anything from 500 to 1 000 ml of bile are secreted each day by the liver; this gradually fills up the *gall bladder* (see Fig. 2.1), which is a pouch specially placed to receive it. If for some reason the bile duct (the tube connecting the liver with the gall bladder) becomes obstructed, or if an individual is infected by the virus of infective hepatitis causing jaundice or what in its milder form used to be called a 'bilious attack', bile accumulates in the blood, producing the characteristic yellowing of the skin and the whites of the eyes, and the feeling of nausea and misery.

Bile itself has little digestive action, but it very greatly increases the extent of the splitting of fats in the small intestine by the pancreatic lipase, partly because it promotes the emulsifying of the fats in the liquid contents of the intestine. These emulsifying properties mean that bile also assists the absorption of fat-soluble vitamins such as vitamin A, vitamin D and vitamin K (see Units 13, 14 and 15). Bile also increases the efficiency of the enzymes which digest carbohydrate and protein.

Additionally, however, bile has a special function as a chemical 'signal' which sets off the digestive process. The orderly way in which the various processes start in the mouth and pass on to the stomach and thence to the intestines is brought about partly by the passage of the food itself down the tract and partly by two more subtle influences. The first is produced by nerve impulses, some passing direct to the digestive tract and others arising from the mental state. Thoughts of food, relaxed contentment, good company and pleasant surroundings improve digestion to a measurable degree, while anger, tenseness, distress and exhaustion hamper it. The second special influence is produced by substances which might be called 'chemical messengers'. Bile plays a part in bringing these messengers into action. The sequence of events is as follows:

First, food put into the mouth, whether aided by the mental state of the eater or not, causes saliva to flow.

Secondly, the food is swallowed and the presence of dextrin, which is starch partially split by the salivary ptyalin, stimulates the secretion of the digestive juices in the stomach.

Thirdly, food leaves the stomach through the pylorus and this initiates a series of muscular contractions passing down the duodenum. These are called *peristaltic waves* and the process, which exerts a 'milking' effect on the intestinal contents and thus carries them along the tract, is known as *peristalsis*.

Fourthly, the peristaltic waves in the duodenum excite a nervous response in the gall bladder, causing *bile* to pass down the bile duct and pour into the duodenum.

The effect of the bile is to cause the cells lining the duodenum to release a substance called *secretin*, which is absorbed into the bloodstream. It is carried in the blood to the pancreas, which it then stimulates to produce the various pancreatic enzymes which bring about digestion in the small intestine. Secretin production is also stimulated by the acid carried into the duodenum with each spurt of partially-digested food released from the stomach.

A note on hormones. We have called secretin a 'chemical messenger' because it is a chemical compound produced by cells in one part of the body (the lining of the small intestine) and carried by the blood circulation to another part (the pancreas) where it has its specific effect, the stimulation of enzyme secretion. Messengers of this kind, of which secretin is one and *insulin* (see Section 3.4) is another are called *hormones*. The word is derived from a Greek term meaning 'to urge on'.

(d) The Large Intestine

The large intestine has three digestive functions:

(*i*) It absorbs any remaining food broken down by the digestive activities of the mouth, the stomach and the small intestine which has not already passed into the bloodstream.

(*ii*) It re-absorbs much of the water which is the major component of the mainly fluid mixture in which digestion takes place in the stomach and small intestine. Waste material and bacterial debris can therefore leave the body in comparatively dry form as faeces.

(*iii*) It serves as an incubator in which certain harmless bacteria can grow. These perform two functions: they break down some of the tougher food components which are resistant to the digestive enzymes, and while doing so and multiplying inside the large intestine the bacteria synthesize some vitamins. Both these functions contribute to the body's total nutritional intake.

Why the Digestive Tract Does not Digest Itself

The enzymes we have discussed, the hydrochloric acid in the stomach and the bile (which in many ways resembles a detergent in its action) are exceedingly powerful digestive agents, quickly breaking down the chemical structure of food components. This being so, it is apparently remarkable that the tissues of the digestive tract itself are not digested. However, certain protective mechanisms are built into it. Mucus, secreted both in the stomach and the small intestine, may exercise a protective lubricating effect. There is also evidence that digestive enzymes cannot pass the outer covering membranes of living cells. But a more subtle biochemical reason is that the powerful enzymes pepsin and trypsin are not produced in the first place in their active form by the cells of the stomach lining and the pancreas, but as inactive precursors called *pepsinogen* and *trypsinogen*. Only when the quite complex sequence of events comprising the digestive process is brought about as we have described, are the appropriate *co-enzymes* released, the enzymes activated and digestion begun.

2.4 Absorption of Nutrients

If the cells of the different parts of the digestive tract are looked at through a microscope, they are seen to differ according to the function which each part performs in absorption. In the mouth and oesophagus which come in contact with solid food, the cells of the lining are *stratified* or layered so that food in the main passes over them and little absorption through this lining takes place. This structure is shown in Fig. 2.2.

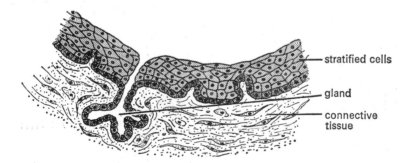

Fig. 2.2 Cells from the lining of the mouth

The structure of the stomach lining must allow the gastric juices to flow through it into the digesting food, and at the same time permit the absorption of some of the products of protein breakdown. The cells here have a columnar structure, and the lining itself is folded so that a comparatively large surface is provided through which the products of digestion can be absorbed (Fig. 2.3).

Most of the absorption of nutrients takes place in the small intestine, and

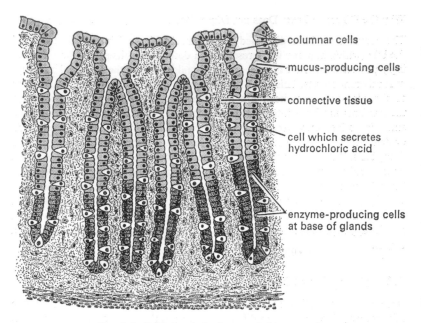

Fig. 2.3 Cells from the lining of the stomach

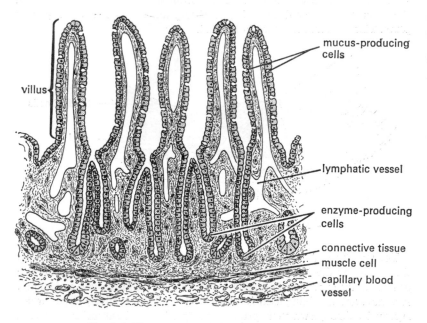

Fig. 2.4 The structure of the small intestine lining

the folded structure of the gut lining is here most pronounced (Fig. 2.4). There is thus available a relatively enormous surface for absorption: it has been calculated to be about 40 square metres. This structure is shown in more detail in Fig. 2.5. The main projections, called *villi*, which expose an enlarged surface to the liquid contents of the intestine themselves possess a surface made up of enormous numbers of *micro-villi*, called the *brush border*. The digested food components penetrate into the blood vessels, which allow some fluid to permeate out so that the cells making up the intestinal wall are bathed in liquid. Some of this collects in the lymph vessels which serve as a drainage

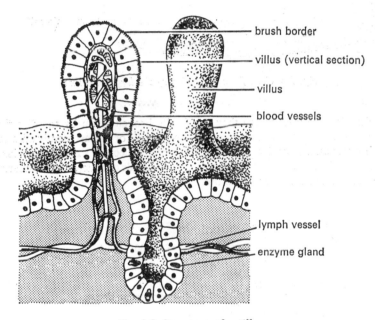

Fig. 2.5 *Structure of a villus*

system by which the liquid in them, called *lymph*, eventually returns to the veins: this lymph also carries some of the fat absorbed in the small intestine (see Section 4.8).

The cells lining the large intestine also have a columnar configuration but they are larger and less closely packed than those of the small intestine (Fig. 2.6). This is because their main function is to allow the absorption of water from the liquid contents of the gut, thus converting the unabsorbed residues of digestion into a firm faecal mass.

Finally, the cells lining the colon again have a stratified configuration (Fig. 2.7), since the organ's function, which resembles that of the oesophagus in some ways, is to convey the solid faeces to the rectum and anus and hence out of the body altogether.

In general, the various components of food are absorbed in the same parts

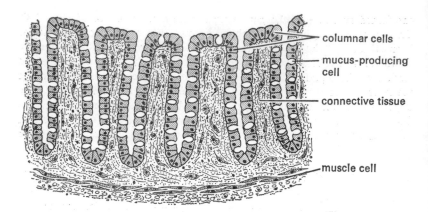

Fig. 2.6 Cells from the lining of the large intestine

of the digestive tract where they are finally broken down by the digestive enzymes into components which are, firstly, soluble or at least readily miscible with water and, secondly, of sufficiently small molecular size to allow them to be absorbed through the lining of the gut wall. We can therefore summarize the process of absorption as follows:

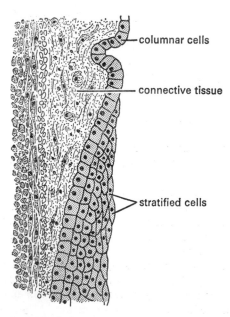

Fig. 2.7 Cells from the lining of the colon

(a) The Mouth

Comparatively little is absorbed in the mouth, although there is some absorption of substances of small molecular size and high solubility such as salt, vitamin C, glucose, alcohol and certain soluble drugs.

(b) The Stomach

While the stomach functions mainly as a storage compartment and mixing vessel for food, the gastric juice also completes the breakdown and consequently permits the absorption of part of its contents. It readily absorbs such soluble substances as alcohol, sugars, salts, water-soluble vitamins and at least some of the products of protein digestion which has been started by pepsin and hydrochloric acid.

(c) The Small Intestine

Sugars from the digestion of carbohydrates, amino acids from the digestion of proteins, soaps, glycerol and other products of fat digestion, together with vitamins and other accessory food substances—all these, as we have described already, are taken into the body in this most efficient organ of absorption.

(d) The Large Intestine

Little absorption of nutrients occurs here except for any small amounts carried through from the small intestine. However, the bacteria which live and multiply here produce vitamins, particularly of the B group, and also small amounts of sugars arising from the breakdown of fibrous material; these substances are absorbed through the large intestine lining.

2.5 The Absorption and Excretion of Water

Water is readily absorbed in the stomach, the small intestine and especially by the large intestine. While the body is specially equipped to absorb and to conserve water, everyone knows that if large amounts of water or of watery beverages like tea or beer are drunk, the excess water quite quickly leaves the body as urine. When, however, a man says that what he has drunk 'passes straight through him', his statement is inaccurate.

We have already mentioned the discovery of the great French scientist Claude Bernard of the necessity for the very life of terrestrial animals (including man) of stability in their internal environment. He called this essential 'la fixité du milieu intérieur'. This means that every living cell must, in order to preserve its normal activity, be surrounded by a fluid of a certain exact chemical composition. It follows, therefore, that if an excessive amount of water is absorbed the blood and other tissue fluids would become diluted, and this composition would change. This change is prevented by the excretion of an appropriate volume of water through the kidneys.

The Kidneys

Every normal individual possesses two kidneys, each weighing about 250 g, situated in the abdominal cavity, one on each side of the backbone. Each of these comparatively small organs is packed with about a million tiny blood-filtration units called *nephrons*. Fig. 2.8 is a diagram of just one of these. As the blood flows through the tangle of narrow capillaries in each *glomerulus* —the main functional element of the nephron—a dilute solution of substances of small molecular size filters through the capillary walls and flows down the tubule. The rest of the blood continues on its way through the circulatory

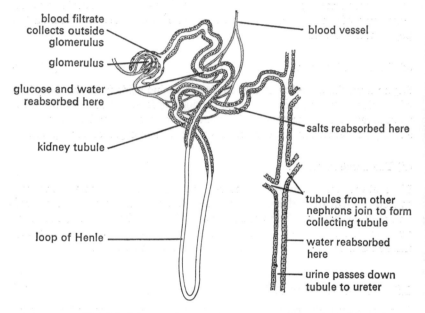

blood filtrate collects outside glomerulus

glomerulus

glucose and water reabsorbed here

kidney tubule

loop of Henle

blood vessel

salts reabsorbed here

tubules from other nephrons join to form collecting tubule

water reabsorbed here

urine passes down tubule to ureter

Fig. 2.8   Diagrammatic representation of a nephron

system. One of the substances filtered out of the blood is the toxic breakdown product of protein, *urea* (see Section 5.2); others include glucose and soluble mineral substances.

The nephrons making up the filtration mechanism of the kidney perform their function in a particularly subtle way. They serve as a filter for removing unwanted substances from the bloodstream, yet they can do this while ensuring a minimum loss of water from the body. After urea and other waste products have been filtered from the blood, much of the water carrying them, together with the glucose, minerals and other soluble nutrients, is quickly reabsorbed into the bloodstream, while the filtrate (soon to become urine) passes on its way down one side and up the other of the *loop of Henle*; the harmful waste products remain to be excreted in the urine. There is a large flow of blood through the kidneys, not only that undergoing filtration in the glomeruli but also in the capillaries which surround the tubules, only a few of which are sketched in Fig. 2.8.

The degree to which the tubules of the loop of Henle and its associated convolutions allow water to be either re-absorbed into the blood or, on the other hand, carried away from the body and excreted as urine, is regulated by a special hormone secreted by the *pituitary gland* at the base of the brain. When water is scarce, the kidneys can carry out their main function of ridding the body of urea from the breakdown of protein while at the same time ensuring the minimum loss of water by re-absorbing much of it. On the other hand, if a great deal of water has been drunk production of the hormone is inhibited, and the tubules become less permeable to water which in consequence passes away along the *ureter* which runs from each kidney into the *bladder*.

The science of nutrition is concerned with the components of food which together constitute a satisfactory diet. These nutrients obviously do no good unless the food of which they form a part is actually eaten. Even then they must be physically broken up by mastication, and chemically transformed into relatively simple compounds by the various processes of digestion. Only then can the nutrients be absorbed into the living tissues of the body and the process of nutrition begin.

Unit Three

Carbohydrate

3.1 Introduction

The primary function of food is to provide the body with the energy it needs to keep life going. Carbohydrate is the principal constituent of almost all normal diets and of all food components it is carbohydrate that generally provides most of the energy. There can be too much carbohydrate in a diet; obviously, if the proportion of carbohydrate becomes so high that the necessary amounts of protein, fat and other essential nutrients cannot be included as well, the quality of the diet as a whole must suffer. But carbohydrates are nevertheless important in nutrition; the main ingredient of bread is a carbohydrate, starch, so that when we pray 'give us this day our daily bread', we implicitly recognize the importance of carbohydrate in maintaining human life.

3.2 The Chemistry of Carbohydrates

Carbohydrates, as their name implies, are a class of compounds made up of *carbon*, *hydrogen* and *oxygen*. The carbohydrates most commonly encountered are made up of sugar units (usually *glucose* although *fructose*, *galactose* and some others are sometimes present). These units of sugar may be uncombined, or they may be chemically bonded in pairs, in small groups, or as elaborate structures built up from thousands of sugar units, like the large multiple molecules of starch.

(a) Monosaccharides

Glucose is the sugar which forms the repeating unit of which starch is composed. In consequence it is the breakdown product of starch digestion, and the main form in which all carbohydrates are used by the body. It has the chemical composition shown below:

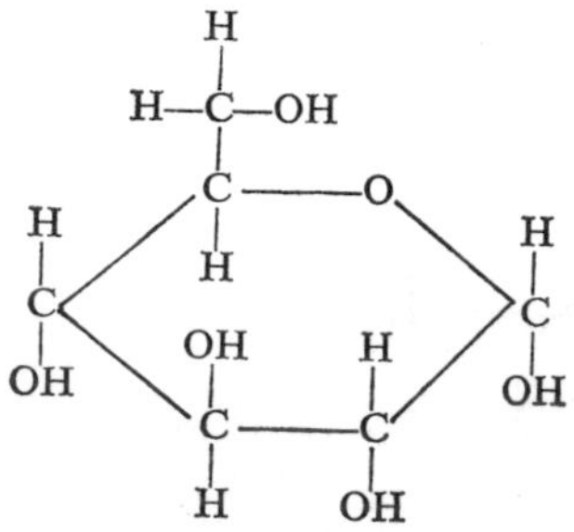

glucose

Glucose is soluble in water and tastes sweet but not as sweet as sucrose, which is what is commonly called 'sugar'. It occurs naturally in grapes and other sweet fruit, onions and unripe potatoes; honey is about 35 per cent glucose. The product called 'liquid glucose' or 'confectioners' glucose', made by treating maize starch with acid, also contains about 35 per cent of glucose.

Fructose has a similar molecular configuration to that of glucose, and is made up of the same numbers of carbon, hydrogen and oxygen atoms. Although it is recognizably different from glucose—

fructose

it is, for example, somewhat sweeter—it was until very recently thought to play a nutritional role identical with that of glucose. We now know, however, that when fructose is eaten it may quite quickly be converted into fat in the blood and hence play some part in the influence which fat has on heart disease (see Section 4.4). Fructose is absorbed very rapidly into the body and is then used more quickly than glucose. Since it is harmless to people with diabetes, and also because it slightly speeds up the rate at which alcohol disappears from the blood, it is sometimes administered when it is thought that these special properties might be useful. Quite recently, however, it has been discovered that if it is eaten in large amounts fructose may produce *acidosis* caused by an increase in lactic acid in the blood, and a raised level of *uric acid* in the blood which is particularly undesirable to people with a tendency to gout.

Fructose may be produced from sucrose (commercial 'sugar'); it also occurs naturally in an uncombined form in honey and in sweet fruits.

The molecules of glucose, fructose and galactose all contain six carbon atoms, and are therefore called *hexoses*. They are all *monosaccharides*, that is to say, they are sugars composed of one ('mono-') sugar unit.

(b) Disaccharides

Sucrose is the commonest sugar in the diet. Both cane sugar and beet sugar consist of purified sucrose and nothing else. Even brown and Demerara sugars are almost entirely composed of sucrose, merely containing traces of colouring matter, mineral residues and moisture. Sucrose is a *disaccharide*, that is, it consists of two monosaccharide sugar units chemically linked together. When disaccharides are eaten the enzymes in the digestive system split the linkage; the two component monosaccharides are absorbed independently, and provide a readily available source of energy.

(glucose unit)   (fructose unit)

sucrose

Sucrose and tooth decay. The main reason for eating sucrose is its sweetness which has, of itself, no nutritional significance. Before it is broken down by digestive enzymes, however, and while it is still in the mouth, sucrose encourages the activity of bacteria which live there, and which attack the teeth and cause them to decay. Recent research clearly demonstrates that *dental caries* (what in America are called *cavities*) is an infectious disease, that is to say it is produced by these particular types of bacteria. Animals which are kept from birth in an environment from which all bacteria are excluded never have decayed teeth.

Lactose. Cows' milk contains about 5 per cent of lactose, a sugar composed

(galactose unit)   (glucose unit)

lactose

of one unit each of glucose and galactose chemically combined together. Human milk contains about 6.8 per cent of lactose. In the small intestine lactose is split into its constituent monosaccharides by the enzyme *lactase*; these sugars are then absorbed and used by the body to produce energy. (But see Section 2.3 (*c*) for a discussion of lactase deficiency.) The chemical configuration of lactose is shown here diagrammatically. The comparatively slight difference in the molecular structures of lactose and sucrose illustrates the remarkable degree of specificity of enzymes, since the enzyme *sucrase* (also called *invertase*) which splits sucrose is incapable of splitting the closely similar disaccharide lactose, which requires its own particular enzyme, lactase.

Maltose. This is the sugar that gives malt extract its sweetness and stickiness. Malt, from which malt extract is derived, is germinated barley which has been heated and dried. During germination, enzymes produced in the barley seed break down the starch which is the major component of the barley, and the product of this process of breakdown is maltose; it can be manufactured industrially by treating starch with acid. A molecule of maltose is composed of two linked glucose units, which during digestion can be separated by the action of the enzyme *maltase*.

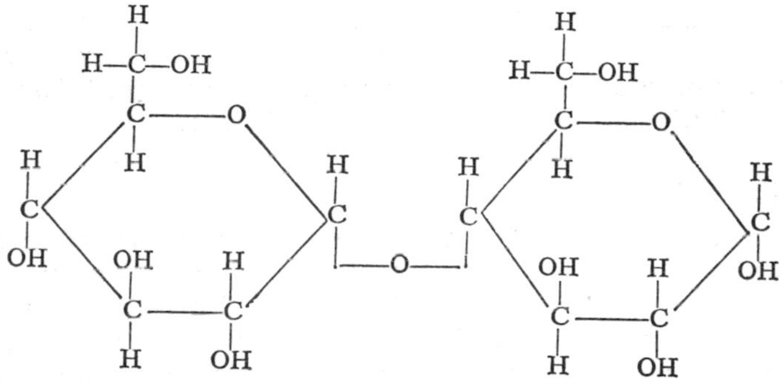

(*glucose unit*)   (*glucose unit*)

maltose

The sugars, sucrose, lactose and maltose, each composed of *two* linked monosaccharide units, are all classified as *disaccharides*.

(*c*) Trisaccharides

Trisaccharides are sugars, the molecules of which are made up of *three* monosaccharide units linked together. They are very much less plentiful in foods than monosaccharides and disaccharides. The principal sources of trisaccharides are beans and peas, and green and root vegetables, and they occur particularly in the more fibrous and stringy parts of these foodstuffs. The relative unimportance of trisaccharides in the diet is not so much on account of any inferior nutritional quality of their constituent monosaccharides, but rather because they are only broken down with difficulty by the processes of digestion. Some of this breakdown is brought about by the micro-organisms present in the large intestine, with a parallel production of gas. The presence of trisaccharides in foods may therefore be one of the causes of flatulence in some people.

Raffinose has a chemical structure in which one unit of glucose, one unit of fructose and one unit of galactose are linked together. Besides occurring in the materials mentioned above, raffinose has also been found in cotton-seed and in the molasses derived from sugar beet. In certain species of eucalyptus trees a curious exudate oozes out when the bark is punctured by insects, and solidifies in the form of a warty crust. These trees are commonly known as 'gum trees' in their native Australia, and the exudate is called *eucalyptus manna*. Although it has little or no nutritional significance, it is of some interest as being nearly pure raffinose.

(d) Tetrasaccharides

Stachyose is an example of a tetrasaccharide. Its molecule contains four monosaccharides, two units of galactose, one of fructose and one of glucose linked together; it has been observed as a contaminant when protein is being isolated from soya beans to make so-called 'meat analogues'. Like trisaccharides, it tends to cause flatulence during its digestion.

(e) Polysaccharides

Starch is the main source of the nourishment from which most of the human race derive the energy they need to maintain life. Primitive hunters obtained their biological fuel from the flesh of the animals they killed, but even then they supplemented their diet with the starch present in such roots as they were able to grub up. The main step towards civilization came with the invention of settled agriculture, which made possible the use of the starch present in seeds of the grass family from which were developed the great cereals of history, rice, wheat, rye, oats and sorghum (millet), later supplemented by maize.

We have already seen that sugars are composed of one, two or, less frequently, three or four monosaccharide units, that is, either glucose, fructose or galactose (there are other monosaccharides, some of which contain fewer carbon atoms, but they are very much less common). Starch, on the other hand, has a very large molecule indeed. It is composed of up to several hundred glucose units linked together into a complex network. As any cook knows, starches from different sources behave differently. For example, maize starch ('corn flour') is better suited as the thickening agent of 'custard powder' than rice starch or wheat starch. One of the reasons for these differences in behaviour is the varying proportions of branched and unbranched chains of linked glucose units in starches of different origins.

Starch is usually a mixture of two substances. The first, *amylose*, has a long, unbranched molecule often made up of several hundred glucose units. The second, which has a branched molecule, is called *amylopectin*. Whatever the proportions of these two substances, all starches are broken down in the digestive system almost entirely into the two-glucose disaccharide, maltose. Maltose is itself broken down into glucose which can then be readily absorbed and used.

Dextrin. When foods containing starch are heated—for example, when bread is toasted or potatoes fried—the very large starch molecules may be broken down into fragments which, though comprising only a fraction of the number of linked glucose units in the original starch, are still quite large molecules. These compounds are called *dextrins*. They are, like starch itself, readily split into maltose and then into glucose by the digestive enzymes.

Glycogen. The starch in cereal grains and in tubers like potatoes is the store of food-energy which the wheat or rice plant, or the potato, draws on in early spring, until the leaves, which will sustain it later on, have developed. Animals, like plants, can also provide themselves with stores of energy, sometimes as fat, which will be discussed in Unit 4, and sometimes as *glycogen*, a substance specially suited for immediate use. Glycogen, which is in fact an animal starch, has a somewhat simpler molecular structure than vegetable starches; its molecule is nevertheless composed of chains of linked glucose units, like that of vegetable starch. Glycogen is stored in the liver, which, when eaten as food, contains about 4 per cent of glycogen. Glycogen is also present in muscle, particularly in those muscles capable of prolonged work such as those constituting horse meat, and the powerful muscles of oysters, which hold their shells tightly closed as you will know if you have ever attempted to open one.

Inulin. The type of starch present in Jerusalem artichokes is different in its chemical composition from those found in other foods, and is called *inulin*. Whereas normal starches consist of chains of glucose units, inulin is composed of chains of 30 or 40 *fructose* units with only a single terminal glucose unit at the end. This might be considered to be a comparatively small variation from the normal chemistry of starch. Nevertheless, small though it may seem, the Jerusalem artichoke and the inulin it contains strikingly illustrate certain of the principles of nutritional science.

The first lesson is that a Jerusalem artichoke is not an artichoke at all. Real, or 'globe', artichokes, *Cynara scolymus*, bear some resemblance to large nettles. Jerusalem artichokes, *Helianthus tuberosus*, which originally came from America, are more like sunflowers. Not only have they nothing to do with artichokes, they have nothing to do with Jerusalem either, the word being an English mispronunciation of *girasole*, the Italian word for a sunflower.

The next lesson is that nutrition is a science that, though to some degree based on chemistry, is itself something much more than chemistry; it is, in fact, a branch of biology. Under favourable conditions and on fertile soil substantial amounts of Jerusalem artichokes can be grown. Yields of up to 50 tonnes per hectare of the underground tubers, which grow rather like potatoes, have been obtained. During the First World War it was suggested that this crop should be cultivated to help feed the British population, whose food supplies were being cut off by the German submarine blockade operating at the time. Fortunately, before this scheme was put into effect, the attention of the authorities was drawn to the fact that, in spite of the similarity of a starch composed of molecular chains of fructose units to normal starch made up of chains of glucose units, the difference was sufficient to prevent the specific enzymes which unlink normal glucose-built starch from unlinking the fructose-built inulin, so that the Jerusalem artichoke would have been useless as a dietary supplement.

A further example of how so apparently small a change in the chemical composition of a food component may affect its nutritional value is the test used by physicians to measure the efficiency of a patient's kidney. We have see already (Section 2.5) how substances being transported in the bloodstream, which of course include the products of digestion absorbed from the intestinal tract, may be filtered out through the glomeruli in the kidney's nephrons. Part or all of such substances which are of use to the body are almost immediately re-absorbed through the tubules of the loop of Henle. It has been found that a convenient way to measure the rate at which a man's kidney is filtering his blood is to inject a measured amount of inulin. Because its chemistry is so similar to that of normal food components it is freely filtered at the glomeruli, but because it is essentially different none of it is re-absorbed by the tubules; the time taken for inulin to appear in the urine can therefore be used to calculate the filtration rate in the kidneys. Because it is not re-absorbed in the kidney tubules, inulin has almost no food value.

Pectin. Pectin, like inulin, is a polysaccharide which has no nutritional value but nevertheless it too has some bearing on nutrition. Pectin is a term which includes several slight variants of the same type of material. It is found in apples, plums, and other fruit and also in turnips and root crops. Whereas inulin is composed of linkages of fructose which itself is a common component of numerous foodstuffs—fructose, remember, is present in honey and fruit and constitutes half the sucrose molecule—pectin is a polysaccharide composed of units of *galacturonic acid*, a compound related to galactose.

Although pectin possesses no nutritional value it is useful in making jam 'set'. Since food needs to be attractive before it will be eaten, it might be argued that pectin has some nutritional usefulness if it contributes thus harmlessly to the palatability of the diet.

Cellulose. Starch, as we have seen, is a large molecule made up of chains of glucose units linked together. The linkage is such that the plant can disengage the glucose units in pairs as maltose, which it can then use as a source of energy. When the starch stored by plants is eaten as human food, as flour or other cereal products, or in potatoes, the digestive enzymes can also unlink the glucose and make use of it when it is absorbed into the body. But plants can also combine glucose into other large complex molecules which serve as structural components by which the stalk of cereals is made stiff, or, in trees, by which the strong scaffolding of wood is formed. These large molecules are *cellulose*; it occurs in food in the fibrous parts of vegetables and the branny fractions of cereals.

The chemical configuration of part of a cellulose molecule, which may contain 3 000 or more glucose units, is shown in Fig. 3.1, for comparison with that of an amylose molecule.

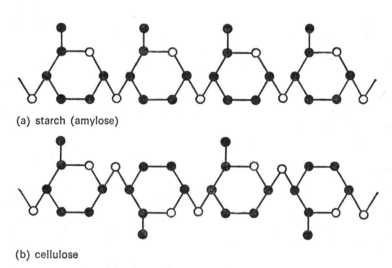

(a) starch (amylose)

(b) cellulose

Fig. 3.1 The configuration of polysaccharides

Whereas in starch the glucose units are linked together all the same way up, so to speak, in cellulose the units are orientated alternately up and down. Here again we find an example of the specificity of the action of enzymes. Those which can break down starch, making it useful to the body—the action we have compared to that of the slide of a zip fastener—can fit on to the starch-linked arrangement. On the other hand, they cannot function at all when faced with the different molecular structure of cellulose.

Cellulose contributes very little food value to the body. All it can provide is what can be released by bacteria in the large intestine which, when they break down cellulose at all, do so only partially and very slowly. Cellulose can be treated chemically to form *methylcellulose*, which also has no nutritional value but is used to increase the bulkiness and viscosity of manufactured foods.

3.3   The Main Sources of Carbohydrate in the Diet

In a normal western diet, the foods contributing the most carbohydrate are cereal products, like flour, bread, rice and oatmeal and the foods made from them, and sugar. Dried fruits contain a good deal of sugar and consequently have a comparatively high content of carbohydrate. However, in assessing the contribution of any particular nutrient made by a foodstuff to the diet, we must always consider not only the concentration of the particular nutrient it contains, but also the amount of the foodstuff eaten in the diet as a whole. It is also important in this context to remember that the figures in a table of food composition relate to a unit weight, for example, 100 g as given in the table in the Appendix, and that different helpings or portions may vary widely in weight. We must bear in mind too that 100 g of a food like milk contain very much more water than 100 g of a dry food like flour. In referring to tables of food composition, therefore, figures for, say, flour cannot be compared with those for, say, bread, without taking into account that bread contains a higher proportion of moisture than flour.

Table 3.1 shows how the proportions of carbohydrate vary in different categories of food.

3.4   Diabetes Mellitus

Diabetes mellitus, commonly known as diabetes, is a rather common disease which affects at least one person in 75 in the population of Great Britain and the United States more or less severely. It is usually due to a lack of *insulin*, a hormone secreted by the pancreas. When glucose, mainly derived from the digestion of carbohydrate, is absorbed through the intestinal tract into the blood, insulin controls the laying down of glucose in the tissues where it is to be used. The pancreas of a healthy person produces the amount of insulin required with such accuracy that after a meal exactly the right quantity of absorbed glucose is taken out of the circulating blood and put where it is needed. When the small steady amount remaining in the bloodstream reaches the kidneys, it is filtered out through the glomeruli and at once re-absorbed by the tubules. When a person develops diabetes this control over glucose is lost. The carbohydrate he eats is absorbed and more and more glucose passes into his blood, but it is not properly taken up by the tissues of the body. A point is reached when his kidney tubules cannot re-absorb all that comes through and some of the glucose is carried off in the urine. But even so, too much remains in the blood.

Although the disease can be effectively treated by giving the patient insulin injections or by certain drugs, this is not a complete substitute for the precise and sensitive control which the pancreas of a healthy person naturally maintains. Patients with diabetes must therefore keep to a diet containing a reasonably uniform amount of carbohydrate. This need not always comprise exactly the same foods; indeed, few people could tolerate so tedious a diet. It is, however, important for those responsible for the diet of a diabetic patient to be aware of the proportions of carbohydrate in the different foods he eats (see Section 19.2(*b*)).

Table 3.1 The carbohydrate content of certain foods

	g per 100 g		g per 100 g
Sugary foods		*Vegetables*	
Sugar	100·0	Potatoes	18·0
Syrup	79·0	Baked beans	17·3
Jam	69·2	Parsnips	11·3
		Beetroot	6·0
Cereals		Cabbage	5·8
Rice (polished, raw)	86·8	Runner beans	2·9
White flour	80·0	Spinach	2·8
Wholemeal flour	73·4		
Oatmeal	72·8	*Dairy produce*	
White bread	54·6	Condensed milk	55·1
Wholemeal bread	46·7	Evaporated milk	12·8
		Milk	4·8
Fruit		Eggs	0
Raisins	64·4	Cheese	trace
Dates	63·9		
Currants	63·1	*Meat and fish*	
Bananas	19·2	Liver	4·0
Grapes	16·1	Meat	0
Apples	12·0	Fish	0
Pineapple	11·6		
Oranges	8·5		

While the concentration of glucose in the blood of diabetic people will rise dangerously high if their disease is untreated, it can fall so low that consciousness is lost if, after having received a routine injection of insulin calculated to be just large enough to deal with the glucose from their normal diet, they happen to miss one of their meals. Under these circumstances they must consume a source of glucose as a matter of urgency. About 10 g of sugar (that is two lumps) is quickly absorbed, and is usually sufficient to raise the concentration of glucose in the blood to a safe level.

3.5 Alcohol as a Food

Although the molecule of alcohol is composed of carbon, hydrogen and oxygen, it is not strictly speaking within the category of carbohydrates, all of which are based on sugar units. Nevertheless, alcohol may have some association with the carbohydrates. It is indeed the residue remaining after sugars have been used for food by living single-celled plants called yeasts. The chemical structure of the alcohol present in fermented beverages, *ethanol* or *ethyl alcohol*, is shown below.

$$
\begin{array}{c}
\text{H} \\
| \\
\text{H}-\text{C}-\text{OH} \\
| \\
\text{H}-\text{C}-\text{H} \\
| \\
\text{H}
\end{array}
$$

ethanol

Alcohol is absorbed directly through all parts of the digestive system. When carried by the circulating blood to the body tissues it can be used for energy production or can be converted into fat, quite apart from its intoxicating effect on the brain.

3.6 The Origin of Carbohydrates and the World's Food Supply

All living things must be able to produce energy in order to keep alive. When they fail to produce the necessary energy, life stops and the creature dies, whether it is a plant, a bacterium, an animal or a man. Energy for living is obtained from food, and, in almost all human diets, carbohydrates provide most of the energy. Among impoverished communities in tropical countries up to 90 per cent of the total energy is supplied by carbohydrates, and even in rich populations such as our own carbohydrates supply 50 per cent of the energy we need.

We obtain carbohydrate from plant foods. In cereal grains, in roots like sugar beet or tapioca, or in tubers like potatoes, the starch and sugar from which we obtain energy were originally laid down as their own energy stores by the respective plants. Carnivorous animals like birds and beasts of prey and predacious fish eat other animals which have themselves obtained their energy from vegetable carbohydrates.

The chemical energy of carbohydrates, which as we have seen usually reaches the body's tissues as glucose, is obtained through a series of intermediate chemical steps until the original glucose molecule, comprising six carbon, six oxygen and twelve hydrogen atoms, is completely oxidized and leaves the body as six molecules of carbon dioxide gas (CO_2) and six molecules of water (H_2O).

Animals can only move and grow provided they consume energy-containing carbohydrates, and they obtain the energy they need from these by oxidizing them to carbon dioxide and water with the oxygen from the air they breathe. Plants also use carbohydrates for their energy needs; but they can also *re-form* glucose from carbon dioxide and water from the atmosphere, at the same time restoring oxygen to the air. Energy is used up in this process, and the plants find the energy they need in the electromagnetic vibrations produced by the sun, which we perceive as light. *Chlorophyll*, the green pigment of leaves, makes the process possible; it acts as a special 'antenna', tuned to pick up the energy from the sunlight. The entire food supply of the world depends upon this system; it is called *photosynthesis* (from the Greek words for 'light' and 'put together'). Fig. 3.2 illustrates the system.

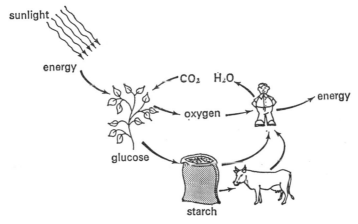

Fig. 3.2 Carbohydrates: formation and use

3.7 New Discoveries in Carbohydrate Nutrition

A general book on nutrition such as this cannot discuss in detail all the new discoveries which are being made about the composition of carbohydrates in food and the biochemical mechanisms by which they are used in the body. It is, however, important that you should always remember that although a great deal is known, knowledge is never complete. This is, indeed, the nature of science. Perhaps the most unexpected recent discovery has been the realization that the particular chemical structure of the sugar, lactose, calls for the presence in the human system of the appropriate enzyme, lactase, capable of dealing with it (see Section 2.3(c)). It now appears that although most adult Europeans possess adequate amounts of lactase in their intestine to enable them to digest and absorb the lactose present in the milk they drink, about 75 per cent of the coloured citizens of the United States and of certain African races are 'intolerant' to lactose and, in consequence, are actually ill if they drink milk. In China, nearly 90 per cent of the population are 'lactose-intolerant', and in Thailand the proportion is nearer 100 per cent.*

For many years, cows' milk has been considered to be a food of exceptionally high nutritional value. We can still accept this in so far as children and adults *in European countries* are concerned. We must now recognize, however,

* For a more detailed discussion see Pyke, M.: *Journal of the Society of Dairy Technology*, **24** (1971), 82.

that for most of the world's adult population, whole milk is actually harmful; it produces diarrhoea and other quite disagreeable symptoms of lactose intolerance.

The lesson to be learned from this, as from other new discoveries mentioned in later units, is that in nutrition, as in all other areas of science, new research may always supplement and modify what is already known.

Unit 4
Fat

4.1 Introduction

It is easy to recognize that *fat* is a different kind of substance from carbohydrates, such as the starches and sugars discussed in Unit 3, or from proteins, dealt with in Unit 5. The everyday concept of fat is a useful and valid one provided it is remembered that foods may contain two forms of fat.

Visible fat is a term sometimes used for the fat contributed to the diet by butter, margarine and other so-called *table fats* and by lard and cooking fats and oils. The term *fat* in relation to nutrition also includes vegetable and animal *oils* (not of course the petroleum oils used industrially for fuel or lubrication; these are *hydrocarbons* and are inedible, of no nutritional value and often poisonous as well). A *fat* is described as such if it is normally solid at room temperature, whereas an *oil* is a fat which remains in the melted state (that is to say, liquid) at room temperature. Both are 'fats' in the nutritional sense.

Invisible fat is an expression used to describe the fat contributed to the diet in fatty foods like meat and bacon. Even though some of this fat can actually be seen and could if desired be cut off and removed, many foods contain a proportion of fat incorporated in their substance. Nuts, for example, contain a considerable proportion of fat, as do herrings and mackerel, eggs and milk. The content of fat in some common foods is shown in the Appendix.

Foods like lard or butter, which the housewife thinks of as fats, do not always consist solely of fat but may contain an admixture of water, protein or other components. Sometimes, too, substances which are properly recognized as 'fat' may be made up of a mixture of different types of fatty compounds. Because this is so, the term *lipid* is used to cover all the diverse groups of chemical compounds which may be found in one or other of the recognizable culinary fats.

4.2 The Functions of Fat in Nutrition

(*a*) The primary function of fat in the diet arises from the fact that it is the most concentrated source of energy of all nutrients. Consequently, fat is a particularly valuable food for people who carry out heavy and exhausting muscular work. For many years, this was considered to be its only function although it was also accepted that fat made the diet more palatable. Bread and butter, besides providing more energy than dry bread, is easier and more agreeable to eat.

(b) Most fats consist of compounds of a number of different fatty acids. While all of these provide the body with energy, certain of them, called *essential fatty acids*, also seem to play a particular part in maintaining health (see also Section 4.5). It follows that a second nutritional function of fats is to provide the appropriate amounts of these essential fatty acids needed for health.

(c) Certain compounds which must be present in the diet in appropriate amounts occur dissolved in fat although they do not form a part of the substance of the fat itself. These are the so-called *fat-soluble vitamins*, vitamin A, vitamin D, vitamin E and vitamin K (see Units 13, 14 and 15). A third nutritional function of fat is therefore to serve as a vehicle for these fat-soluble vitamins.

(d) Besides these nutritional considerations, the stored fat in the body also has a protective function. Some organs—for example, the kidneys—are protected from accidental injury by the layers of fat which surround them; additionally, the sheet of fat cells (*adipose tissue*) which lies just below the skin in healthy people protects the body from excessive heat loss by acting as an insulator.

4.3   The Chemistry of Fats

(a) Triglycerides

Edible fats are in the main composed of compounds of *glycerol* (a sweet sticky colourless liquid popularly called ' glycerine') combined with *fatty acids*. The principal reason why one fat differs from another, that is to say, why olive oil is different from lard and both are different from butterfat, is because different fatty acids are combined with the glycerol which forms the backbone of their molecules, or if the same fatty acids are present, because they occur in different proportions. The chemical structure of glycerol, of three common fatty acids and of the way three molecules of fatty acids combine with one of glycerol to form fat, are shown below. It is because each molecule of fat contains *three* fatty-acid units that such fats are called *triglycerides*.

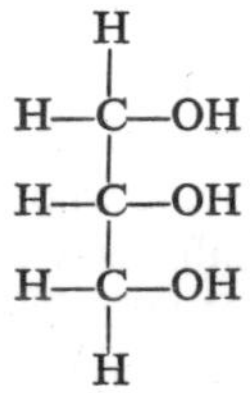

$$
\begin{array}{c}
\text{H} \\
|\\
\text{H--C--OH} \\
|\\
\text{H--C--OH} \\
|\\
\text{H--C--OH} \\
|\\
\text{H}
\end{array}
$$

glycerol

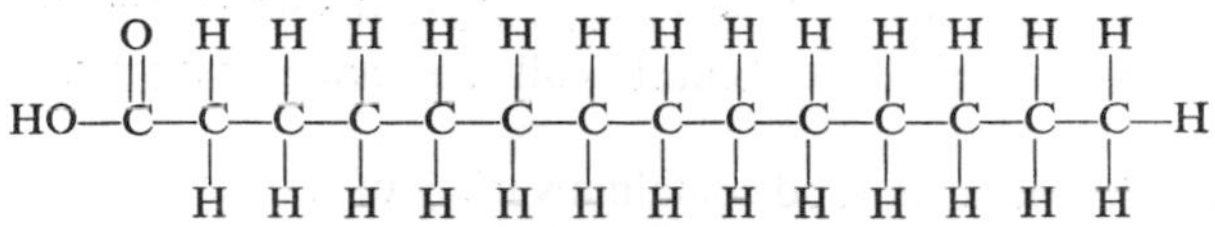

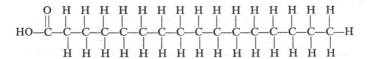

myristic acid

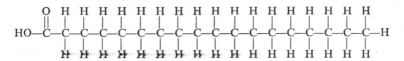

palmitic acid

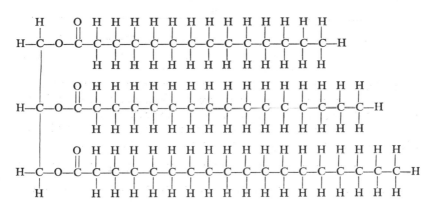

stearic acid

a molecule of fat

A molecule of fat may be composed of glycerol combined with three different fatty acids, with two the same and one different, or with three molecules
of the same kind. The diagram above shows glycerol combined with a molecule each of *myristic acid, palmitic acid* and *stearic acid*. However, numerous
other fatty acids are found in different kinds of fat.

Saturated fatty acids. The three fatty acids shown in the diagram each contain
a long, straight chain of carbon atoms. The end carbon atom, to which the
oxygen atom and the hydroxyl (HO—) radical are attached to form a *carboxyl
group*, gives the molecule its acid nature. Each of the other carbon atoms
(except that at the other end of the chain) has two hydrogen atoms attached

to it. The presence of these pairs of hydrogen atoms along the whole length of the chain is characteristic of what chemists call a *saturated* fatty-acid molecule.

The common fats which occur in food contain a variety of saturated fatty acids.

Table 4.1 The saturated fatty acids

Name of acid	Total number of carbon atoms	Characteristic
Butyric	4	present in butter
Caproic	6	present in numerous fats; these fatty acids
Caprylic	8	possess a smell reminiscent of goats, hence
Capric	10	their names (*caper* is Latin for goat)
Lauric	12	widely distributed in common fats; the
Myristic	14	longer-chain fatty acids tend to be present
Palmitic	16	in higher proportions in harder fats such as
Stearic	18	lard

Unsaturated fatty acids. Although the saturated fatty acids are the main components of most common fats, a proportion of *unsaturated fatty acids* is also present. Three of these, like stearic acid, contain 18-carbon-atom (C_{18}) chains, but unlike stearic acid, not all the carbon atoms of the middle links of the chain are 'saturated' by having two hydrogen atoms linked to them; in these acids, two, four and six respectively of the carbon atoms each have only one attached hydrogen atom. The structures of these, together with that of a 20-carbon-atom (C_{20}) unsaturated fatty acid, are illustrated below:

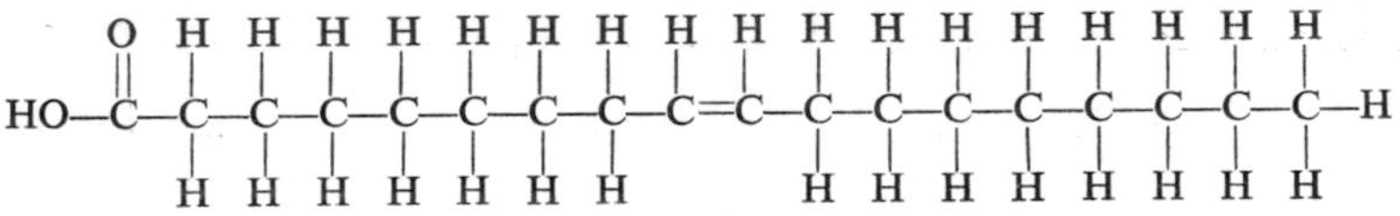

```
      O  H  H  H  H  H  H  H  H  H  H  H  H  H  H  H  H  H
      ‖  |  |  |  |  |  |  |  |     |  |  |  |  |  |  |  |  |
HO—C—C—C—C—C—C—C—C—C=C—C—C—C—C—C—C—C—C—H
         |  |  |  |  |  |  |        |  |  |  |  |  |  |  |
         H  H  H  H  H  H  H        H  H  H  H  H  H  H  H
```
oleic acid

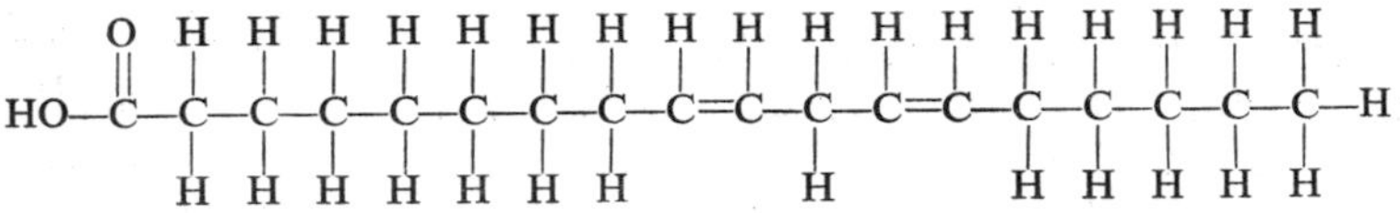

```
      O  H  H  H  H  H  H  H  H  H  H  H  H  H  H  H  H  H
      ‖  |  |  |  |  |  |  |  |     |  |     |  |  |  |  |  |
HO—C—C—C—C—C—C—C—C—C=C—C—C=C—C—C—C—C—C—H
         |  |  |  |  |  |  |        |           |  |  |  |  |
         H  H  H  H  H  H  H        H           H  H  H  H  H
```
linoleic acid

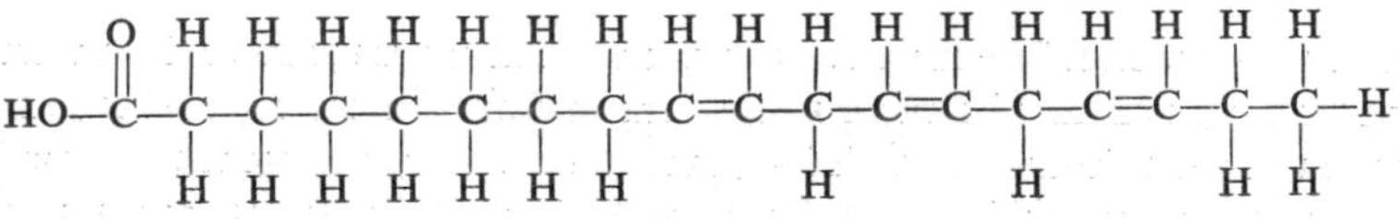

```
      O  H  H  H  H  H  H  H  H  H  H  H  H  H  H  H  H  H
      ‖  |  |  |  |  |  |  |  |     |  |     |  |     |  |  |
HO—C—C—C—C—C—C—C—C—C=C—C—C=C—C—C=C—C—C—H
         |  |  |  |  |  |  |        |        |        |  |
         H  H  H  H  H  H  H        H        H        H  H
```
linolenic acid

$$\text{HO}-\overset{\displaystyle O}{\overset{\|}{C}}-\overset{\displaystyle H}{\underset{\displaystyle H}{C}}-\overset{\displaystyle H}{\underset{\displaystyle H}{C}}-\overset{\displaystyle H}{C}-C\overset{\displaystyle H}{=}C-\overset{\displaystyle H}{C}-C\overset{\displaystyle H}{=}C-\overset{\displaystyle H}{C}-C\overset{\displaystyle H}{=}C-\overset{\displaystyle H}{C}-C\overset{\displaystyle H}{=}C-\overset{\displaystyle H}{C}-\overset{\displaystyle H}{C}-\overset{\displaystyle H}{\underset{\displaystyle H}{C}}-\overset{\displaystyle H}{\underset{\displaystyle H}{C}}-\overset{\displaystyle H}{\underset{\displaystyle H}{C}}-H$$

arachidonic acid

Fatty acids in different types of fat

(*i*) *Vegetable fats and oils*. Oils derived from maize, peanuts, palm kernels, wheat germ and other plant seeds are mainly composed of C_{14}, C_{16} and C_{18} saturated fatty acids (myristic, palmitic and stearic) together with substantial proportions of the unsaturated fatty acids—oleic and linoleic and sometimes linolenic acids. Coconut oil is exceptional in being mostly made up of saturated fatty acids, including the C_{12} *lauric acid*.

(*ii*) *Animal fats*. Palmitic acid is the predominant fatty acid in most animal fats. Oleic acid is also present; although this is an unsaturated fatty acid it only contains one so-called *unsaturated double bond* in its molecular structure. As Table 4.2 shows, the main difference between the animal and vegetable fats is that the animal fats contain much less of the more unsaturated linoleic acid, with two unsaturated double bonds, and no linolenic acid with three unsaturated double bonds.

(*iii*) *Dairy fats*. Butterfat contains C_4, C_6, C_8, C_{12} and C_{14} fatty acids as well as the more common C_{16} and C_{18} fatty acids.

(*iv*) *Marine oils*. Fish oils and oils and fats from marine animals contain, besides the common fatty acids, the more unsaturated fatty acids, linolenic and arachidonic acid containing three and four unsaturated double bonds in their molecules.

Table 4.2 shows the amounts of the more important fatty acids present in a number of different vegetable, animal and marine fats and oils; however, other fatty acids also occur in smaller proportions.

The figures in Table 4.2 can only be taken as a rough indication of the proportions of the different fatty acids to be expected in an *average* sample of an oil or fat. The composition of a particular specimen of a vegetable fat will be affected by the weather, the soil and cultural conditions in general, while the composition of animal and marine fats is influenced by the nature of the diet of the animal concerned, the total availability of food, the physiological state of the animal and the temperature of its environment.

(*b*) Fatty Compounds other than Triglycerides

Triglycerides are the main components of fat. There are, however, other fatty compounds which are present both in foods and in the body.

Phospholipids. These are present in vegetable oils and in the fats of animal tissues, in blood and in egg yolk. Up to 2–3 per cent of phospholipids may be found in crude soya-bean oil or maize oil, although most of this will be

Table 4.2   The percentage of the principal fatty acids in various fats and oils

| | Saturated fatty acids | | | | Unsaturated fatty acids | | | |
	lauric (C_{12})	myristic (C_{14})	palmitic (C_{16})	stearic (C_{18})	oleic	linoleic	lino-lenic	arachi-donic
Vegetable fats								
Coconut oil	48	17	9	2	6	3		
Cottonseed oil		1	29	4	24	40		
Linseed oil			6	4	22	16	52	
Maize oil			13	4	29	54		
Olive oil			16	2	65	15		
Palm oil		1	48	4	38	9		
Peanut oil			6	5	61	22		
Sunflower oil			8	3	13	75	1	
Sesame oil			10	5	40	43		
Soya-bean oil			11	4	25	51	9	
Sunflower-seed oil			11	6	29	52		
Wheatgerm oil			13	4	20	55	7	
Animal fats								
Beef fat		3	25	24	42	2		
Butterfat (cow)	4	12	29	11	25	2		
(goat)	6	12	28	6	21	4		
Lard		3	24	18	42	9		
Mutton fat		5	25	30	36	4		
Fat in egg yolk*			32	4	43	8		
Marine fats								
Cod-liver oil		6	8	1	20	29	25	10
Herring oil		7	12	1	12	20	26	22
Menhaden oil		6	16	1	15	30	19	12
Pilchard oil		5	14	3	12	18	18	14
Sardine oil		6	10	2	13	14	26	29
Whale oil		9	16	2	14	37	12	7

* Fat in egg yolk also contains 13% of a C_{22} saturated fatty acid.

removed from refined oil. Their molecular structure comprises a glycerol stem to which two fatty-acid units are linked. In place of the third fatty acid which would be found in a triglyceride, the remaining linkage is taken up by a *phosphate* radical, with which in turn a variety of quite complex substances can be combined. Phospholipids have various functions in the body concerned with the absorption of fat and its transfer from one site to another, and also with the functioning of the nerves and other physiological mechanisms. While these biologically active substances are mostly produced within the body itself, the fact that they also occur in foodstuffs (being, of course, a part of the functioning system of the animals and plants used as food) makes it important for nutritionists to be aware of their existence. *Lecithin*, a phospholipid prepared from soya-bean oil or egg yolk, is added to many manufactured foods, including margarine, chocolate and cooking fats, where its emulsifying properties are useful in preventing fatty ingredients from separating out.

While phospholipids are necessary for the body's function, they are apparently produced without difficulty in the body itself and do not need to be specially provided in the diet. Nor is there evidence that any harm arises from eating foods particularly rich in phospholipids. Although it has nothing to do with nutrition, it is nevertheless interesting that cobras and some other poisonous snakes have a special kind of enzyme in their venom. This enzyme, *lecithinase A*, can split off one of the two fatty acids in the lecithin molecule, which, thus subtly altered, is able in some way not fully understood to break down the red blood cells of the cobra's victim and thus kill him.

Sterols. These are fatty substances with quite a complicated molecular structure, which are found in a concentration of 1 per cent or less in animal and vegetable fats. They do not occur linked to glycerol but they are able to form chemical linkages with fatty acids. There are several classes of sterol, differing in detail from one another, but they all possess the characteristic four-ring framework of carbon atoms shown below.

sterol skeleton

Sterols play a part both in nutrition and in physiology. That is to say, some of them are essential constituents of the diet: *vitamin D*, for example, is derived from a sterol. Others, like *cholesterol*, which can be manufactured in the body, can occur in excessive amounts in the diet and may be harmful. Other sterols again, such as *progesterone* and *testosterone*, have no dietary significance but function as sex hormones, either when produced naturally by the body or when given in medicinal preparations.

4.4 Saturated Fatty Acids, Cholesterol and Heart Disease

There are a number of causes of heart disease. Two of the most important are high blood pressure (*hypertension*) and so-called hardening of the arteries (*atherosclerosis*). Atherosclerosis is known to be associated with an increased concentration of cholesterol in the blood (*hypercholesterolaemia*). Both these conditions are connected with obesity (overweight), and are therefore also in some degree the result of too much to eat and too little exercise and are thus a factor of nutrition (see Unit 8).

Although cholesterol is produced naturally in the body, and its production is also affected by exercise and overweight, the level of cholesterol in the blood is also influenced in a very direct way by the amount of fat in the diet and by the kind of fat which is included. Hypercholesterolaemia is associated with the consumption of a diet containing large amounts of those fats which are mainly composed of saturated fatty acids.

A reduction in the cholesterol level of the blood is brought about by eating fats containing several unsaturated double bonds in their molecular structure. These fatty acids in which two or more double bonds occur are called *poly-unsaturated*; the commonest examples are linoleic, linolenic and, in fish oils, arachidonic acids.

Using Table 4.2, you can see now why it is that an excessive consumption of animal fats—that is the fat from beef, mutton and pork, from egg yolk which is itself comparatively rich in cholesterol, and from butter, all of which contain only small amounts of polyunsaturated fatty acids—should be avoided by people susceptible to heart disease and who take little exercise. On the other hand, the consumption of vegetable oils and particularly marine oils, both of which (except for coconut oil and palm oil) contain significant amounts of the polyunsaturated fatty acids, has been shown to reduce the level of blood cholesterol. Oleic acid, however, the molecule of which contains only one double bond, has little effect one way or the other on hypercholesterolaemia.

A comparison of diets containing mainly saturated fatty acids and those with a good proportion of polyunsaturated fatty acids in them, and of the liability of the people eating them to die of heart disease, was made in a study carried out in Finland between 1959 and 1971. The inmates of two separate institutions were studied; altogether these provided nearly 30 000 'person–years' of experience by the time the trial was over. The experiment consisted simply in recording the number of those who died of heart attacks during the twelve years of the trial. During the first six-year period of the trial, the normal diet was served to the people in one institution while in the other the proportion of fats containing saturated fatty acids was reduced and that of fats containing polyunsaturated fatty acids increased. At the end of the first six years the situation was reversed: the proportion of fats rich in polyunsaturated fatty acids was increased in the first institution and the normal diet restored at the second.

The experimental diet differed from that normally eaten in two important respects and two only:

(*a*) Ordinary milk was replaced by skim milk to which was added an amount of soya-bean oil equivalent to the butterfat content of the cream that had been removed. (This kind of mixture when homogenized is called *filled milk*.)

(*b*) Butter and the standard margarines normally used were replaced by a special soft margarine made with fats containing polyunsaturated fatty acids.

The average concentration of cholesterol in the blood plasma of the people in the first institution at the end of the first period was 270 mg per 100 ml, compared with only 235 mg per 100 ml at the end of the second period. On the other hand, the average cholesterol level of the people in the second institution was 230 mg per 100 ml at the end of the first period, but had risen to 272 mg per 100 ml at the end of the second. Furthermore, when appropriate adjustments were made to allow for any differences in the average ages of the inmates during the two six-year periods, it was found that while the normal diet was high in fats containing saturated fatty acids, the average death-rate from coronary heart disease was 14.08 per 1 000 person–years for men and 7.90 per 1 000 person–years for women. During the time when fats containing polyunsaturated fatty acids were being used, the death-rates were 6.61 and 5.21 per 1 000 person–years for men and women respectively. (Normal death-rates from coronary heart disease are always considerably lower for women than for men of the same age.)

In the United States, nutritionists have been seriously concerned at the rate at which coronary heart disease had been increasing; 666 000 people died there from this cause in a year. The Food and Nutrition Board of the National Research Council and the American Medical Association in fact recommended in 1972 that there should be a 'partial replacement of the dietary sources of saturated fat with sources of unsaturated fat' and 'a reduction in the consumption of foods rich in cholesterol'. The ways in which more unsaturated, and particularly more polyunsaturated, fats can be obtained by substituting vegetable and fish oils for animal fats can readily be seen from Table 4.2. Table 4.3 shows how the direct intake of cholesterol can be reduced by restricting the consumption of eggs, and especially dishes containing egg yolk, and avoiding such foods as brains, oysters, sweetbreads and fish roe. In short, since cholesterol only occurs in foods of animal origin, the amount of cholesterol eaten can be reduced by increasing the proportion of cereals, vegetable fats and oils and fruit and vegetables in the diet.

However, in spite of all the circumstantial evidence associating dietary fats with coronary heart disease, positive proof of the association is still lacking; nor do all investigators agree what inferences should be drawn from the studies so far reported (see also Section 4.7).

4.5 Essential Fatty Acids

The three most widely distributed polyunsaturated fatty acids, linoleic acid, linolenic acid and arachidonic acid, are often described as *essential fatty acids* (EFA); we have already discussed the importance of their effect on the concentration of blood cholesterol. When the term 'essential fatty acid' was first coined, evidence of their activity was based on experiments carried out on animals. In the absence of EFA from their diet, young rats grew more slowly than normal, and they developed a form of eczema. Other symptoms were also detected in a variety of creatures, including mice, dogs, calves, pigs, chickens and certain kinds of insects, when they were fed on diets entirely lacking in EFA. In a number of experimental trials carried out on human beings, however, it has not so far been definitely proved that any specific

Table 4.3   The cholesterol content of certain foods

Dairy produce	mg per 100 g	Fish	mg per 100 g
Egg yolk	1 500	Roe	300 or more
Whole egg	550	Oysters	200 or more
Egg white	0	Lobster	200
Butter	250	Crab	125
Cheese	100	Shrimps	125
Milk	11	Fish (most fillets)	70
Meat and meat 'offal'		Other foods	
Brains	2 000 or more	Lard	95
Kidney	375	Margarine (made partly	
Liver	300	from animal fat)	65
Sweetbreads	250	Margarine (made solely	
Heart	150	from vegetable fat)	0
Veal	90	Cereals and all other	
Pork	70	foods of vegetable	
Beef	70	origin	0
Mutton	65		
Chicken	60		

symptoms occur in man similar to those found in animals when these fatty acids are deficient in the diet.

4.6   The Main Sources of Fat in the Diet

The total amount of fat in the diet that people eat depends to some extent on their wealth; the food eaten in richer countries and by the more prosperous people in any particular country tends to contain a higher proportion of fat than does that of poorer people. This is due to the fact that in a conventional western diet, the categories of food listed below contribute the proportions of the total fats shown.

Table 4.4   The proportion of the total dietary fat contributed by different categories of food

	per cent
Butter, margarine, cooking fats and oils	40
Meat, bacon, poultry, fish	32
Milk, cheese and eggs	18
Bread, flour and other cereals	6
Miscellaneous	4

The contribution of fat made by different foods to the diet as a whole obviously depends both on the amount of any particular food eaten and the percentage of fat in the food. Table 4.5 lists the proportions of fat in a number of the more widely used foods.

Table 4.5   The fat content of certain foods

	g per 100 g		g per 100 g
Fats and oils		*Cereal products*	
Frying oil	99·9	Oatmeal	8·7
Lard, dripping, cooking		Wholemeal bread	3·1
fat	99·3	Barley	1·7
Margarine	85·3	White bread	1·7
Butter	82·5	Spaghetti	1·0
		Rice	1·0
Meat		Cornflakes	0·5
Bacon	28·2–61·1		
Pork	23·2–50·3	*Fruit and nuts*	
Lamb	20·4–52·5	Desiccated coconut	62·0
Beef	10·5–32·1	Brazil nuts	61·5
Duck	23·6	Almonds	53·5
Calf's liver	8·1	Walnuts	51·5
Chicken	6·7	Peanuts	49·0
Veal	2·7	Olives	8·8
		Avocado pears	8·0
Fish		All other fruits	trace
Fatty fish:			
herring	18·1	*Vegetables*	
kipper	11·4	Potatoes	trace
mackerel	8·5	Green vegetables	trace
canned salmon	6·0	Peas and beans	trace
Non-fatty fish:			
plaice	1·8		
sole	1·3		
cod	0·5		
haddock	0·5		
Dairy produce			
Cream	48·0		
Cheddar cheese	34·5		
Gorgonzola cheese	31·1		
'Processed' cheese	30·0		
Edam cheese	22·9		
Eggs	12·3		
Condensed milk	9·2		
Milk	3·8		

The figures in Table 4.5 can be used only as a rough indication of the percentage of fat in different classes of food. The proportion of fat actually present in a particular sample of, for example, pork or lamb may be much more or much less than the figures given. Again, the amount of fat in fish like herring or mackerel varies with the season of the year, and is also affected by the maturity and physiological condition of the fish at the time it is caught. It must also be remembered that the fat content of what is eaten as, say, potato or fish will be changed if any fat is added during the course of cooking; the way in which cooking affects the composition of food is discussed in Section 19.2(c). Finally, it is worth repeating that the significance of the figures given in the table depends on the *amount* of any particular food that is commonly eaten. For example, one obtains 18.5 g of fat in drinking 500 ml (about a pint) of milk which contains 3.7 per cent of fat, but only 7.7 g of fat from the 15 g of walnuts in a slice of cake, even though the walnuts contain 51.5 per cent of fat.

4.7   Desirable Proportions of Fat for Good Nutrition

Fat in the body, as people with a tendency to obesity know all too well, can be produced from a surplus consumption of carbohydrate. Since it is not entirely certain whether human beings require a supply of essential fatty acids (EFA) in their diet (Section 4.5), it cannot be asserted definitely that any fat at all is absolutely *necessary* in the diet to satisfy the strictly nutritional demands of the body. On the other hand fat is valuable not only as a concentrated source of energy, a source of EFA and a vehicle for fat-soluble vitamins (see Section 4.2), but also as an essential factor in good cooking in both western and tropical countries.

(*a*) To provide the minimum amount of fat to produce a palatable diet, sufficient must be present to contribute about 20 per cent of its energy value (this term is explained in Section 6.2).

(*b*) The diet eaten by wealthier people, both in eastern and in western countries, usually contains sufficient fat to provide 40 per cent of the energy value.

(*c*) People doing heavy muscular work and consequently requiring a diet high in energy value can be recommended to obtain a high proportion of their total kilojoules from fat. It has been suggested that those expending less than about 12 500 kJ a day should eat an amount of fat providing up to 20–25 per cent of their total kilojoules, but that people needing more than 12 500 kJ a day may safely obtain 30–35 per cent as fat.

It is interesting that in 1968, the United States National Academy of Sciences recommended that in order best to avoid coronary heart attacks middle-aged men should restrict the amount of fat in their diet to that providing 25 per cent of the total energy value; however, the proportion provided by fat in the United States, Denmark and Great Britain—all rich countries in which heart attacks are a serious public-health problem—are actually 42, 38 and 36 per cent respectively.

4.8   Some Special Features of the Absorption of Fat

Since the functions of the body are carried out almost entirely in an *aqueous medium*—that is to say that, derived as we are from remote ancestors who lived in the sea, our blood and the living tissues through which it runs operate in *water*—it follows that fat, which is insoluble in water, must be dealt with by the body in some special manner. We saw in Unit 2 how a fat can be broken down chemically into *soaps* of its constituent fatty acids, together with free *glycerol*. Both soaps and glycerol are water-soluble and can, therefore, be readily absorbed through the intestine and transported to appropriate storage depots or used for energy. This, however, is not the only way in which dietary fats are absorbed into the system; indeed, we have not yet enough information to say exactly how fats are absorbed and used, but we know of at least three mechanisms for this purpose.

(*a*) Some of the fat consumed is split up by *pancreatic lipase*, converted into glycerol and free fatty acids which are then converted by the alkali present into soaps (the process of *saponification*), absorbed through the intestinal lining and almost immediately re-synthesized into triglyceride fat (see Section 2.3).

(*b*) Part of the fat is split by lipase, not completely into free fatty acids but to form compounds called monoglycerides and diglycerides, in which one or two fatty acids respectively remain linked to glycerol. These are powerful *emulsifying agents* as are the *bile salts* which are also present, and their effect is to cause a proportion of the undigested fatty material to become so finely dispersed as almost to become soluble.

(*c*) Part of the long-chain fats pass into the body actually in the form of minute droplets, the so-called *chylomicrons*. These are stabilized and prevented from separating out and merging into one another by the phospholipids. For some time after a fatty meal has been eaten, these droplets are visible as a milky coloration of the liquid in the *lymph ducts* constituting the *lymphatic system* (see Fig. 2.5).

4.9 New Knowledge about Fats

Modern research is continuously throwing new light on the nutritionist's understanding of fats. The significance of polyunsaturated fatty acids, their influence on the level of cholesterol in the blood and their function, if any, for man as 'essential fatty acids' are all under close scrutiny at present. Again, even though the chemical structure of triglyceride fats is well established, it now appears that not all of the fat occurs in the form of these so-called *glycerol esters*. A limited proportion occurs as *ethers*: that is to say, the ester group, $>C-O-\overset{\displaystyle O}{\overset{\|}{C}}-CH_2-$, is replaced by the ether group, $>C-O-CH_2-$, in these molecules.

It is also interesting to find that the main fatty acids making up common fats contain only even numbers of carbon atoms (see Table 4.1), and indeed until recently it was believed that *no* fatty acids containing odd numbers of carbon atoms were present in natural fats (odd-numbered fatty acids do occur in synthetic fats). But, although there is little information about their nutritional importance, it is now clear that a small proportion of these fatty acids is actually found in most natural fats.

Further new information suggests that the polyunsaturated fatty acid *linoleic acid* may be closely involved in brain development, and that damage may be caused by an inadequate supply of this compound during the period when the brain is growing very rapidly, during the weeks just before birth and for a few months afterwards.

Again, the lesson remains that nutritional knowledge is constantly becoming more detailed and complete for those who take the trouble to keep in touch with the progress of research.

Unit Five
Proteins and Amino Acids

5.1 Introduction

A man or woman cut off from all supplies of food or drink is in urgent need of *water* in order to stay alive—although, as we have said, water may reasonably be excluded from our definition of food and equally from the definition of nutrients, the food components which provide the nourishment needed to maintain the function and well-being of the living body. Water is rather the medium in which the life of the cells of the body goes on. The next most urgent need of the starved man would be some source of *energy*. This could be one or other of the digestible carbohydrates, such as starch or dextrins or one of the sugars; alternatively, it could be fat (Unit 6 deals with this topic in detail). Protein would also serve as an immediate source of energy but this is not the primary reason for its importance in the diet.

In many respects the different kinds of carbohydrates and fats are interchangeable so far as their nutritional value is concerned. If there is only a very little butter available, one can make up much of the nutritional value of the diet by eating more bread. Both carbohydrates and fats are in the main composed of carbon, hydrogen and oxygen. Protein is different; although much of a protein molecule consists of a carbon-atom framework (as do, indeed, all organic substances), each sub-unit of a protein molecule contains one or more atoms of *nitrogen* as an essential part of its structure.

5.2 The Chemistry of Proteins

Protein is what chemists call a *polymer*. That is to say, each molecule consists of a three-dimensional network of several thousand sub-units linked together in a pattern which is characteristic not only of the animal or plant of which the protein is a part, but characteristic also of each particular tissue within the living creature. The molecule can be visualized as being rather like a piece of sponge rubber looked at through a microscope, although that is a very much simplified picture. The complexity of protein can be appreciated when it is compared with man-made polymers like nylon, polyethylene or perspex. Although we are familiar with these in a wide variety of textures and consistencies, they are each composed of only one or two different sorts of repeating sub-units. Consider therefore the variety of different kinds of structure and composition possible in proteins, the molecules of which are built up out of up to 23 different kinds of sub-units. All the thousands of words in the dictionary are made up from just 26 different units, which can be arranged and rearranged in one dimension only, for the letters are always printed flat on the page, side by side along a straight line. In contrast, protein molecules are not only different because of the order in which the sub-units are arranged like links in the chains which make up the molecule, but also because the chains themselves may be twisted and convoluted up, down and across as well as along. The sub-units or links, the *monomers* from which the protein polymer is built up, are molecules of compounds called *amino acids*.

The Amino Acids which Make Up Proteins

An amino acid is an organic compound which contains in its molecular structure both the amino group, —NH$_2$, and the acidic carboxyl group, —CO$_2$H. The molecules of the particular amino acids which make up proteins all contain these two groups linked to the *same* carbon atom: that is, they all contain the grouping

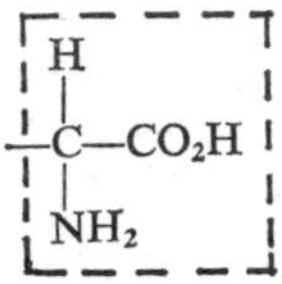

$$\begin{array}{c} H \\ | \\ -C-CO_2H \\ | \\ NH_2 \end{array}$$

The importance of this particular arrangement lies in the fact that it allows the individual amino acids to link together into an almost infinite number of different configurations. The amino acids which are most frequently found in food proteins have the following structures:

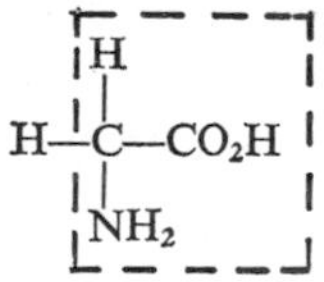

$$H-\overset{\overset{\displaystyle H}{|}}{\underset{\underset{\displaystyle NH_2}{|}}{C}}-CO_2H$$
glycine

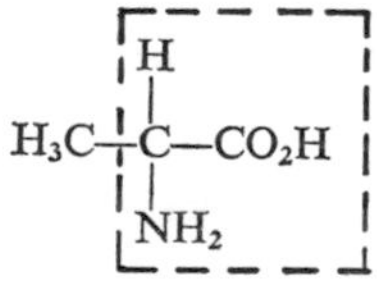

$$H_3C-\overset{\overset{\displaystyle H}{|}}{\underset{\underset{\displaystyle NH_2}{|}}{C}}-CO_2H$$
alanine

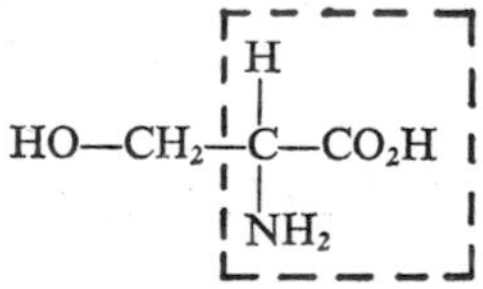

$$HO-CH_2-\overset{\overset{\displaystyle H}{|}}{\underset{\underset{\displaystyle NH_2}{|}}{C}}-CO_2H$$
serine

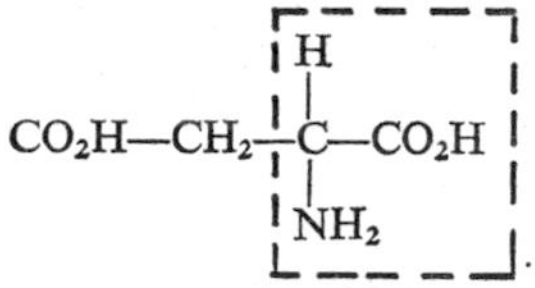

$$CO_2H-CH_2-\overset{\overset{\displaystyle H}{|}}{\underset{\underset{\displaystyle NH_2}{|}}{C}}-CO_2H$$
aspartic acid

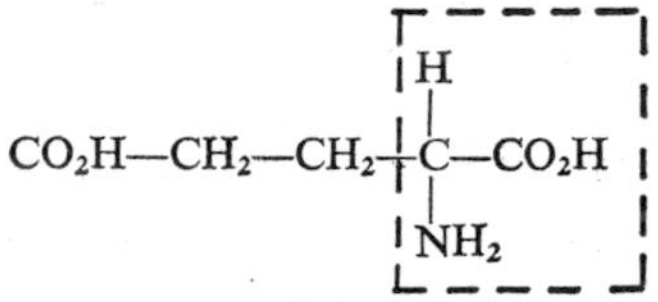

$$CO_2H-CH_2-CH_2-\overset{\overset{\displaystyle H}{|}}{\underset{\underset{\displaystyle NH_2}{|}}{C}}-CO_2H$$
glutamic acid

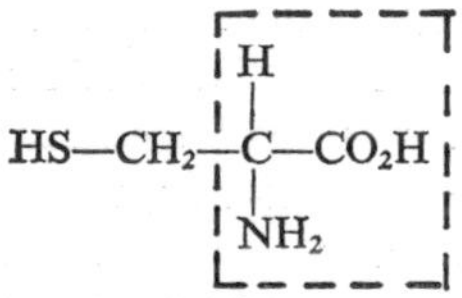

$$HS-CH_2-\overset{\overset{\displaystyle H}{|}}{\underset{\underset{\displaystyle NH_2}{|}}{C}}-CO_2H$$
cysteine

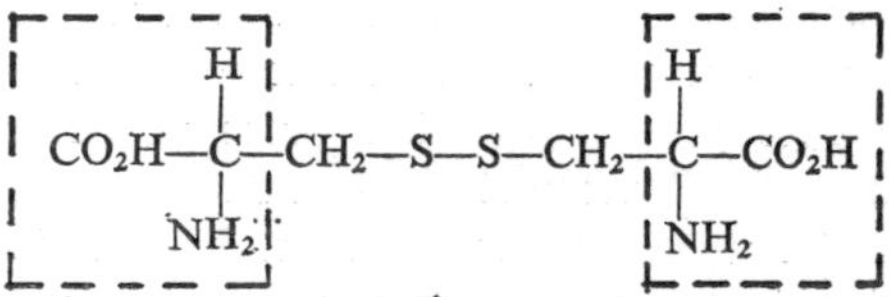

$$CO_2H-\overset{\overset{\displaystyle H}{|}}{\underset{\underset{\displaystyle NH_2}{|}}{C}}-CH_2-S-S-CH_2-\overset{\overset{\displaystyle H}{|}}{\underset{\underset{\displaystyle NH_2}{|}}{C}}-CO_2H$$
cystine

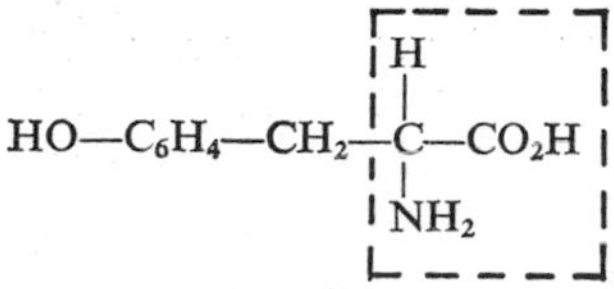

HO—C$_6$H$_4$—CH$_2$—C—CO$_2$H
 | H
 | NH$_2$

tyrosine

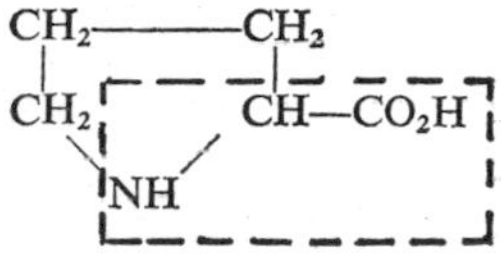

CH$_2$———CH$_2$
CH$_2$ CH—CO$_2$H
 NH

proline

To these must be added a second group called the *essential amino acids* (for a reason discussed below):

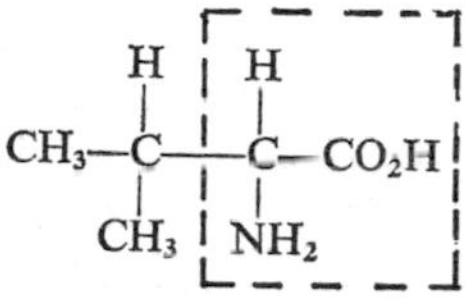

CH$_3$—C—C—CO$_2$H
 | CH$_3$ | NH$_2$

valine

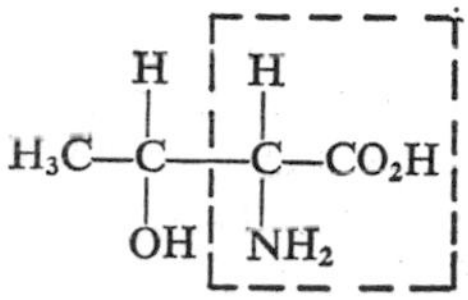

H$_3$C—C—C—CO$_2$H
 | OH | NH$_2$

threonine

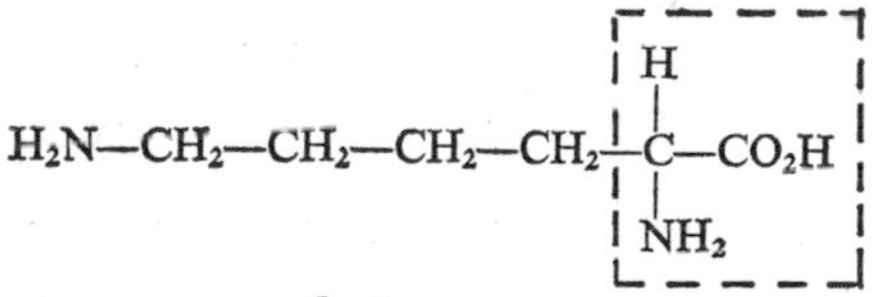

H$_2$N—CH$_2$—CH$_2$—CH$_2$—CH$_2$—C—CO$_2$H
 | NH$_2$

lysine

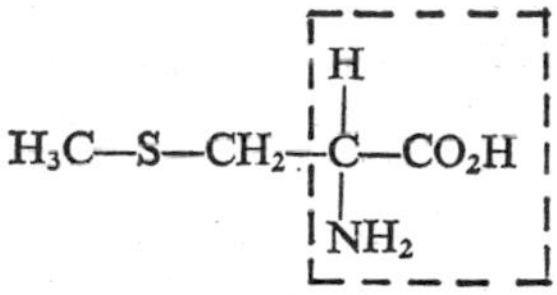

H$_3$C—S—CH$_2$—C—CO$_2$H
 | NH$_2$

methionine

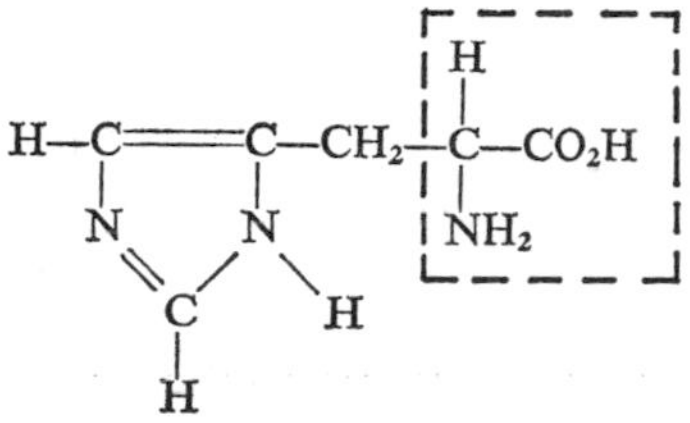

H—C══C—CH$_2$—C—CO$_2$H
 N   N   NH$_2$
   C   H
 H

histidine

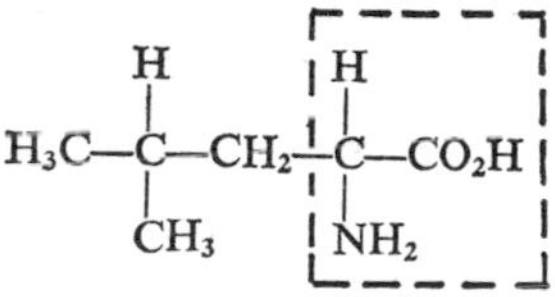

H$_3$C—C—CH$_2$—C—CO$_2$H
 | CH$_3$ | NH$_2$

leucine

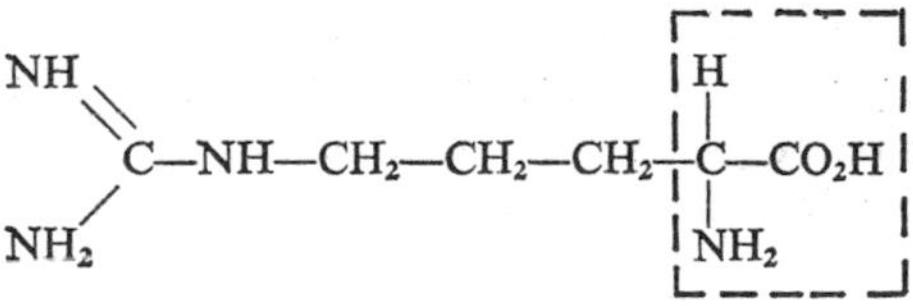

NH
  C—NH—CH$_2$—CH$_2$—CH$_2$—C—CO$_2$H
NH$_2$ NH$_2$

arginine

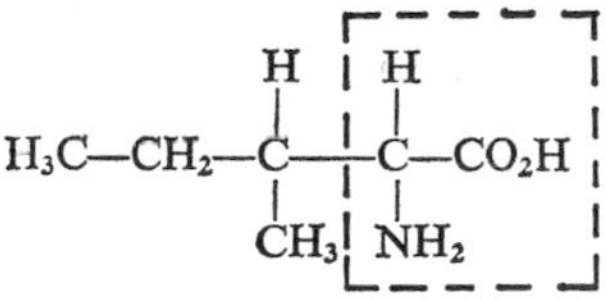

H$_3$C—CH$_2$—C—C—CO$_2$H
 | CH$_3$ | NH$_2$

isoleucine

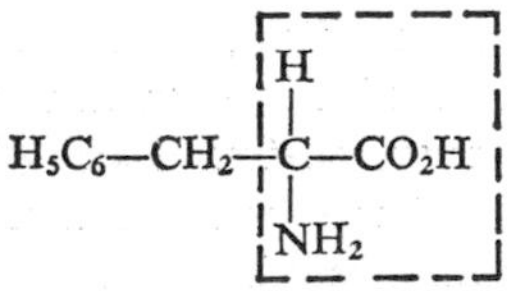

H$_5$C$_6$—CH$_2$—C—CO$_2$H
 | NH$_2$

phenylalanine

H—C
H—C   C══C—CH$_2$—C—CO$_2$H
   C   C—H   NH$_2$
     N
 H

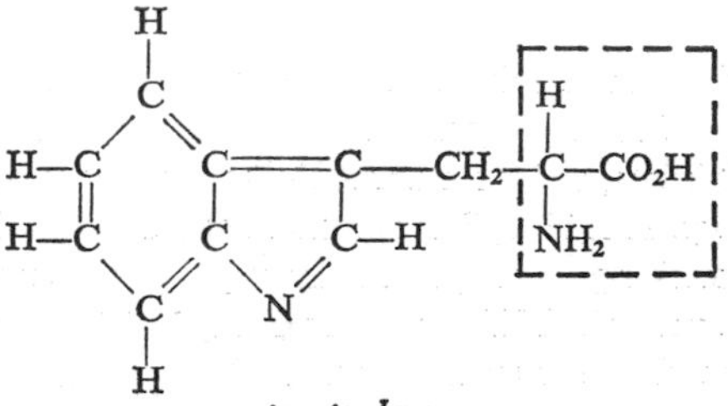

tryptophan

When proteins are eaten, they are split up by the digestive enzymes into their constituent amino acids. This is done partly by pepsin in the stomach and partly by trypsin and peptidases in the small intestine. The amino acids are then absorbed into the bloodstream and carried in it to various parts of the body, where one of three things may happen to them:

(a) They may constitute a 'pool' from which the various proteins needed for the growth or repair of the body's own tissues are built up. Just as the protein of lean chicken is obviously different from that of lean beef or white of egg, so also the compositions of the proteins of human brain or muscle tissues are different again. These differences are due to the varying proportions and arrangements of the different amino acids in the protein molecule.

(b) If this 'pool' in the tissues does not contain the right proportions of the different amino acids needed to build up the body proteins, some of them can be broken down and reconstituted into any of those named in the first list on pages 52–3. Those in the second list, however, cannot be produced quickly enough in the body to allow it to function properly. Sufficient of each of them must therefore be provided by the diet. This is why they are called *essential amino acids*. It is important to remember, however, that the term 'essential' is only relative.

(c) Some of the amino acids may be broken up, the carbon framework used as a source of energy and the nitrogen combined with carbon to form the soluble compound, *urea*, which is then filtered out of the blood by the kidneys and excreted in the urine.

$$O{=}C\underset{\diagdown NH_2}{\overset{\diagup NH_2}{}}$$

urea

If you are not particularly familiar with chemistry, you may well wonder why it is that protein, the basic building material of living creatures, is made up of the particular amino-acid units we have mentioned. In particular, you may be curious as to the nature of the special significance of the characteristic configuration,

$$-\overset{\overset{\textstyle H}{|}}{\underset{\underset{\textstyle NH_2}{|}}{C}}{-}CO_2H$$

found in all the nutritionally important amino acids.

Undoubtedly the chemistry of the amino acids is particularly significant in Nature, and is fundamental to the mechanism of life process on earth. As long ago as 1913, a German chemist named W. Löb observed that when an electric discharge was passed through a mixture of carbon monoxide gas (CO), ammonia (NH_3) and water (H_2O) (all of which may have been present in the earth's atmosphere before life began), the simplest of the amino acids, *glycine*, was formed. Forty-two years later, S. L. Miller in the United States, using the more advanced analytical methods then available, found that a mixture of *glycine, glutamic acid, aspartic acid, alanine* and three or four other amino acids were all produced together in these conditions. Later still, in 1964, S. W. Fox in Florida found that up to 14 amino acids are all formed simultaneously when an electric discharge is passed through a mixture of simple gases. It seems that when atoms of carbon, hydrogen, oxygen and nitrogen react together under these circumstances they have some inherent tendency to orientate themselves into the structure of one or other of the biologically important amino acids; but the mechanism by which this takes place is still unknown.

5.3 The Structure of Proteins

An important characteristic of the molecules of amino acids is that they are able to link themselves together into chains, and the chains themselves readily combine with each other either into a form similar to chain-mail armour or into an even more complex structure resembling a pot-scourer or a tangled ball of wool. This is why proteins are found in such different forms as hair, which is springy and resistant, the tough flexible material we call gristle, or the viscous liquid of egg white.

When several amino acids link together, the combination is called a *peptide* and has the kind of chemical structure shown below.

$$
\begin{array}{ccccc}
\text{H} & & \text{H} & \text{O} & \\
| & & | & \| & \\
\text{H—C—CO}_2\text{H} + \text{NH}_2 & \longrightarrow & \text{H—C——C——NH} & + \text{H}_2\text{O} \\
| & | & | & | & \\
\text{NH}_2 & \text{H—C—CO}_2\text{H} & \text{NH}_2 & \text{H—C—CO}_2\text{H} & \\
& | & & | & \\
& \text{H} & & \text{H} &
\end{array}
$$

glycine	glycine	glycylglycine
(two molecules of amino acid)		*(one molecule of a peptide)*

Two amino-acid molecules having linked together, the product (a *dipeptide*) can then readily link with a third amino-acid molecule, and so on until a structure of several thousand amino acids has been put together. This structure is a protein molecule: three different kinds of protein molecules are shown diagrammatically in Fig. 5.1.

Fig. 5.1 gives only a very simplified impression of the complexity of the chemistry of all the different proteins which go to make up a living body. When the second half of the twentieth century is discussed by future historians, it may well be celebrated as the time when scientists discovered how the particular kinds of protein are put together to make up a living creature. Each individual begins as a single cell, containing the molecule which carries with it all the influences of its heredity. This molecule, called *deoxyribonucleic acid* (DNA), has the form of two long interlocking corkscrews held together like the two halves of a zip-fastener. The pattern of the 'teeth' of this zip-fastener arrangement acts as a guide by which the amino acids, both those derived from food and the others produced from them, are linked together

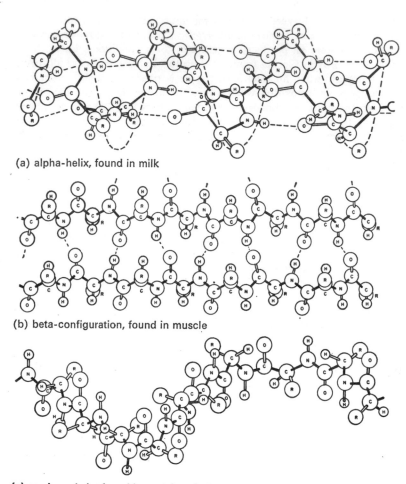

(a) alpha-helix, found in milk

(b) beta-configuration, found in muscle

(c) random chain, found in protein solutions

Fig. 5.1 Protein structures

in such a way that from one cell the proteins are built up so as to produce a mouse, and from another (containing DNA of a different pattern) there grows a man.

The remarkable discovery of the role of DNA in the building up of proteins of subtly different constitution has led us to further insight into the way a child grows in such a manner that its various tissues enlarge in a harmonious relation to each other. Even more marked than the differences between proteins from different parts of an individual are the differences between proteins from different people; as you will probably know, elaborate precautions are necessary if protein is to be transferred from one person to another, as in a kidney transplant. Differences between the proteins of different kinds of animals are still more marked, and of course the differences between proteins from animals and plants are greater still. All these differences arise from the various code patterns of the DNA which guides the building up of the proteins. Although it is interesting for its own sake to know something of the structure of different types of protein, and it is of practical importance to food technologists and cooks to understand the physical properties of the proteins of meat or milk, the special behaviour of egg proteins or of the protein gelatin, these are only of incidental significance to nutritionists. This is because these protein structures eaten as food are broken down by the enzymes of the stomach and small intestine (Section 2.3) and the resulting fragments are absorbed into the tissues as separate amino acids.

5.4 The Protein Content of Different Foods

Meat, cheese, fish, peas, beans and nuts are all commonly described as 'protein' foods. This, however, is an over-simplification. Almost all foods contribute some protein to the diet, except refined foods like cooking oils or sugar, important constituents of western diets, which contain none at all, and sago and tapioca, important in the east, which contain very little. Representative figures are shown in Table 5.1.

Again we must emphasize that the figures in this table can only give a general idea of the proportion of protein likely to be present in a particular type of foodstuff. The composition of an individual helping of any product may be different. For example, the fat content of meat or fish may vary from sample to sample. The exact moisture content will also affect the proportion of protein expressed as a percentage of the total weight. Also, in considering the significance of percentage figures, the total weight of food likely to be eaten must be taken into account. For example, a person will probably eat a greater weight of white bread (containing 8.3 per cent of protein) than egg (containing 11.9 per cent of protein). Bread may therefore contribute more to the *total* protein content of the diet than an egg.

5.5 The Main Sources of Protein in the Diet

An individual in a western community will probably obtain the protein he needs from various kinds of foods roughly in the proportions given in Table 5.2.

The figures given in this table imply that 47 per cent of the total supply of protein in a particular diet from which the calculations were made was derived from *animal* sources (dairy produce, meat, fish, poultry and egg) and the remaining 53 per cent from *vegetable* sources. Animal protein is generally of greater nutritional value than vegetable protein, for reasons discussed in Section 5.6. It follows, therefore, that the proportion of the total protein derived from animal sources is a matter of nutritional importance: that is, there are problems in designing a diet of good nutritional value from plant

Table 5.1   The protein content of certain foods

Meat	g per 100 g	Pulses and nuts	g per 100 g
Corned beef	22·3	Soya flour	40·3
Rabbit	21·0	Peanuts	28·1
Chicken	20·8	Lentils	23·8
Whale	20·6	Dried peas	22·1
Veal	19·2	Haricot beans	21·4
Calf's liver	16·5	Brazil nuts	13·8
Beef (fresh)	14·8	Walnuts	12·5
Lamb	13·0	Desiccated coconut	6·6
Pork	12·0	Chestnuts	2·3
Fish		Cereals	
Lobster	21·2	Oatmeal	12·1
Whiting	19·9	Wholemeal flour	11·6
Crab	19·2	White flour	10·0
Salmon	19·1	Maize	10·0
Cod	18·0	Wholemeal bread	9·6
Herring	16·0	White bread	8·3
Haddock	15·9	Rye	8·0
Plaice	15·3	Barley	7·7
Eel	14·4	Rice	6·2
Dairy produce		Fruit and vegetables	
Dried egg	43·4	Green peas	5·8
Dried skimmed milk	37·2	Cauliflower	3·4
Dried whole milk	26·6	Spinach	2·7
Cheese	25·4	Potato	2·1
Egg	11·9	Dates	2·0
Condensed milk	8·5	Cabbage	1·5
Evaporated milk	8·2	Bananas	1·1
Liquid milk	3·3	Turnip	0·8
Butter	0·5	Apple	0·3

Table 5.2   The proportions of the total dietary protein derived from different categories of food

	per cent
Bread, flour and other cereal products	40
Dairy produce	20
Meat	17
Fish and poultry	6
Potatoes	6
Eggs	4
Miscellaneous	7

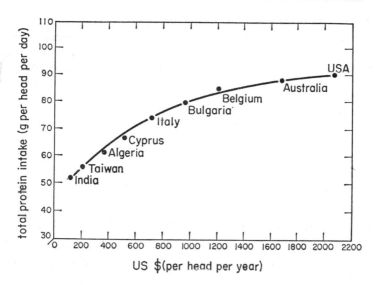

Fig. 5.2 Effect of income on total protein intake

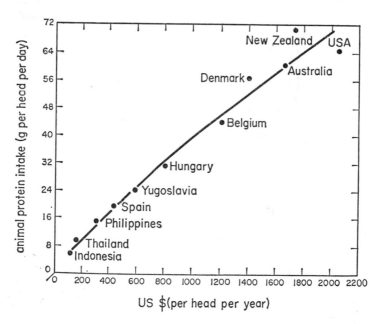

Fig. 5.3 Effect of income on animal protein intake

and vegetable foods alone, or, to put the matter a little differently, diets containing little or no animal protein tend to be nutritionally unsatisfactory. The practical implications of the relationship between the total protein intake, the proportion of animal protein in this total, and the influence of poverty or wealth on this proportion can be seen from Figs 5.2 and 5.3. These statistics, collected in 1964, indicate that in a country where the average income per person amounted to only $200, as little as about 17 per cent of dietary protein was of animal origin. When the income was $600, the proportion of animal protein rose to 36 per cent. With an income of $1 200, animal protein made up 55 per cent of the total, while in affluent countries like Australia and the USA with incomes around $1 800 a head, about 70 per cent of the larger total amount of protein consumed was derived from animal sources.

5.6   The Nutritional Value of Different Proteins

The chart in Fig. 5.4 shows the relative proportions of eight essential amino acids in two kinds of animal protein, those from milk and meat, and in two vegetable proteins, those from wheat and maize.

The chart shows that the two animal proteins both contain several times as much *lysine* as either of the two vegetable proteins. This is one of the main reasons why most animal proteins are of higher *biological value* (that is to say, they are more nourishing) than vegetable proteins. The proportion of *tryptophan* in maize protein is evidently also very small, and the amount of

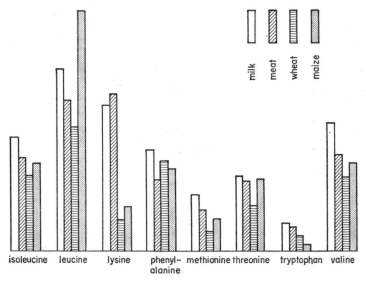

Fig. 5.4 Composition of different proteins

methionine in both the cereal proteins is little more than half that present in the animal proteins. Although students of nutrition are not expected to memorize the amounts of the different essential amino acids present in various proteins, it is interesting to see from Table 5.3 how amino-acid contents vary.

Table 5.3 The amounts of essential amino acids in certain proteins (mg per g of nitrogen)

	isoleu-cine	leucine	lysine	phenyl-alanine	methio-nine	threo-nine	trypto-phan	valine	protein score as measure of excellence
Amino-acid combination estimated as ideal for man	270	306	270	180	144	180	90	270	100
Egg protein	428	565	396	368	196	310	106	460	100
Beef	332	515	540	256	154	275	75*	345	83
Milk protein	402	628	497	334	190	272	85*	448	80
Fish	317	474	549	231	178	283	62*	327	70
Oat protein	302	436	212*	309	84*	192	74*	348	79
Rice protein	322	535	236*	307	142*	241	65*	415	72
Flour protein	262*	442	126*	322	78*	174	69*	262	47
Maize protein	293	827	179*	284	117*	249	38*	327	42
Soya protein	333	484	395	309	86*	247	86*	328	73
Pea protein	336	504	438	290	77*	230	74*	317	58
Potato protein	260*	304	326	285	87*	237	72*	339	56
Cassava	118*	184*	310	133*	22*	136*	131	144	22

* Less than the estimated ideal proportion.

Although Table 5.3 clearly indicates how cereal proteins lacking in lysine could be supplemented with soya and other bean protein, the 'score' of each protein given in the last column is based on somewhat imprecise tests of what biological excellence is. These values are derived from a variety of feeding tests, some carried out on experimental animals and some on people. There are two basic difficulties, however, in measuring in exact terms the nutritional quality of any particular protein. The first is that, as we have already pointed out, 'essential' amino acids are only essential because the rate at which they can be manufactured in the body is too slow to keep up with the need for supplies of them to combine with those which are more readily available, in order to make up a pool of amino acids which contains the proper proportions for building up the proteins the body needs. The second difficulty is that the biological value of a particular protein will be affected by the *total* amount of the protein present in the diet. Obviously, if very little protein is available, what there is will serve the body best if it contains the right proportion of amino acids. If, however, there is ample protein in the diet and some to spare there may be sufficient of any particular amino acid, simply because of the quantity of protein eaten. When the diet's protein content is derived from a good mixture of protein-containing foods, it will have a higher biological value than if the same amount of protein were derived from a single food. This capacity of proteins to make good one another's deficiencies is known as their *supplementary* or *complementary* value.

The biological value of protein is most commonly expressed in one of two ways:

(*a*) *The protein efficiency ratio* (*PER*) is measured by feeding young rats on a diet in which the only source of protein is the particular food, the protein quality of which is being tested. Conditions are quite carefully controlled and the diet is made up to contain exactly 10 per cent of protein. The PER is defined as the average gain in weight of the rats per gram of protein eaten.

(*b*) *The net protein utilization* (*NPU*) is also measured by feeding experimental animals, usually rats; but instead of assessing the animals' growth, this index of protein quality is measured by weighing the amount of the test food eaten and determining the weight of nitrogen in it by chemical analysis. This weight is taken as a measure of the amount of protein consumed; it is then compared with the amount of nitrogen retained in the rats' bodies, calculated from measurements of the amount of nitrogen which is excreted in the urine and faeces of the rats over the test period.

Tests of this sort, although in some ways inexact, do provide a means of comparing the biological values of different proteins, and this is the way that 'scores' like those quoted in Table 5.3 are established.

In summary, we can see that the nutritional value of animal proteins is usually higher than that of vegetable proteins. Their superiority is due to the fact that the proportions of the various amino acids, and particularly those designated as 'essential amino acids', are closer to those needed to build up human protein. In particular, cereal proteins contain low proportions of lysine.

It is important to remember that not all animal proteins have a high nutritional value. For example, gelatin is an animal protein yet it contains almost no tyrosine, cystine or tryptophan; consequently, it cannot support the growth of young rats if it is used as the sole source of protein, and it therefore has a NPU of zero.

On the other hand, proteins derived from vegetable sources may have almost as good a biological value as animal protein. As Table 5.3 shows, some cereal proteins and the protein from soya beans have a nutritional value superior to that of some animal proteins, as does the small amount of protein in green vegetables, with a 'score' of about 70.

5.7   The Nutritional Significance of Protein

(*a*) Growth

Since protein is a major constituent of the body's tissues, then clearly the amount of protein in an adequate diet must be enough to supply both the total amount of amino acids and also sufficient of the 'essential amino acids' for the reconstruction of the necessary amount of its own proteins. Because this is the primary nutritional function of protein, foods containing a high proportion of protein are often called 'body-building' foods.

The amount of protein required is usually assessed in terms of the weight of protein in grams per kilogram of body weight. Obviously, an infant eats less food than a grown man and obtains less protein from it. Nevertheless, the infant is growing very rapidly and 'putting on flesh', whereas an adult 'grows' only to the extent of replacing the comparatively small amounts of nitrogen lost when skin is rubbed off, hair and nails are cut, and in other minor ways. The protein requirement of the infant *per kilogram of its body weight* is therefore very much greater than that of the man.

Women, when they are pregnant and more particularly when they are nursing a baby, need extra protein from which their bodies can manufacture the growing foetus and the milk to feed the infant when it is born. Boys and girls also require rather more protein in their diet during the period when they undergo a sudden spurt in growth as they become adolescent. This is at approximately 12 years old for girls and 15 for boys.

The United Kingdom Department of Health and Social Security recommended in 1969 that, in general, an adult's diet should contain at least 10 per cent of protein. However, the actual amount of protein needed each day to maintain good health and (in children) adequate growth cannot be stated as a definite figure for any individual. This is because the protein we eat is almost always in a mixture derived from a variety of foods and its amino-acid pattern will vary from day to day in the degree to which it approaches the perfect amino-acid combination for the build-up of replacement proteins. The composition of the pool of amino acids already contained in the body may also vary from one individual to another, so that people's need for different amounts of any particular amino acid also varies. We cannot so far measure the extent of these variations, however; and the conclusions reached about the amounts of mixed dietary protein required by different categories of people are by no means precise, as Table 5.4 indicates. It must also be said that sometimes scientific conclusions about nutrition are influenced by the kind of diet the people being studied are accustomed to eat.

(b) Protein and Children

Healthy, well-fed children always grow; if a child is receiving insufficient protein of the amino-acid composition which its body needs, its growth may be affected in one or more of the following ways:

(i) **Restriction in growth.** Children who are not given enough protein to eat will not grow as quickly and, if the deficiency is at all prolonged, will not grow to the same stature as those who receive an adequate diet. One reason for the varying estimates of what *is* an ideal protein consumption for children is that it is by no means certain that a child fed so as to grow as fast as possible, like a pig being fattened for market, necessarily becomes the healthiest adult.

Table 5.4   Estimates of the amounts of protein needed by different categories of people

	g of protein needed per kg of body weight	estimated intake per day of protein (g)
Infants	2·6–4·0	36– 40
Children		
1–3 years	2·1–3·3	25– 40
4–6 years	1·5–2·8	27– 50
7–9 years	1·3–2·2	35– 60
10–12 years	1·5–1·9	54– 70
Girls 13–15 years	1·2–2·1	59–102
Boys 13–15 years	1·3–2·1	64–102
Lactating women	1·3–1·9	75–111
Pregnant women	0·9–1·8	50–102
Boys 16–19 years	0·9–2·1	59–130
Girls 16–19 years	0·8–1·7	41– 93
Women	0·7–2·0	38–109
Men	0·6–2·1	46–146

There is indeed some evidence, although it is not very conclusive, that *very* rapid growth in infancy and childhood may be associated with some degree of shortening of life in old age.

(*ii*) **Kwashiorkor.** This is a deficiency disease, also called *protein-calorie malnutrition*, which occurs when a child, often fed satisfactorily in infancy on its mother's milk, is suddenly weaned, and then given too little food containing too little protein. The muscles of a child with kwashiorkor waste away but its limbs and body often become bloated with fluid, a symptom called *oedema*. It fails to grow, becomes irritable and apathetic, its liver becomes damaged and, if the condition is not relieved in time by an improved diet providing the amino acids it needs, the child dies.

(*iii*) **Mental deficiency.** A child's brain grows very quickly during the first months of its life after birth and by the time it is 18 months old the brain is approximately 80 per cent as big as it is ever going to be. When there is an acute shortage of protein in the early months after weaning the brain, like the rest of the body, cannot grow properly, so that the child grows up mentally defective and remains so for the rest of its life. This effect results from *severe* malnutrition associated with a general shortage of food as well as a lack of protein. The child may suffer from kwashiorkor as well. If there is only a moderate shortage of protein, or if the shortage occurs later on in life when the brain's development is virtually complete, a child's growth will be checked but, depending on the degree of deficiency, it may or may not attain its full stature later on if it then receives an adequate diet. In such circumstances, however, its brain will not be harmed and its intellectual capabilities will be undamaged.

(c) Protein and Adults

The evidence for the existence of protein deficiency in different parts of the world is almost always provided by children: that is to say, protein deficiency is for the most part a condition of childhood. In its extreme form it appears as kwashiorkor; under less severe circumstances it causes a restriction in growth. It may therefore be inaccurate to describe an entire community as suffering from lack of protein because children with kwashiorkor are found among them. The disease may be due to their having been fed on a badly designed diet after having been weaned and sent away from home to live with an aunt or grandmother, as often happens in African populations. Of itself, however, it says nothing about the nutritional status of the adults in the community. In fact, protein deficiency is comparatively uncommon among adults although there are, of course, people who do not obtain enough to eat (see Section 7.1(d)). The symptoms of protein deficiency in adults, when it does occur, may take the following forms:

(*i*) **Anaemia.** Both the *red blood cells* and the yellow fluid in which they are suspended, the *plasma*, contain specialized proteins. When the diet is seriously lacking in protein for a time the proper production of plasma protein is first affected; if the deficiency is severe and prolonged, the synthesis of the protein portion of the red haemoglobin of the blood cells will also be affected, and the condition known as *anaemia* (that is, a shortage of haemoglobin in the blood) will occur.

(*ii*) **Hunger oedema.** When there is a severe and prolonged shortage of food, which may amount to famine, there will also be a serious shortage of protein. When the diet has been inadequate for a long time the plasma-protein concentration falls, so that the blood becomes 'thin', to use a colloquial and not altogether accurate expression. At the same time, the muscles waste away so that the skin becomes loose. In a manner not fully understood, this leads to a seepage of fluid from the blood which causes first the legs, then other parts of the body, to become swollen with liquid, or 'water-logged'. This is *hunger oedema*. Although protein deficiency is not its only cause, this is certainly involved in its appearance.

(*iii*) **Injury, inactivity and protein loss.** When a person suffers an injury such as a broken leg or serious burns, or when he undergoes a surgical operation, a significant amount of his body protein is broken down—as much as 60 g or more a day. This is shown by the loss of weight that occurs and by the escape of nitrogen in the form of *urea* excreted by the kidneys. Some body protein is broken down and lost in this way when people merely stay in bed, or when men are cooped up for a week or so in a semi-recumbent posture in a space capsule. Under all these conditions, therefore, it must be recognized that the nutritional requirements of adults for protein are increased.

(d) **Protein, Energy and Muscular Work**

Although the particular nutritional importance of protein arises from the part that amino acids play in building up the 'patterned brickwork' of our human tissues, most of the protein consumed by people who have enough to eat is broken down, its nitrogen excreted through the kidneys as urea (see Section 5.2) and the remaining part of the protein molecules simply used as a source of energy to keep the body's machine going (see Unit 6). When protein is used in this way its nutritional function is little different from that of carbohydrate or fat.

There is a quite widespread popular belief that meat is of particular nutritional value to men who do heavy muscular work. Obviously a big plate of meat with plenty of fat on it provides a strenuous worker with a palatable meal which is a very useful source of the energy he needs to do his work. However, there is still no evidence for the notion that more *protein* is required by people who do muscular work than by those who do not.

5.8   The Specificity of Protein

We have said that protein has two nutritional functions:

(a) It provides *amino acids* from which the body structure is built up. Some of these contribute to a pool held within body tissues from which the body's needs are met directly, and these are largely interchangeable; others, the so-called *essential amino acids*, must each be obtained from food in its appropriate proportion.

(b) It contributes *energy* for the general requirements of the processes of life.

It is important to remember that the diet provides the body with *amino acids* and that any protein that is eaten *must* be broken down by the processes of digestion before it is absorbed and taken into use. The proteins of each species of living creature, animals and plants alike, are characteristic of that species. If complete protein molecules or even large peptide fragments from another species gain entry into the body tissues, the results are disastrous and can be even fatal; the same kind of effect occurs if incompatible blood is accidentally injected during a transfusion.

Coeliac disease is a condition which occurs when a person, usually but not always a child, is incapable of using *gluten*, a protein found in wheat. Although the precise cause of this defect is not fully understood, one explanation which may be part of the truth is that there is a deficiency of a particular enzyme in the small intestine which splits the peptides derived from gluten. When this enzyme is lacking these peptides are absorbed into the blood without being split into their component amino acids. The reactions that follow include inflammation of the intestinal cells which produce mucus. This interferes with the absorption of fat and a number of other nutrients including vitamins, minerals and some carbohydrate and protein components as well. Children with coeliac disease fail to thrive, lose their appetite and become pot-bellied.

The only way to protect them against the harm resulting from the entry of the undigested peptide is completely to exclude wheat flour, wheat products and all other foods containing gluten from their diet. The student of nutrition has a lesson to be learned from coeliac disease. The chemical structure of protein, like that of carbohydrate and fat, the two other major components of food, can be understood for what it is. Beef, mutton, cheese and chicken supply animal protein; peas and beans, nuts, oatmeal and, particularly in western countries, wheat provide vegetable protein. We can add these together to assess the total protein intake, and mix foods in various combinations to provide an acceptable and varied diet. Almost always, this amount of nutritional knowledge is enough: on rare occasions, it is not. Coeliac disease is one example of a condition in which, for reasons still unknown, the unacceptability of a commonplace protein from a foodstuff as basic as wheat—and this particular protein only— reminds us how subtle is the special molecular configuration of each of the innumerable types of protein on which our bodies depend, and how delicate is the complex mechanism we use to benefit from our daily bread.

Unit Six
Metabolism, Work and Energy

6.1 'La vie est une fonction chimique'

The science of nutrition as we now understand it owes its foundation to the work of the French scientist Antoine Lavoisier, towards the end of the eighteenth century. Within a few years of his identification of the element oxygen and his discovery that combustion—that is the burning of a substance, with the production of energy in the form of heat and light—is a *chemical process*, Lavoisier had the genius also to deduce that the energy of living creatures is also produced by a kind of combustion. This led him to make the statement at the head of this section, that 'life is a chemical process'.

Combustion, or burning, is certainly a chemical process. The reaction involves the combination of *oxygen* with a substance capable of being *oxidized*. Such substances—which in nature are almost always carbon compounds—are said by chemists to be in a *reduced* state. When the reaction takes place, energy is released. It is this kind of energy, stored up as *chemical energy* in the special fuel compounds which can be used as food, that keeps life going.

The Various Forms of Energy with which Nutrition is Concerned

(*a*) **Electromagnetic radiation.** Such radiation may be recognized as, for example, radio waves, X-rays, microwaves or light. These waves are all of the same nature; they differ in that their wavelengths, and consequently many of their properties, are different. As we explained in Section 3.6, it is the energy of the light waves of the sun, transmitted through the molecules of the chlorophyll of green plants, that is transformed into the stored *chemical* energy of plant carbohydrates from which almost all living creatures directly or indirectly obtain their food, and which is therefore responsible for maintaining all the life on earth.

(*b*) **Chemical energy.** All the main food components, the carbohydrates, fats and proteins, as well as certain other compounds like alcohol, serve as biological fuels, that is, as sources of chemical energy. Of course, just as the 'combustion' of this biological fuel in living tissues is very different from that which occurs when a piece of wood is burned, so also the chemistry of these two processes is different, although the end results are the same. Biological 'combustion', which is an important part of *metabolism*—that is, the sum total of biological changes taking place within a living organism—has to take place in a special way so that it can proceed within the physiological limits outside of which life is impossible (Section 1.3). In fact, when the most important fuel, *glucose*, is broken down to yield its energy to the body, the biological process takes place as a series of many interlocking stages, although the net results are the same as when a lump of glucose is burned in the laboratory. Furthermore, while it is necessary to heat glucose to about 700 °C before it will catch fire and yield up its energy in a burst of flame, in living tissues the appropriate *enzymes* unlink the structure of the glucose molecule piece by piece at the body temperature of 37 °C so that its chemical energy is released in a manageable steady flow.

The sum total of this chemical reaction in both burning and living can be written:

$$C_6H_{12}O_6 \;+\; 6O_2 \longrightarrow 6CO_2 \;+\; 6H_2O \;+\; \text{ENERGY}$$

glucose	oxygen	carbon	water	
	(*from the air*)	dioxide	vapour	
		gas		

This complete breakdown is accomplished in the living tissues of higher animals and human beings via a complex pathway requiring the formation and subsequent breakdown of *phosphate compounds*, the intermediary production of *pyruvic acid* and *lactic acid*, both with three carbon atoms in their molecules, a group of compounds with four-carbon-atom structures and many others. The elucidation of this chemical mechanism is one of the major triumphs of biochemistry. Understanding these reactions is not only interesting in itself but may also be directly useful in nutrition. For example, as we shall describe in detail in Unit 16, several of the B-group vitamins help to maintain health by contributing to the action of certain enzymes concerned in the intermediate stages of the energy-release system. Perhaps the best example is that of *thiamine* (see Section 16.1), also known as vitamin B_1. This substance is concerned with the breakdown of the three-carbon-atom pyruvic acid to the fully oxidized one-carbon-atom carbon dioxide. We now know that beri-beri, a disease which appears when thiamine is lacking from the diet, is in fact due to an accumulation of pyruvic acid by which certain sensitive tissues become poisoned.

(c) **Mechanical energy.** Nutritionists have traditionally measured energy in terms of *heat*, and have used *Calories* (units of heat energy) as energy units for almost 30 years. This convention is now being abandoned. A moment's thought makes it clear that the use of a heat unit is entirely arbitrary, since food is used by a hungry man for many biological functions besides the production of heat. Energy, of course, may appear in various forms, and can be converted from one form to another. For example, the *chemical* energy stored in a shovelful of coal is released as *heat* energy when the coal is burned. If it is burned in the fire-box of a steam locomotive, part of the heat energy is converted into the *mechanical* energy by which the train is driven along. Another part of the heat energy is converted into the mechanical energy by which the lighting dynamos in the train are operated, and is further manifest as *electrical* energy. Again, part of this electrical energy passes through the lamp filaments and is translated into *heat*, some of which appears as *light* when the filaments become incandescent.

The concern of the nutritionist in mechanical energy arises from the fact that the complex series of biochemical changes occurring during the oxidation of glucose can bring about the shortening of the muscle fibres which extend as elastic bands across the joints which connect two bones. This conversion of *chemical* energy into *mechanical* energy produces a force which acts across the joint and produces a movement of the limb or other part of the body.

(*d*) **Thermal energy.** When mechanical energy is used to do work, some of it is always dissipated as *thermal energy*—that is, as *heat*. Indeed we are all well aware of this phenomenon taking place when we use mechanical energy produced from the chemical breakdown of fuel in the body (which is, as Lavoisier said, a *chemical* engine, and quite different from a *heat* engine like that in a steam locomotive): we all know that chopping wood or going for a brisk walk makes one warm.

(*e*) **Electrical energy.** The biochemical system by which food is metabolized and the chemical energy in it released is, as we have already indicated, subtle and complex. While some of the energy is used for *mechanical* purposes so that a man can keep his lungs pumping, his heart beating and his muscles pulling, some of it appears as *heat* and some of it is converted as fat or glycogen into stored *chemical* energy, a small amount is also constantly being transformed into *electricity*. When a doctor studies a patient's heartbeat with an electrocardiograph he is merely using an instrument to pick up and register electrical discharges emitted every time the heart muscle contracts. An electroencephalograph similarly measures the electrical discharges of the brain. Certain animals have evolved in such a way that these natural discharges of electricity have become considerably exaggerated. For example, the electric eel possesses specialized organs by which it can discharge enough electrical energy to electrocute its prey.

6.2   Units for Measuring Energy

As we mentioned in the last section, it has been customary for many years to measure the energy value of foods and the energy cost of different kinds of activity in terms of *Calories*. This custom is being abandoned nowadays, as part of a trend towards the general adoption of standardized units. People accustomed to thinking of the 'Calorie value' of diets are instead recommended to speak of *energy values*. This has some logical advantage since a Calorie is a unit of heat and only a proportion of the energy value of what is eaten is in fact converted into heat. On the other hand, the term *energy* is not entirely explicit. While when used about food it refers to the value of such food when employed as a biological fuel, it is important to bear in mind that the word is not synonymous with *vigour* when it is used in this sense. It is misleading to describe a chocolate bar, for example, as providing 'energy', illustrating the statement by a picture of athletes bounding about.

A calorie is the amount of heat required to raise the temperature of 1 gram of water by 1 °C.

The Calorie heretofore used in nutrition (which conventionally should always be written with a capital C) is strictly designated a *kilocalorie*, that is 1 000 calories, or *the amount of heat required to raise the temperature of 1 000 grams (1 litre) of water by 1 °C.*

A *joule* (the unit of energy which has now taken the place of the Calorie in nutrition) is defined as *the amount of work done or heat generated by an electric current of 1 ampere acting for 1 second against a resistance of 1 ohm,* or, alternatively, *by a force of 1 newton acting through a distance of 1 metre.* This unit is too small for most practical purposes in nutrition. It is, therefore, more convenient to use the *kilojoule* (written kJ) or the *megajoule* (MJ).

1 kilojoule = 1 000 joules, and 1 megajoule = 1 000 000 joules

The relationship between calories and joules is as follows:

1 calorie = 4·184 J (joules)
1 kilocalorie = 4 184 J = 4·184 kJ (kilojoules)
1 000 kilocalories = 4 184 000 J = 4·184 MJ (megajoules)

Although these conversions from Calories to joules appear to be rather clumsy, the use of joules is no more difficult than was that of Calories in the past. For example, a man's daily energy intake given as 3 000 Calories can equally well be expressed as 12 550 kJ.

6.3 The Energy Value of the Nutrients in Foods

The basic work on nutrition initiated nearly 200 years ago by Lavoisier and followed up by a series of distinguished successors established that when a certain weight of carbohydrate or fat is burned in the laboratory it releases almost exactly the same amount of energy (measured as heat) as it does when it is given to an animal, or to a man, to eat and metabolize in his tissues.

Protein may also be used as fuel to produce energy and, as we have said, most of it is used in this way. Even quickly growing infants only use a small proportion of the protein in their food for the formation of new cells. But whereas when protein is burned in the laboratory all its substance is available for oxidation, before it is oxidized in the body the nitrogen and some of the carbon in it is split off and excreted by the kidneys as urea. Less energy is therefore produced from protein metabolized in the tissues than from protein burned in the laboratory.

Table 6.1 lists the amounts of energy available from different nutrients.

The energy value of *alcohol*, which makes a significant contribution to that of beer, wines and spirits, is 7·0 Calories, or 29 kJ, per gram.

Table 6.1   **Energy values of nutrients**

	heat of combustion		energy available as food-value	
	(Calories per g)	(kJ per g)	(Calories per g)	(kJ per g)
Carbohydrate	4·1	17	4·0	17
Protein	5·6	24	4·0	17
Fat	9·4	39	9·0	37

6.4   The Energy Value of Foods

Foods provide the body with energy, as measured in terms of kilojoules, in proportion to the amounts of fat, protein and carbohydrate—and sometimes also alcohol—they contain. Since 1 g of carbohydrate or protein produces 17 kJ in the body whereas 1 g of fat produces 37 kJ, the foods with the highest energy values are those containing the largest proportion of fat. Water, as we have said, provides no nourishment to the body but is rather the medium in which the biochemical processes of life take place. The energy value of a food is therefore *inversely proportional* to its water content; that is to say, the more water a food contains the fewer units of energy are provided by each gram of food consumed. A soup kitchen in a disaster area could serve 100 refugees with a pan of soup designed for 50, if the soup is diluted with an equal volume of water; but clearly the dilution does not change the food value of the soup, and so the 100 receive only half of the kilojoules they should.

The energy values of a number of common foods are shown in Table 6.2.

Table 6.2 is intended to illustrate a number of important points having a bearing on nutrition. First of all it shows the great difference between the high energy value of foods rich in fat and low in moisture, such as cooking fat, or, to a lesser degree, high in carbohydrate and low in moisture, such as cereals and cereal flours, and the low energy value of foods like fruit and vegetables that contain a high proportion of moisture and little or no fat. It is, for example, interesting to see that 100 g of turnip, usually considered as a *solid* food, contribute fewer kilojoules to the body than 100 g of beer which is not commonly regarded as a food at all and is certainly considered to be a *liquid*.

A second factor which must always be borne in mind when the significance of such a table of energy-value figures is studied, is that since each figure applies to 100 g of edible material, its practical importance can only be judged in relation to the amount of each food likely to be eaten. For example, although 100 g of raisins contribute 1 032 kJ of energy compared with the 318 kJ provided by 100 g of potatoes, potatoes are likely to be a much more important energy source than raisins, in spite of their lower value per 100 g, since most people eat a great deal more potatoes (by weight) than raisins.

Finally, we must repeat that although the figures listed in the table are characteristic of the various foods named, individual samples may vary quite widely. The fat content of one specimen of meat may differ quite largely from

Table 6.2   The energy value of some common foods (per 100 g of edible portion)

	Calories	kJ
Cereals		
Oatmeal	400	1 676
Barley	360	1 508
Rice	359	1 504
White flour	348	1 458
Wholemeal flour	343	1 433
White bread	253	1 060
Brown bread	237	993
Fats		
Salad oil	899	3 767
Cooking fat	894	3 746
Margarine	769	3 222
Meat		
Bacon	476	1 994
Pork	408	1 710
Pork sausages	369	1 546
Lamb	331	1 387
Beef (fresh)	313	1 311
Corned beef	224	939
Calf's liver	139	582
Veal	108	450
Kidney	105	440
Fish		
Herring	273	1 140
Kipper	201	840
Salmon	190	794
Mackerel	150	630
Whiting	90	376
Cod	82	342
Plaice	79	330
Haddock	71	297
Dairy produce		
Butter	745	3 122
Dried egg	580	2 424
Dried whole milk	492	2 061
Cheese	412	1 726
Dried skimmed milk	329	1 379
Condensed milk	322	1 349
Evaporated milk	166	696
Eggs	158	662
Fresh milk	65	272

Table 6.2—continued

	Calories	kJ
Legumes		
Soya-bean meal (defatted)	326	1 363
Dried peas	275	1 149
Haricot beans	256	1 073
Baked beans	92	385
Fruit		
Dates	248	1 039
Raisins	247	1 032
Dried figs	213	892
Dried apricots	182	763
Dried prunes	161	675
Canned peaches	88	369
Bananas	76	318
Apples	46	193
Pineapple	46	192
Oranges	35	147
Plums	32	134
Blackcurrants	28	117
Melon	23	96
Vegetables		
Potatoes	76	318
Green peas	63	264
Cabbage	28	117
Cauliflower	24	101
Onions	23	96
Carrots	23	96
Spinach	21	88
Turnips	17	71
Watercress	14	59
Tomatoes	14	59
Lettuce	11	46
Miscellaneous		
Mayonnaise	718	3 001
Plain chocolate	541	2 261
Sugar	394	1 651
Honey	288	1 207
Jam	262	1 098
Whisky	245	1 025
Beer	25	105

that of another and the energy value will be affected accordingly. Similar, if less drastic, differences occur in fish. While the fatty fish like salmon, herring and mackerel always have a higher energy value per 100 g than 'white' fish like cod and haddock, the proportion of fat in them is affected by the season and the stage in the breeding cycle when they are caught. Tables like this one, or like that given in the Appendix, allow the composition of the diet eaten by a particular *group* of people to be assessed. Should it be necessary, however, to make a closer investigation of a particular individual, specimens of the actual food he eats would have to be analysed in order to determine the proportions of carbohydrate, protein and fat it contains. The energy value could then be calculated from the factors, 17, 17 and 37, the number of kilojoules produced by each gram of carbohydrate, protein and fat respectively.

6.5   The Make-up of the Energy Value of a Normal Western Diet

We have already said that the proportions of fats and proteins which people eat tend to increase as they become richer and to fall when they are poorer (Sections 4.6 and 5.5). It follows, therefore, that the proportion of energy contributed to the diet by foods like meat, fats and dairy produce tends to be greater in prosperous communities than it is in needy ones. The approximate proportion of the total energy value derived from the main classes of food by people in what might be called modest circumstances is however shown in Table 6.3.

Table 6.3   **Proportion of the total energy value likely to be derived from different types of food**

	per cent
Bread and flour	36
Fats	15
Meat	14
Dairy produce	10
Sugar	10
Potatoes	6
Other foods	9

Unit Seven
Energy Requirements and Energy Intake

7.1 Energy Expended by the Body

The fundamental purpose for which people eat food is as fuel to keep their bodies going; or we can put this statement in another way by saying that as long as the body is alive it is an energy-using machine. A living man must have energy available to keep his heart beating to pump blood through his circulatory system, to keep his lungs working so that the blood flowing through them can pick up oxygen from the air for the oxidation of food to maintain his energy supply, and to keep his muscles in their appropriate state of tension. The process of biological 'combustion' forms part of the enormously complicated series of changes which together comprise *metabolism*. The fuel that is metabolized may be derived immediately from the food in the daily diet or from energy stores like glycogen or fat. Should the supply of food be cut off for a time, part of the body's own substance will be used to provide energy. During a famine, a man may metabolize up to about 40 per cent of his original body weight as fuel to keep the living engine going, but beyond this point no more fuel is available, the engine stops and the man dies of starvation.

Basal metabolism is the term used to describe the biochemical changes which take place while the individual is lying down, still, relaxed and warm. The rate at which energy is used up while the body is in this condition is defined as the *basal metabolic rate* (BMR); for example, the average basal metabolic rate of a young man of average build and temperament, weighing 70 kg, is about 293 kJ per hour.

(a) The Effect of Body Size on the Basal Metabolic Rate (BMR)

It is not surprising that, other things being equal, a big man requires more energy to keep his body going than a small man does. At one time it was considered that the BMR was proportional to the area of the body surface. Since, however, a big body surface may in part be due to excessive fatness, it is now recognized that what matters is the weight of the lean body, disregarding the fat. The average effect of body size on the BMR is indicated in Table 7.1.

Although in assessing the adequacy of a diet provided for a *group* of people, it is sensible to accept the best available estimate of the *average* energy required for basal metabolism, namely 7 030 kJ per day, Table 7.1 makes it clear that one particular individual who happened to be tall and heavy might require 7 560 kJ per day whereas another, a smaller and slighter man, might

Table 7.1   The average difference in BMR due to difference in body size above and below a conventional standard of 70 kg weight and 183 cm in height

weight (kg)	height (cm)	basal metabolic rate			
		per hour		per day	
		(kJ)	(Calories)	(kJ)	(Calories)
80	188	313	75	7 560	1 798
75	185	304	73	7 280	1 747
70	183	293	70	7 030	1 680
65	180	282	67	6 650	1 613
60	178	270	64	6 470	1 546

only need 6 470 kJ each day to keep the basic functions of his body in operation.

It is generally accepted that whereas an average 70-kg *man* requires 293 kJ an hour for his basal metabolism, an average 55-kg *woman* has a BMR of 251 kJ per hour (6 020 kJ per day). The BMR of a woman will like that of a man depend on her body size, again measured as the *lean body mass* (see Glossary, page 215).

(b) **The Effect of Age on Basal Metabolic Rate**

(i) **Adults.** The basal metabolic rate of both men and women tends to fall as they become older; Table 7.2 shows the approximate magnitude of this change.

Table 7.2   The average fall in BMR that occurs as people become older

age (years)	men				women			
	per hour		per day		per hour		per day	
	(kJ)	(Calories)	(kJ)	(Calories)	(kJ)	(Calories)	(kJ)	(Calories)
20	293	70	7 030	1 680	251	60	6 010	1 440
30	280	67	6 820	1 608	247	59	5 930	1 418
40	276	66	6 580	1 584	245	59	5 880	1 414
50	272	65	6 520	1 560	242	58	5 800	1 392
60	267	64	6 420	1 536	234	56	5 620	1 344
70	259	62	6 210	1 488	226	54	5 420	1 296
80	251	60	6 010	1 440	218	52	5 230	1 248

(ii) **Children.** Of course, a child uses less energy for basal metabolism than an adult does, because children are smaller than adults. On the other hand a child's *rate* of metabolism for each unit weight of lean body mass is greater than that of normal adults. If we take the BMR of an average 70-kg man as an arbitrary value of 100 per unit of lean body mass per hour, the comparative BMR of children is given in Table 7.3.

Table 7.3   The comparative BMR per unit of lean body mass of girls and boys in relation to that of an adult man

age (years)	boys	girls
1	137	137
3	133	132
5	127	125
7	123	117
9	117	111
11	111	109
13	109	104
15	106	95
17	105	94
19	102	92
20	100	91

(c) The Effect of Specific Dynamic Action on the BMR

The total energy requirement of a moderately active man during the 24 hours of a day and a night may amount to 12 000 kJ (Section 7.1(g)). The energy required for maintaining basal metabolism, which will be about 7 030 kJ, is therefore a significant part of the whole, amounting indeed to 58 per cent. Although the average values for BMR given for *groups* of men and women and boys and girls of different heights and weights and of different ages are generally representative, there are other factors which may affect the BMR of an *individual*. One of these is called *specific dynamic action* (SDA).

When a meal is eaten and especially when protein is consumed, a phenomenon occurs somewhat analogous to what happens when the door of the fire-box of a steam locomotive is opened and the stoker shovels in coal. While in due course this maintains the continuous supply of power to the locomotive, its immediate effect is to cause the fire to flare up. Similarly, when protein is absorbed and its metabolism in the tissues begins, there is an increase in the metabolic rate which may amount to 30 per cent of the BMR. This increase in energy output, which appears in the form of *heat*, is *specific dynamic action*.

If SDA takes place when the body is already warm—for example, when a lavish business lunch rich in beefsteak protein is eaten in a heated room, and the consumer's forehead is seen to be bedewed with sweat—the energy so released is wasted. On the other hand, if the heat produced by SDA can be used to maintain the body temperature, it does make a contribution to the body's needs. Clearly, it is quite a complicated matter to assess the exact amount of energy required to meet the needs of any specific individual.

(d) The Effect of Undernutrition on the BMR

We have already seen that the BMR of a particular individual is proportional to the amount of living tissue in his body so that a big man, having more lean body mass than a small one, also has a higher BMR. If this man is starved, that is to say, if he has too little to eat over an extended period of time, some of his lean body mass will waste away and thus, at the same time as he *eats less* and obtains less energy from his food, he will actually come to *require less* to keep his body going in its reduced state. Besides this, it has been found that when people are compelled to remain in a state of under-nutrition, their BMR falls. In experimental underfeeding as well as in conditions of shortage a man's BMR may fall as much as 40 per cent below its normal level; this decrease in metabolic rate can act as a valuable protective mechanism in times of famine. Whereas a well-fed individual may require 293 kJ an hour to maintain his body in equilibrium while he is lying still and warm, the same person forced to live on, say, half as much food as he would like to eat, may re-establish a condition of equilibrium at a BMR of only 176 kJ an hour. This biological adjustment partly explains how it is that people can live—as many are compelled to do—all their lives without having what they would describe as 'enough to eat'. The fact that this is so, and that the physiological mechanisms controlling appetite and also those which regulate the weight and fatness of the body are equally as complex as those controlling metabolism, make it extraordinarily difficult to decide *what is enough to eat.*

(e) Metabolic Rate and the Thyroid Gland

Tables 7.1, 7.2 and 7.3 are intended to indicate the *average* BMR of groups of people of different size, age and sex. There are wide differences between individuals, as so commonly happens in nutrition. Lively, excitable people constantly on the move usually have higher BMRs than stolid, phlegmatic people. The organ that controls an individual's BMR, operating in a manner analogous to that of a thermostat in a gas cooker, is a small gland situated in the neck. This is the *thyroid gland*, which is further discussed in Unit 12.

The functions of the thyroid gland are complex, but its main action is to maintain the BMR at an appropriate steady level. To do this, it discharges a controlled concentration of an iodine-containing hormone (see Section 2.3(c)) called *thyroxine* into the bloodstream.

Even among normal healthy people there are some in whom the thyroid gland is more active than in others. These people have a higher BMR and are usually more lively and active, or sometimes more tense, than those more slow-moving people whose thyroid glands produce less thyroxine.

(i) The effect of thyroid deficiency.

Sometimes the variations in thyroid activity exceed what can be considered to be normal. There are people whose thyroid gland is abnormally inactive, their BMRs are always very low, and this is accompanied by a slowing down of the body and of the mind as well, often associated with an accumulation of fat which makes the body gross and unwieldy and the face and hands swollen. In an adult man or woman, this condition is called *myxoedema*. Should the thyroid gland fail at or before birth, or in childhood, the condition is known as *cretinism*. Besides his low

BMR, a cretin often fails to grow properly, and unless thyroxine is supplied artificially the unfortunate child may survive only as an idiot dwarf.

(*ii*) **The effect of thyroid excess.** There are occasions when the activity of the thyroid increases well above the limits of normal fluctuations. When this occurs the BMR increases by as much as 20 per cent, or even more. The individual becomes excessively excitable, physical and mental activity increase, the pulse beats quicker and very often the eyeballs protrude. The high BMR causes sufferers from this condition, called *hyperthyroidism*, to use up their bodies' stores of fuel and become thin and drawn. Because of this, it was once thought that injections of thyroxine, inducing a kind of artificial hyperthyroidism, might be used as a method of slimming for people who wished to lose weight. It is now generally recognized, however, that this is a dangerous procedure accompanied by a risk of serious side-effects. Nevertheless, it was based on the valid principle that BMR, that is, the rate at which fuel derived from the diet is oxidized in the body at rest, is controlled by the thyroid gland.

(*f*) **The Energy Requirement of Various Activities**

The BMR is a measure of the amount of energy that must be expended to keep the bodily engine 'ticking over'. When the engine is, as it were, 'put into gear', that is, when the body becomes physically active, the rate of energy expenditure required to do work immediately increases above that required for basal metabolism alone. For the performance of every kind of muscular activity there is therefore an energy demand measurable in kilojoules (or Calories) which in due course must be obtained from food or, if food is lacking, from the tissues of the body itself.

The amount of energy expended in the performance of a wide variety of activities has been measured by numerous investigators at different times and with different people as experimental subjects. The figures shown in Table 7.4 are representative of the values that have been obtained. But although they may be accepted as characteristic values, we must emphasize yet again how great the differences may be between one person and another. There are several reasons for this. Some people's bodies carry out a task more smoothly and with greater mechanical efficiency than others; for example, a trained athlete expends less energy running on a track than a middle-aged man of the same size running at the same rate to catch a train. Most of the activities listed in the table could be done more economically by a dexterous individual. But in spite of individual differences of energy expenditure, the average values given below enable the nutritionist to obtain a rough idea of the energy expenditure for the different categories of activity listed.

The important point to observe in these figures is that often 'hard work' as measured in terms of human mechanics and reflected in the body's energy expenditure is not the same as what is generally assumed to be hard work in the industrial sense. In general, Table 7.4 shows that activities which involve

Table 7.4   The average energy requirements for various activities

	energy per hour (kJ)	(Calories)
Light work		
Sitting	63	15
Writing	84	20
Standing (at ease)	84	20
Typing	67–167	16–40
Typing quickly	230	55
Sewing	125–368	30–80
Dressing	138	33
Undressing	138	33
Drawing	167–209	40–50
Lithography	167–209	40–50
Violin playing	192	46
Tailoring	209–350	50–84
Washing dishes	247	59
Ironing	247	59
Bookbinding	180–376	43–90
Moderate work		
Shoemaking	343–481	82–115
Sweeping floors	351–460	84–110
Dusting	460	110
Washing clothes	518–894	124–214
Charring	339–646	81–157
Metal working	489–589	117–141
Carpentering	585–752	140–180
House painting	606–669	145–160
Walking	523–1 003	130–240
Hard work		
Polishing	727	174
Joinery	815	195
Blacksmithing	1 154–1 667	276–351
Riveting	1 154	276
Marching	1 170–1 672	280–400
Cycling	752–2 508	180–600
Rowing	501–2 508	120–600
Swimming	836–2 926	200–700
Very hard work		
Coalmining (average for a shift)	1 338	320
Stonemason's work	1 379	330
Sawing wood	1 756	420
Climbing	1 672–3 766	400–900
Fast walking	2 362	565
Ski-ing	2 090–4 013	500–960
Running	3 344–4 184	600–1 000
Wrestling	4 096	980
Walking upstairs	4 184	1 000
Fast rowing	5 183	1 240
Sprinting	5 183	1 240

moving the body about, like walking and running and especially walking upstairs, call for the expenditure of a good deal of energy. Nowadays, walking and running are gradually disappearing from everyday life as more and more people come to own motor-cars or use other mechanically propelled vehicles. At work, there is a tendency for people to sit down, while the objects they are working on come to them on travelling conveyors; other people sit down to drive fork-lift trucks or cranes rather than pushing wheelbarrows. People's daily energy requirements are therefore significantly less than they used to be, and it follows that if the energy content of the food people eat is not reduced in parallel with the amount of energy they expend, the result must inevitably be obesity (see Unit 8).

(g) The Assessment of the Daily Energy Expenditure

(i) **Men.** The total energy expended during the course of 24 hours, which must be balanced by the energy value of the total amount of food and drink consumed, is made up of the sum of the energy expended on each type of activity. For example, the daily energy used up by a tailor would be made up as follows:

		kJ	Calories
24 hours	basal metabolism	7 030	1 680
1 hour	dressing and undressing	138	33
1 hour	walking slowly	481	115
2 hours	light exercise, say	711	170
4 hours	sitting	251	60
8 hours	tailoring	2 675	640
		11 286	2 698

If it is assumed that the day's miscellaneous activities of, say, a worker in an engineering plant are the same as those of the tailor, but 8 hours metal working at 585 kJ per hour (amounting to 4 675 kJ in all) are substituted for 8 hours tailoring at 2 675 kJ, the plant worker's daily energy output becomes 13 283 kJ.

A coalminer's day might be assessed as follows:

		kJ	Calories
24 hours	basal metabolism	7 030	1 680
1 hour	walking to and from work	836	200
8 hours	leisure	1 338	320
8 hours	coalmining	10 701	2 560
		19 905	4 760

(ii) **Women.** As a general rule women's energy expenditure is less than men's. This is primarily due to their basal metabolism being less than that of men, partly because on average women are smaller than men, and partly because their BMR per unit weight of lean body mass is actually somewhat lower as well. The energy expenditure of women is calculated in the same way as that of men; thus, for example, a woman engaged in light work as a typist might use up energy as follows:

		kJ	Calories
24 hours	basal metabolism	6 019	1 440
3 hours	light exercise, say,	1 003	240
5 hours	domestic activity, say,	690	165
8 hours	typing	1 003	240
		8 715	2 085

The sum total of the energy used up by a charwoman might comprise the following:

		kJ	Calories
24 hours	basal metabolism	6 019	1 440
1 hour	walking	836	200
2 hours	sitting	125	30
5 hours	domestic activity	960	165
8 hours	charring	5 016	1 200
		12 956	3 035

(h) Individual Variability

Once again, it has to be accepted that individuals vary quite widely from each other in the amount of energy they use to perform the same tasks and carry out the same activities. Anyone who has owned two motor-cars of the same make and paid close attention to their performance will know that no two will perform alike or travel the same distance on a gallon of fuel. People differ far more from each other than motor-cars of equal horsepower. They differ in weight, size, body conformation, the mechanical efficiency and dexterity with which they achieve their results, and in temperament and personality.

Individual variability may be substantial. In a careful study carried out some years ago, Dr Elsie Widdowson studied 20 young men, 18 years old, all of whom were doing much the same kind of work and living approximately the same kind of lives. The exact energy value of the diet of each was determined and a wide spread of intake was found. This ranged from 9 773 kJ, for the men who ate the least, to 25 113 kJ, for the men who ate the most. The average intake was 14 325 kJ.

While it is convenient to have standards for the *average* energy requirement for different *groups of people*, that is to say, for growing children, sedentary men and women, people doing heavy physical work, or expectant mothers, the fact that a particular individual—or even a particular group of individuals —eats less than the recommended value, or eats more, does not *necessarily* imply that this individual or this group is under- or over-nourished.

7.2   Assessing the Energy Intake Necessary for Health

(a) Estimated Average Requirements

The basic nutritional function of food, as we have said already, is to supply the person who eats it with the energy he or she needs. Should the diet supply too little energy, the person in question will not be having enough to eat; should the energy value be excessive, he or she will be eating too much. It may come as a surprise to you that even now, almost 200 years after Lavoisier discovered the basic principles of nutritional energetics, it is still by no means easy for a nutritional scientist to know precisely what will be the ideal energy value of the diet eaten by any particular individual.

A number of expert committees have done the best they could to make recommendations about what a so-called 'reference man' or a 'reference woman' or 'reference children' of various ages should ideally eat. The fact that these recommendations have varied from one committee to another and that individual committees have revised their recommendations over the years indicates how difficult the problem is. The figures given in Table 7.5 are those recommended in 1969 by an expert committee of the British Department of Health and Social Security.

In general, if we need to calculate how many units of energy are needed from the food supply for a community—perhaps a nation, a regiment of soldiers or a school—a reasonable estimate will be obtained by assessing how many sedentary, moderately active and very active men there are, how many women who are leading normal lives, or who are very active, pregnant or nursing, how many boys and girls of various ages, and then multiplying each category by the figures set out in Table 7.5 and adding the answers all together. Although this procedure may not lead to a very precise result, it is probably the best that a conscientious nutritionist can do.

The 'reference man' and the 'reference woman' are useful statistical abstractions but they cannot claim to be real people. The aim of optimum nutrition, of which *enough to eat* is an essential part, is health; and health, as we said at the beginning of this book, is defined as 'complete physical, mental and social well-being and not merely the absence of ill-health and infirmity'. It is thus asking much to expect that what satisfies a 'reference man' in all these points will accord with the needs of everyone.

(b) The Ideal Body Weight

The human body is a biological machine in which the energy content of the food consumed can be used to perform work. If the amount of food eaten provides more units of energy than the body requires for its various activities, the unused part may be stored in the form of fat. On the other hand, if the diet eaten provides insufficient energy, fat already stored in the tissues or, eventually, part of the body substance itself can be consumed to provide the energy needed to perform the work. In brief, if an individual eats too much in terms of units of energy, he will become fat; or, if he eats too little, he will

Table 7.5   Recommended daily energy intake for 'reference' people

	body weight (kg)	energy intake (kJ)	(Calories)
Boys and girls			
0 up to 1 year	7·3	3 300	800
1 up to 2 years	11·4	5 000	1 200
2 up to 3 years	13·5	5 900	1 400
3 up to 5 years	16·5	6 700	1 600
5 up to 7 years	20·5	7 500	1 800
7 up to 9 years	25·1	8 800	2 100
Boys			
9 up to 12 years	31·9	10 500	2 500
12 up to 15 years	45·5	11 700	2 800
15 up to 18 years	61·0	12 600	3 000
Girls			
9 up to 12 years	33·0	9 600	2 300
12 up to 15 years	48·6	9 600	2 300
15 up to 18 years	56·1	9 600	2 300
Men			
18 up to 35 years			
sedentary	65	11 300	2 700
moderately active	65	12 600	3 000
very active	65	15 100	3 600
35 up to 65 years			
sedentary	65	10 900	2 600
moderately active	65	12 100	2 900
very active	65	15 100	3 600
65 up to 75 years			
sedentary	63	9 800	2 350
75 years and over			
sedentary	63	8 800	2 100
Women			
18 up to 55 years			
most occupations	55	9 200	2 200
very active	55	10 500	2 500
55 up to 75 years			
sedentary	53	8 600	2 050
75 years and over			
sedentary	53	8 000	1 900
pregnant 3–9 months		10 000	2 400
nursing		11 300	2 700

become thin. If a person remains the same weight, we can conclude that the energy value of the diet taken into the body is equal to the energy expenditure of the body's activity. This does not necessarily imply, however, that a diet of ideal energy value is being eaten. It may be that the individual concerned eats too much and is consequently overweight. The surplus food is burned up in maintaining the metabolism of a certain amount of excess lean body mass and as wasted specific dynamic action. On the other hand, people obtaining much less than they need may nevertheless do the work they have to do, and thereafter maintain themselves in equilibrium after having lost weight and at a reduced BMR.

The most direct way of finding out whether an individual's energy intake is nutritionally adequate is to ask him whether he has enough to eat. If he says 'yes' and if his body weight is satisfactory, his energy intake is satisfactory too.

(*i*) **Different kinds of bodies.** Human beings differ almost as much from one another in body build as do dogs. Among dogs, there are bull terriers, greyhounds and alsatians; among people, there are *endomorphs, mesomorphs* and *ectomorphs* and infinite combinations of all three (see Fig. 7.1).

    An endomorph is a round-faced, round-bodied person who, if he or she becomes fat, tends to develop double chins and a paunch.
    A mesomorph is a thickset, square individual, the type capable of taking up heavyweight wrestling, weight-lifting or tossing the caber.
    An ectomorph is a tall, thin individual with long arms and fingers and, if a man, often possesses a prominent Adam's apple.

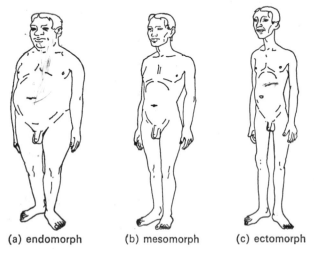

(a) endomorph   (b) mesomorph   (c) ectomorph

Fig. 7.1 Different kinds of body shape

Since these types and all the diverse mixtures of them are fixed by genetical inheritance, a nutritionist obviously cannot establish any single set of figures to indicate whether the energy value of any individual's diet is exactly that required to maintain an ideal body weight. The ideal weight for a short, stocky, thickset mesomorph, say an Eskimo 145 cm tall, will be different from that of a slight, slim-built ectomorph, perhaps a slender Indian, of the same height.

Because there are so many body shapes, even though all of them can be classified as mixtures of the three main types, it is common practice among nutritionists to compare the body weights of the people they may be studying with a single standard. While this is a convenient way of estimating whether people are overweight or underweight, and consequently whether the energy value of their diet is too great, too small or exactly right, we must recognize that the standard may not necessarily represent the ideal for the health of any one person. For example, standard measurements may be derived from an underfed community where the people are accustomed to having too little to eat and have become used to it. On the other hand, if the standards are those of the sort of community from which American women tennis players and competitors in the Miss World competition are drawn, the figures may indicate some degree of overfeeding. Table 7.6 shows figures derived from a large number of measurements made by various workers.

(*ii*) **The influence of social ideas on the ideal body weight.** Table 7.6 provides the nutritionist with a standard for the detection of *marked* deviations in the energy intake of a group of people either above or below satisfactory nutrition. As we have said, however, it might be seriously misleading if it were used to assess whether a particular individual is eating too much or too little. Variations from the standard could arise from body conformation differing significantly from the average, or from a marked difference in BMR due to a thyroid gland which is more or less active than usual. There is, however, another factor which a nutritional scientist must always bear in mind.

The purpose of good nutrition is health and health, let us repeat, can be defined as 'complete, physical, mental and social well-being and not merely the absence of ill-health and infirmity'. Different communities have different ideas about what they consider to be the appropriate body weight desirable for *complete social well-being*. Although, as we shall explain later, there are certain technical methods for measuring *obesity*, which is a sign of malnutrition, there is a margin within which individuals can choose *what kind of people they would like to be*.

A community which thinks a great deal (perhaps, in fact, too much) about health and nutrition and how its members look, who like their children to be big and their young men and women plump and buxom, may accept certain body weights as standards of optimum nutrition. In another community with a different idea of 'complete social well-being', where people consider that children should work, young men and women overcome strict tests before being accepted as full members of society, and adults think little of their appearance and more of some duty or purpose, considerably lower body

Table 7.6   Not too fat, not too thin—an estimate of ideal body weight

Height (cm)	men (kg)	women (kg)
140		44·9
141		45·4
142		45·9
143		46·4
144		47·0
145	51·9	47·5
146	52·4	48·0
147	52·9	48·6
148	53·5	49·2
149	54·0	49·8
150	54·5	50·9
151	55·0	51·0
152	55·6	51·5
153	56·1	52·0
154	56·6	52·5
155	57·2	53·1
156	57·9	53·7
157	58·6	54·3
158	59·3	54·9
159	59·9	55·5
160	60·5	56·2
161	61·1	56·9
162	61·7	57·6
163	62·3	58·3
164	62·9	58·9
165	63·5	59·5
166	64·0	60·1
167	64·6	60·7
168	65·2	61·4
169	65·9	62·1
170	66·6	
171	67·3	
172	68·0	
173	68·7	
174	69·4	
175	70·1	
176	70·8	
177	71·6	
178	72·4	
179	73·3	
180	74·2	
181	75·0	
182	75·8	
183	76·5	
184	77·3	
185	78·1	
186	78·9	

Height (cm)	boys (kg)	girls (kg)
110		18·8
112	19·7	19·6
114	20·6	20·4
116	21·3	21·2
118	22·1	22·0
120	22·9	22·8
122	23·7	23·6
124	24·5	24·5
126	25·4	25·4
128	26·4	26·4
130	27·3	27·4
132	28·2	28·5
134	29·2	29·5
136	30·2	30·6
138	31·4	31·6
140	32·5	32·8
142	33·7	34·0
144	35·1	35·3
146	36·2	36·5
148	37·4	37·7
150	38·6	38·8
152	40·0	39·8
154	41·4	42·0
156	43·1	43·9
158	44·7	46·4
160	46·5	49·7
162	48·2	52·7
164	50·2	
166	52·5	
168	54·8	
170	57·0	
172	59·4	

weights may be accepted as normal. Yet, though it is difficult for a nutritionist to judge, both may be equally healthy although the members of one community may obtain more units of energy in their diet than those of the other.

(c) The Measurement of Subcutaneous Fat

There are a number of ways, besides weighing a man, to measure whether he is obtaining too much or too little food for the work he has to do and for the maintenance of his body. Perhaps the simplest and most informative of these is to measure the thickness of the layer of tissue which lies just below the skin, which is partly made up of fat. This can be done by pinching up a fold of skin at the back of the upper arm, which is called the *triceps* area. In order to obtain uniform results, the thickness of this skinfold is best measured with

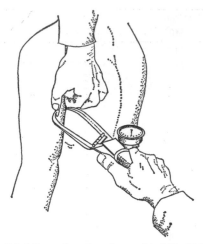

Fig. 7.2 Measuring the triceps skinfold thickness

a pair of specially constructed spring-loaded calipers. Again, as with body weight, the measurement can be compared with standard reference measurements to determine whether a particular person is too fat, normal or too thin; but individual variations still have to be borne in mind, and care is needed when comparing people from different communities who may well have different ideas of what constitutes 'normality'. Besides this, the skinfold

Table 7.7 Triceps skinfold thickness standards taken as representative of optimum nutrition (mm)*

age	male	female
1	10·3	10·2
2	10·0	10·1
3	9·3	9·7
4	9·3	10·2
5	9·1	9·4
6	8·2	9·6
7	7·9	9·4
8	7·6	10·1
9	8·2	10·3
10	8·2	10·4
11	8·9	10·6
12	8·5	10·1
13	8·1	10·4
14	7·9	11·3
15	6·3	11·4
adults	12·5	16·5

* As quoted by Jelliffe, D. B.: *The assessment of the nutritional status of the community*, World Health Organization, Monograph series 53 (Geneva, 1966).

thickness of an ectomorph, a mesomorph and an endomorph are different even when all three are equally well nourished.

The way the measurement is made is shown in Fig. 7.2; Table 7.7 lists some 'standard' figures for skinfold thickness measured in this way. In Section 8.2, the way these measurements are used to indicate the onset of obesity is discussed.

Unit Eight
Appetite and Obesity

8.1 Appetite and Energy Intake

During a man's life he will eat on aggregate tons of food, and at various times his way of life will involve widely varying degrees of activity, so that sometimes, in the summer, for instance, he may take a great deal of exercise and at other times very little. It is remarkable that throughout this long period the energy value of what he eats matches the energy expenditure of what he does so precisely that his body weight may remain almost exactly the same.

For many years no one knew why an individual seated at the table abruptly pushed back his chair at the end of a meal and decided that he had had enough. Even today there is more to be discovered about the physiological mechanisms controlling appetite. The factors most closely concerned, however, are now well known.

(a) The Hypothalamus

This is a small region at the base of the brain which acts as the regulator of appetite. In deciding whether or not we are 'hungry', the hypothalamus is thought to take various factors into account. Some of those which have been suggested are the level of glucose and free fatty acids in the blood (these are chemical stimuli), the degree of distension or contraction of the stomach (nervous stimulus) and the temperature of the blood (thermal stimulus). While there is apparently some justification for each of these—eating sweets before meals reduces the feeling of hunger; stomach contractions indicate that it is lunch time; we tend to eat less when we are hot—no complete picture has yet been produced which entirely accounts for the feeling of hunger.

In normal people, who maintain a constant body weight without any trouble and are almost unconscious of the existence of a problem in others, the hypothalamus 'switches off' the appetite exactly when the energy intake matches the energy output. This control does not necessarily operate on a day-to-day basis. If the energy intake suddenly rises, for example over the Christmas holidays, or on the other hand if the energy output falls, there may be a brief period when the body weight rises. However, equilibrium will soon be re-established and the appetite regulated so that the previous body weight is regained.

The hypothalamus in people *with a tendency to become overweight* appears to be 'set' in such a way that it fails to 'switch off' the appetite as soon as the energy value of the food eaten is exactly equal to the energy requirements of the day's activities. Such people therefore remain hungry and retain their appetite just too long. As a result, if they go on eating until they are satisfied (as people naturally do when food is available) they become overweight. Alternatively, if they wish to avoid being overweight they must leave the table *while they still feel hungry*—and this is a difficult thing to do.

The appetite-control mechanism *in people who take very little exercise* loses its ability to regulate energy intake in proportion to energy output. Whereas, as we have said, the hypothalamus usually regulates appetite with remarkable accuracy in accordance with the varying amounts of energy expended on work, this precision is lost when people become almost entirely sedentary. It follows that when energy expenditure becomes very low, people are inclined to eat a diet providing more kilojoules of energy than they need. Under these circumstances they consequently tend to put on weight.

(b) Psychological Factors

It is well known that the flow of hormones produced by the so-called *endocrine glands*, of which the hypothalamus is one, is affected by psychological factors. The flow of digestive juices, for example, is not only influenced by the sight of food and the taste and smell of food in the mouth and nose, but also by the *thought* of food even when no food is there. Similarly, anger, worry or apprehension can actually take away a man's appetite. There is a well-documented psychological disease called *anorexia nervosa* in which the patient, who is frequently a young woman, develops a kind of melancholia and loses her appetite so completely that she becomes thin and emaciated and, unless she can be successfully treated, may actually starve to death. On the other hand, a girl who feels neglected or frustrated may eat to excess in an attempt to comfort herself and relieve her need, and in consequence she may become fat.

Appetite is also psychologically affected by people's deeply ingrained ideas of what is acceptable to eat and what is regarded as repugnant. For example, people eagerly accept and enjoy tripe when they are accustomed to it, but those to whom it is unfamiliar may prefer to go hungry rather than eat it. In some countries dog or horseflesh is accepted with relish, while in other communities it is refused with disgust.

8.2 Overweight (Obesity)

Obesity is the condition that exists when the body is overloaded with excessive fat; it is the commonest of all types of malnutrition in industrialized countries. While it is not easy to determine precisely the point at which the amount of fat on any particular individual can be said to be excessive, it is usually accepted that obesity definitely exists when the body weight has increased to 10 per cent more than a standard level.

Some American nutritionists consider that the triceps skinfold measurement is a more reliable indication of obesity than excess weight. This is logical since the skinfold thickness is a direct measurement of the layer of fat lying under the skin. Figures accepted as indicating the beginning of obesity among white Americans are shown in Table 8.1. These can be compared with values in Table 7.7, which refer to normal non-obese people.

Table 8.1 Triceps skinfold thickness measurements indicating the start of obesity in white Americans (mm)*

age (years)	males	females
5	12	14
6	12	15
7	13	16
8	14	17
9	15	18
10	16	20
11	17	21
12	18	22
13	18	23
14	17	23
15	16	24
16	15	25
17	14	26
18	15	27
19	15	27
20	16	28
21	17	28
22	18	28
23	18	28
24	19	28
25	20	29
26	20	29
27	21	29
28	22	29
29	22	29
30–50	23	30

* Seltzer, C. C., and Mayer, J.: *Postgraduate Medical Journal, 38* (1965), 2.

(a) The Causes of Obesity

Obesity is always caused by overeating, that is to say, it arises when the amount of food consumed each day provides more units of energy than the energy expended to maintain the body's mechanism (the BMR) and in the general activities of the day and the demands of muscular activity in work and sport. When this occurs, a proportion of the surplus energy in the diet is stored in the form of fat and if the consumption of food of surplus energy value is prolonged the individual concerned becomes obese. The cause of obesity thus appears to be simple, but as we have said the situation is more complicated than it at first seems. This is because the *causes* impelling a person to overeat and hence to become obese may involve a number of different factors, which may be classified under the following five headings.

(*i*) **Hereditary.** What kind of an individual he is; whether he has inherited from his ancestors a type of body structure that is more or less likely to become fat. For example, endomorphs, the people who have a round-bodied build, become fat more readily than the lankier ectomorphs.

(*ii*) **Hormonal.** Whether his hypothalamus is overactive; whether his other endocrine glands are producing other hormones in quantities likely to disturb the natural balance within the body. The action of the hypothalamus may be disturbed if it is damaged, either accidentally or by surgical operation.

(*iii*) **Psychological.** Whether he suffers from any kind of psychological disturbance which can induce a hormonal imbalance that may itself disturb his appetite control, and hence induce obesity.

(*iv*) **Socio-economic.** Whether the type of community in which he lives, his position in the social scale or the kind of meals he is expected to eat may influence any tendency to obesity which he may have—for example, whether he may be expected to accept food, or more often drink, whenever it is offered even if he is neither hungry nor thirsty.

(*v*) **Exercise.** Whether his daily routine includes sufficient exercise to keep his hypothalamus functioning properly, and to keep the balance between his energy intake and energy output correctly maintained.

(*b*) **Dangers of Obesity**

(*i*) **Earlier death.** Statistics collected in the United States imply that people who are overweight do not live as long as those who are not. A man of 45 who weighs 10 kilograms more than the standard weight for his height can on average expect to live only about three-quarters the number of years of a man of standard weight.

(*ii*) **Coronary heart disease.** Obesity is associated with a raised concentration of cholesterol in the blood which is probably related to coronary heart disease (see Section 4.4). Furthermore, people who are overweight are more likely to die of a heart attack if they have one.

(*iii*) **Expectant mothers.** Obese women are more subject to complications of pregnancy, particularly toxaemia, and are more likely to have difficult deliveries.

(*iv*) **Miscellaneous effects.** Obese people are more liable to varicose veins, high blood pressure and certain kidney diseases; their chances of developing diabetes in middle age are somewhat increased and they are more subject to abdominal hernias. On the other hand they are less likely to contract tuberculosis or to commit suicide.

(*v*) **Psychological difficulties.** Many people suffer unhappiness and distress from the thought that they are fat. Although obesity undoubtedly ranks as a state of malnutrition and although the deviations from health we have mentioned are undoubtedly real, the feeling of revulsion at being fat and the constant effort required to achieve, and then to maintain, a more desirable weight represent significant and continuing additional hardships for the obese.

(c) The Treatment of Obesity

(i) **Diet.** The only way for an obese person to lose weight is to eat less than he has done before, or to increase his energy expenditure by taking more physical exercise without increasing his food intake, or to do both.

When a person loses weight, a proportion of the adipose tissue of his body disappears. Adipose tissue consists mainly of fat, but it also comprises some protein. Fat itself has an energy value of 37 kJ per gram and that of adipose tissue is approximately 32 kJ per gram. It follows, therefore, that in order to lose about 1 kg of body weight a week, which is a reasonable target, an obese person must eat a diet which provides each week the energy equivalent of 1 kg of adipose tissue *less than his physiological requirement*. (This means that he must eat this much less than he needs, *not* this much less than he was eating before.) The energy value of 1 kg of adipose tissue is $32 \times 1\ 000 = 32\ 000\ kJ$; this implies a cut in his energy intake of roughly 5 000 kJ each day. We have seen (Section 7.2(*a*)) that an obese sedentary man can be expected to need 11 300 kJ each day; he must therefore restrict his daily energy intake to 6 300 kJ if he is to lose weight at a reasonable rate. Similarly, an obese sedentary woman whose average daily needs are 9 200 kJ must reduce her intake to 4 200 kJ per day if she is to treat her obesity effectively.

A so-called *reducing diet* can be constructed in a variety of ways; but certain principles must be borne in mind.

1. Select food items from which reasonable meals can be made.
2. The total weight of all the food items in the diet, including snacks and drinks—in fact, anything eaten or drunk whether or not it is called a meal—multiplied by the energy value of each must not exceed the target figure, for instance 6 300 kJ, as in the example above. If the energy value is to be kept down to this level, and yet the food left is to be enough for the preparation of something still recognizable as a meal, it is obviously sensible to limit drastically high-energy-value foods such as sugar and starchy foods of comparatively low moisture content like bread, cake and pastry. Fat is of all foods the one of highest energy value. It is possible to avoid altogether high-fat commodities like suet pudding and mayonnaise, and to limit severely the use of butter or margarine, so as to reduce significantly the energy value of the diet as a whole; but such a diet may well prove so unpalatable and unsatisfying that the obese man or woman may rebel, and abandon the reducing diet altogether.
3. Bulky food of low energy value, green salads, melon and most other fruits, vegetables like cabbage—all these can be included without making any major contribution to the energy value of the daily intake.
4. It is important to make sure that although the diet is limited in energy value and therefore to some extent in quantity, it is not impossibly restricted in variety and interest. Thus, for example, either meat or fish will provide animal protein; either fruit or green vegetables will contribute vitamin C (see Unit 17).

From time to time exaggerated claims are put forward for the special efficiency of reducing diets composed on some novel or bizarre basis. Proposals have been made for diets high in fat, for diets in which protein is eaten at one meal and starch at another but never the two together, and many others. None of these claims has been justified. Two principles only have been shown to have some justification. When the energy intake is provided mainly by protein there is a possibility that some energy may be dispersed in the form of specific dynamic action. And when the day's diet is consumed as seven meals or more rather than three meals or less, there is some evidence that there is an economy in usable energy value.

The essential feature of all reducing diets is that they have a *restricted energy value*. This means that no matter how ingeniously their reducing diets are constructed or how attractively they are served, people who wish to lose weight will still be hungry when they leave the table, and as the price of their success must face for a prolonged period the disagreeable necessity of resisting the temptation to enjoy satisfying their appetite. This degree of fortitude in the face of the continual feeling of hunger is difficult to maintain, which is why the treatment of obesity is so often unsuccessful or, if it does at first succeed, short-lived. For this reason, clubs where overweight people can meet together and give each other encouragement, after the principle of the Alcoholics Anonymous organization, may serve a useful nutritional purpose.

(*ii*) **Exercise.** Physical exercise is in two respects as important as diet in the treatment of obesity. When obese people live an almost entirely sedentary life, as frequently happens, the hormonal control which in normal people maintains a delicate balance between energy intake and energy expenditure is disturbed. Quite a slight increase in the amount of exercise taken by a sedentary overweight person may therefore exert a disproportionately favourable response. Over and above this, regular daily exercise, combined with the maintenance of a diet providing only the energy value physiologically desirable, makes it easier to attain a desirable body weight. For example, a man who takes an hour's walk expends about 1 250 kJ in doing so. This is equivalent to using up 40 g of adipose tissue, which in itself seems very little; but if this same man keeps up his daily walk, without increasing the energy value of his diet, he will lose 14·6 kg in body weight in a year.

(*iii*) **Drugs.** Many of the drugs and nostrums claimed to reduce appetite and thus make it easy to lose weight are as ineffective as are the vibrating machines and other patent devices put out for the same purpose. There are drugs, however, which do have an effect on appetite. The best known of these are the *amphetamines*. Their depressing effect on the appetite is, however, temporary and they sometimes produce undesirable side-effects. They can, therefore, only be obtained on a medical prescription and their usefulness is very restricted. *Fenfluramine*, a compound related to the amphetamines, has recently received some publicity: it affects the uptake and metabolism of glucose and free fatty acids, rather than stimulating the central nervous system as the amphetamines do, and it is also less habit-forming. However, until research workers can develop a drug acting directly on the hypothalamus, it is unlikely that obesity will be effectively treated by appetite-limiting drugs.

Certain other drugs, which increase the BMR and thus accelerate the rate at which the body uses up energy, have been tested in an attempt to reduce body weight. These have caused disastrous side-effects, including blindness, and have consequently been abandoned.

Preparations of *methylcellulose* are sometimes used as slimming aids. Methylcellulose is not a drug but a chemically inert compound which cannot be digested. When taken with fluid, these add bulk to the stomach contents, so distending the stomach walls, and giving a feeling of fullness.

(d) Obesity in Children

All mothers are pleased to see their children growing quickly. If a child is to grow properly, his diet must contain an adequate proportion of protein to produce muscular tissue (see Unit 5) and enough calcium and phosphorus to enable the bones to grow (see Unit 10); it must also have an adequate energy value. The measure of adequacy, however, for a child as for an adult is the extent to which it balances the child's energy expenditure on muscular activity, basal metabolism and growth. Children will become obese if they are pressed and persuaded to eat more than they need and if, furthermore, they take little exercise, as may easily happen nowadays when many children no longer walk to school but are driven in motor-cars, and when some of them run about and play less than children used to do because they sit watching television instead.

There is an extra disadvantage for an obese child not shared by most obese adults. When an adult becomes fat, the fat accumulates in adipose tissue, in the specialized cells lying under the skin, in the abdominal cavity and elsewhere. In adults, an increase in girth is largely due to the consequent swelling of these cells, rather than to an increase in their number. In a growing child that is eating too much the *number* of such cells increases. If an obese child recovers, and regains a normal weight, he may therefore find that in adult life there is a tendency for him to become fat rather easily and for his obesity to be unexpectedly serious, since he already possesses an abnormally large number of adipose cells.

Unit Nine

Mineral Substances and Nutrients

9.1 Introduction

A number of mineral (inorganic) substances are important either in the structure or in the functioning of the body and must therefore be provided by the various foods which go to make up the diet. These chemical elements can be divided into three groups according to their physiological function.

(a) Minerals in the Body Tissues

Among these are *phosphorus, iron, sulphur, zinc, copper* and many others, some of which, although essential to the body, are necessary in minute amounts only. They are found in the muscles, the blood corpuscles, the liver and elsewhere.

(b) Soluble Minerals in the Body Fluids

The function of these is concerned with the maintenance of a constant environment for the living cells of the body. The most important substance in this category is common salt, *sodium chloride*. If the level of salt in the blood plasma varies, even by a tiny amount, from its normal concentration of approximately 0.9 per cent, the functioning of the body is immediately disturbed, and unpleasant symptoms appear.

(c) Mineral Components of the Bones and Teeth

The hard, rigid structures of bones and teeth obviously consist of different materials from those which make up flesh and blood. Whereas the soft tissues of the body are built up of organic polymers, predominantly protein, which all contain large carbon-atom networks, bones and teeth are mainly mineral structures. This is why when the tissues of the body decay after death (in fact, their substance becomes the food for bacteria), the skeleton survives. The principal elements composing bones and teeth are *calcium, phosphorus* and *magnesium*, with some other elements in lesser amounts.

In addition to these, other mineral elements have special roles in nutrition. *Iodine*, for example, is a component of thyroxine, the hormone controlling the BMR of the body. *Fluorine* plays a part in the formation of enamel, the inner hard tissue of the teeth. *Manganese, cobalt, zinc* and others all exercise essential functions in the physiological operation of the body (see Section 9.3).

Many of these minerals occur in the body in the form of *ions* or ionic compounds (an ion is an atom or a group of atoms carrying an electric charge due to its having gained or lost one or more electrons). It is important to remember that the properties of ions are very different from those of the free element(s). For example, chlorine occurs in body tissues and in foods in the form of chloride ions, that is, chlorine atoms which have each gained an electron and hence carry a negative charge. The element chlorine is never found free in nature; it is a yellowish gas with a choking smell, which is so toxic that it was used as a poison gas in the First World War.

9.2 The Maintenance of the Uniformity of the Body's Internal Environment

Early in the history of life on earth land-dwelling creatures did not exist; the primitively simple organisms from which human beings have evolved lived in the warm sea. These creatures were not able to carry their internal environment about with them, as we do. The membranes which enclosed them allowed the soluble components of the surrounding sea water to diffuse freely in and out of their constituent cells, with the result that the soluble mineral elements were present in the same concentrations in the cells as in the sea water. These early forms of life evolved into more complex creatures until at last, in the form of primitive amphibians, they became capable of leaving the sea and maintaining life on land; they then took with them tissue fluids of the same proportional composition as that of the sea water in which their bio-chemical mechanisms had evolved. Even though, during the long ages since then, modified and specialized functions have evolved in higher animals and man, the mineral composition of the fluid in which the body's cells function—called *extracellular fluid*—has definite similarities to that of the sea, not so much as it is now but as it was many millions of years ago. The most important elements in this fluid are chlorine, sodium, magnesium, calcium, sulphur, potassium, bromine, iodine and iron, and all these elements, with the possible exception of bromine, contribute to human nutrition. However, the sea contains many more minerals than these, even though the concentration of some of them is minute, and it is interesting that it has recently been discovered that some of these other minerals have a part in nutrition.

(a) Salt (sodium chloride)

The body of a 'reference' man weighing about 65 kg contains about 200 g of salt. The amount of salt which people consume each day varies very widely; it can fluctuate from 5 g up to 20 g or more. This is made up partly of the salt which occurs naturally in foods or which is added to commodities like cheese and bread during manufacture, and partly from salt which may be added as a condiment, either in cooking or at the table. The relative amounts of salt present in the different types of food which make up a normal diet are shown in Table 9.1.

Under normal circumstances the body can maintain the salinity of its extracellular fluid with great precision. This control is regulated by hormones produced by the *adrenal glands*, which lie close to the kidneys. Most normal mixed diets provide more salt than the body requires, and the surplus is excreted in urine by way of the kidneys.

Table 9.1   The approximate salt content of certain foods

	g per 100 g
Foods rich in salt	
Ham	5·0
Corned beef	3·3–4·2
Cheese	1·7–3·8
Sausages	1·8–3·2
Bacon	1·9–3·0
Cornflakes	1·7–2·2
Butter	0·5–2·5
Kippers	2·5
Foods containing moderate amounts of salt	
Celery	0·4
Green and root vegetables	0·02–0·3
Eggs	0·3
Meat (beef, mutton, pork)	0·12–0·3
Fish	0·02–0·2
Milk	0·1
Oatmeal	0·1
Foods containing little or no salt	
Fresh fruit	0·02
Nuts	0·02
Prunes	0·02
Rice	0·02
Flour	trace
Sugar	trace
Lard and cooking fat	trace
Unsalted butter	trace

There appears to be little or no nutritional reason for adding salt to one's food; this is best explained as a matter of taste or custom. When the Arctic explorer Stefansson lived for a year with the Eskimos on a diet composed almost entirely of meat, his health remained good, but he complained that the only disagreeable feature of the whole dietary study was his craving for the taste of salt, a desire apparently not shared by his Eskimo companions. Normally the kidneys can readily get rid of any excess of salt consumed for reasons of taste. However, patients with certain types of heart disease and some kinds of kidney failure require a diet with a low salt content.

Salt loss. Under certain circumstances the body can lose a considerable proportion of its salt content, especially if a great deal of fluid is being lost.

(i) *Diarrhoea.* Substantial amounts of salt may be lost when diarrhoea persists for an extended period. This may occur in certain infectious diseases and under conditions of serious undernutrition including kwashiorkor (Section 5.7(b)).

(*ii*) *Sweating.* Sweat contains from about 0.2 to 0.4 per cent of salt. A man doing heavy work under hot conditions, such as a boilerman working in the engine room of a ship in the tropics or a furnaceman in a steelworks, may lose up to 4 litres of sweat a day, or sometimes even more. This represents the excretion of about 14 g of salt.

Salt deficiency causes muscular cramps, and it is important that people known to be at risk receive adequate salt in their diet and perhaps have salted drinks freely available as well.

(*b*) Potassium

Potassium has chemical properties which are similar in many respects to those of sodium and, like sodium, occurs in foods as positively charged ions. Like sodium, potassium is present in most ordinary diets in adequate amounts and any potassium which is consumed in excess of the body's needs is readily excreted by the kidneys. Potassium plays an important part in maintaining the constancy of the body's internal environment; but it behaves differently from sodium in that whereas sodium (as salt) is found for the most part in the extracellular fluids (as can be recognized by the saltiness of blood, sweat and tears) potassium occurs mainly within the cells themselves. The contributions of potassium to the diet made by various foods are shown in Table 9.2.

Under normal circumstances the body regulates its potassium uptake to suit its needs, but since most of the element is held within the body's cells, it is not at all easy to assess whether the current diet is supplying adequate potassium. Most ordinary western diets provide ample potassium so that it is rarely necessary for a nutritionist to pay any particular attention to the exact amount provided by the different foods consumed.

Severe injury and other conditions resulting in breakdown of cellular proteins may lead to excessive potassium loss in the urine. The same condition may occur in certain rare diseases or in some kinds of kidney failure. Raised levels of potassium in the blood are sometimes found when there has been leakage of potassium from the cells into the blood as a result of shock after injury. Perhaps more important, it has been realized that prolonged diarrhoea, as in diseases like cholera, may lead to potassium depletion which can result in heart failure.

Potassium deficiency in the diet is uncommon in industrialized countries, but it is sometimes found in tropical areas where sago and tapioca form a major part of the diet and where there may be too little of any kind of food to eat. The symptoms of potassium deficiency are mental apathy and muscular weakness, which can be associated with attacks of paralysis lasting 24 hours or more.

(*c*) Other Minerals Contributing to the Constancy of the Internal Environment

Besides sodium and potassium ions, *calcium* and *magnesium* ions must also be present in appropriate concentrations to maintain a uniform internal

Table 9.2   The potassium content of certain foods

	mg per 100 g
Good sources of potassium	
Soya flour	1 660
Dried milk	1 300
Dried fruit	860
Potatoes	570
Nuts	400–600
Chocolate	250–350
Meat (beef, mutton, pork, chicken)	350
Fish	250–350
Bacon	250–280
Green and root vegetables	250
Golden syrup	240
Eggs	160
Milk	160
Bread	70–140
Fruit	120
Cheese	116
Cornflakes	114
Rice	113
Poor sources of potassium	
Honey	35
Tapioca	20
Butter	15
Stewed tripe	9
Margarine	5
Cooking fat	5
Sago	5
Sugar	2
Lard	1

medium within the body. These are in balance with chloride, phosphate, sulphate and carbonate ions carrying *chlorine, phosphorus, sulphur* and *carbon dioxide*. Of these, *calcium* and *phosphorus* are of most direct interest to a practising nutritionist, and are discussed in more detail in Unit 10. *Magnesium* occurs in comparatively large concentrations in the tissues and also in the bones; the body contains about 25 g of magnesium altogether. Like potassium, most of the body's magnesium content is held within the cells. Magnesium is quite widely distributed in foods and particularly in green vegetables, where it is a constituent of the green pigment, chlorophyll. The chances of a deficiency of magnesium in the diet under normal circumstances are therefore small, but it has been known to occur, causing depression, muscular weakness and sometimes even convulsions, when prolonged diarrhoea has led to serious loss of magnesium from the body.

9.3   Trace Metals of Nutritional Significance

Besides the minerals discussed in Section 9.2, others have special significance even though they are present in foods only in minute quantities. Of these, *iron* is dealt with in detail in Unit 11 and *iodine* and *fluorine* in Unit 12. The remarkable advances that have taken place in analytical chemistry in recent years have led to the discovery that a number of other mineral elements also contribute to well-being. This is, perhaps, not altogether surprising when we recall our distant ancestors living in the prehistoric sea in the water of which, then as now, mineral elements of many sorts were to be found.

(a) Copper

Although there have been no reports of diets harmfully deficient in copper, this metal is known to be essential to health. The reasons why symptoms of nutritional deficiency do not normally appear are that the amount required is very small indeed, and that most foods contain at least a trace of copper.

Copper is essential for the normal development of the nervous system and plays a part in maintaining the myelin sheath which forms a kind of insulating layer around each nerve. Copper is also a component of several of the enzymes important in metabolism.

(b) Zinc

Like copper, zinc occurs in trace concentrations in most foods. It is known to be essential for tissue growth, and like copper it forms part of a number of enzymes. There is some evidence that zinc is concerned with some of the processes involved in the development of the foetus during pregnancy.

Zinc deficiency is uncommon, but it has recently been suggested that this may be the cause of a particular kind of stunted growth seen in some children in the Middle East. It also seems possible that a deficiency of zinc may arise through interference in zinc absorption by phytic acid, present in unfermented cereal products (compare Sections 10.4(b) and 11.3(a)).

(c) Cobalt

Cobalt is another metal needed in the diet in exceedingly small amounts, probably even smaller than the necessary quantities of copper and zinc. Since traces of cobalt are widely distributed in foodstuffs and may even occur in the atmosphere it is hardly surprising that symptoms of cobalt deficiency have not been observed in people, although they have been demonstrated in sheep. Cobalt however forms part of the molecular structure of *cyanocobalamin* (vitamin B_{12}) (see Section 16.5) and deficiency of cyanocobalamin may occur with serious results when people eat certain unusual kinds of vegetarian diet.

(d) Manganese

Manganese is present in the blood and also in the liver. Although the picture is not entirely clear, it is probably necessary for nutritional health in people, since it forms a part of certain enzymes; besides, shortage of manganese has been shown to affect bone growth in several species of experimental animals, and also to impair the reproductive performance of mice and rats. It is widely distributed in foods with the interesting exception that it is entirely lacking from milk (which is also deficient in iron and copper). This emphasizes that milk, although it is a useful food for infants, is *not* a 'perfect' food, as is sometimes claimed.

(e) Selenium

Nutritionists can learn a useful lesson from selenium, although the element is unlikely to be of practical importance to them since it is only required in the very small amounts which most food combinations certainly supply. Many of the minerals needed in trace quantities for good nutrition may at the same time be poisonous if present as major contaminants of food: copper is one such example. Selenium, however, first came to the attention of nutritionists *because* of its toxicity. In certain areas of America, the soil contains appreciable amounts of selenium, which, passing into the herbage of the pastures, makes it poisonous to livestock. It is used nowadays in manufacturing such products as electrical rectifiers and paints, and it is known as a serious industrial hazard. Yet careful experiments with animals have shown that about 0.01 to 0.04 mg of selenium per kilogram of diet is required as a nutrient if young animals are to grow properly and adult ones are to remain healthy. So far as is known, selenium is concerned with the action of vitamin E, which is discussed in Unit 15. Yet while exerting this beneficial influence when only a trace is present in the diet, there is also evidence to suggest that when present in much larger amounts selenium may have a carcinogenic (cancer-producing) effect. This is no cause for special alarm; it demonstrates, however, how important it is in nutrition always to consider facts in relation to the circumstances.

(f) Chromium

The intake of chromium each day from a normal diet is about 0.07 mg and of this quantity only approximately 1 per cent is apparently absorbed: that is to say, as far as we know at present, a man's daily intake of chromium is about 0.000 7 mg. Yet in spite of this very small amount consumed each day in food, there is good evidence that chromium is important in maintaining the appropriate glucose level in the blood. Diabetic patients appear to have a need for chromium which is different from (and probably greater than) that required by normal people. Some old people have been found to have difficulty in bringing the glucose concentration in their blood back to a normal level after eating carbohydrate-containing food. It is possible that they absorb chromium less efficiently than normal people and their disability may in some way be due to a shortage of chromium, although this is by no means certain.

9.4   Minerals in the Diet

Nutritionists concerned with the practical problems of providing satisfactory diets for those for whom they are responsible need to ensure that the amounts of sodium (as salt) and potassium, calcium and phosphorus, iron, iodine and fluorine are sufficient for their needs. The other mineral elements discussed in this Unit can all be expected to be present in the minute quantities required in almost any combination of food likely to be chosen as a normal diet. Apart from the intrinsic interest of understanding the way in which these substances play a part in metabolism, and thus becoming equipped with information which might provide the key to some unexpected emergency, this knowledge has another value. It is obviously important that foodstuffs, many of which are manufactured on a large scale and distributed to great numbers of people, should be wholesome, pure and free from harmful contaminants. There is, however, a danger that by drawing up unnecessarily stringent specifications—for example, that all foods must be entirely free from selenium which is more toxic than arsenic when too much is eaten—the nutritional value of food may actually be harmed by an insistence that it should be too 'pure'.

A further point arises from this discussion of trace minerals. It is that, since science can never pretend to provide all the knowledge there is to know but always shows that there is more to be discovered, it is prudent to recommend that diets should wherever possible be made up of a *variety* of different foods. In nutritional science, as in other aspects of life, there is safety in numbers.

Unit Ten
Calcium and phosphorus

10.1 Introduction

In the last 50 years, for the first time in history, great numbers of people have been able to live out their lives without the fear that they, their children or their friends would die from the infectious diseases against which all previous generations had been helpless. Smallpox, typhus, yellow fever, typhoid, malaria—great killing diseases of humanity—and in our own generation tuberculosis and poliomyelitis have all become preventable. These triumphs in the ceaseless battle against human misery have been due to advances in the sciences of bacteriology and virology and an increasing understanding of the mechanism by which the body can acquire immunity to infection. A scientific achievement of equal importance has been made between 1920 and the present time with the virtual disappearance of *rickets* in northern industrialized countries and in some of the crowded cities of India as well. This, however, was brought about by discoveries in the science of nutrition.

Rickets is a disease of infancy and childhood, in which calcium and phosphorus are not laid down as usual by the child's body to form the structure

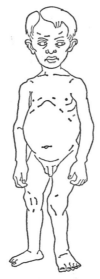

Fig. 10.1 A child with rickets

of the bones. The result is that the legs become bent and deformed, the ribs grow malformed to give a pigeon chest and the pelvis becomes misshapen (see Fig. 10.1); these and other disfigurements cannot be corrected except by major surgery, and accompany the victims to the end of their days. Until about 1900, up to 75 per cent of all working-class children in many great industrial cities, particularly those of northern countries—London, Glasgow, Vienna, Paris—suffered more or less severely from rickets. A glance round the playground of any urban school is enough to demonstrate that this state of affairs has been entirely changed by the continued application of nutritional knowledge; but the disease occasionally re-appears in poorly fed children, and it is therefore important that students of nutrition should be familiar with the functions of calcium and phosphorus in the diet.

While rickets is primarily due to calcium deficiency (phosphorus, discussed in Section 10.7, is readily available from many sources and is often harmlessly consumed in excess), a second factor, *cholecalciferol* (vitamin D), is also involved; this compound is discussed in Unit 14.

10.2   Functions of Calcium in the Body

(*a*) Formation of the Skeleton

An average man's body contains approximately 1.5 kg of calcium. Of this, more than 99 per cent goes to make up the principal structure of the bones and skull, mainly in the form of *calcium phosphate*. Not all the calcium is fixed; the bones are living structures just as the fleshy tissues are. They also act as stores of calcium, from which it may be drawn for use elsewhere, in the body.

(*b*) As a Component of Blood

The roles of calcium in various metabolic processes require that a steady concentration of about 10 mg of calcium per 100 ml of blood plasma is maintained consistently. This uniform calcium concentration is controlled with remarkable precision by the *parathyroid glands*. These are small bodies, of which there are normally four, which lie close to, or actually embedded in, the thyroid gland in the neck.

(*c*) Blood Clotting

Calcium is one of the several substances involved in the mechanism of blood clotting, by which haemorrhage (loss of blood) from a wound or injury is stopped.

(*d*) The Contraction of Muscles

Calcium is concerned with the ability of muscles to contract in a controlled fashion and also with the transmission of the nerve signals to the muscles which initiate this orderly movement. A drop in the normal concentration of blood calcium, even a comparatively small one, produces cramp in the muscles, and a characteristic muscular twitching called *tetany*. A lowering of blood calcium may arise from absolute reduction, for example, through injury and consequent malfunction of the parathyroid glands, in severe rickets, or in malnourished women who are breast-feeding infants and consequently losing calcium in their milk. Alternatively, an effective fall in the calcium level may be brought about if the normal alkalinity of the blood is increased. This may happen when severe vomiting has caused a loss of hydrochloric acid from the stomach, or it may be deliberately produced by 'over-breathing'. If a person breathes unnecessarily fast and continues doing so for some little time, a considerable amount of carbon dioxide gas is pumped out of his system by way of the lungs, and the carbon dioxide concentration in the blood falls in consequence. Now dissolved carbon dioxide is, in effect, an acid; in fact, at one time the solution was called 'carbonic acid'. Loss of carbon dioxide, that is, a loss of acid, from the blood, means that the blood becomes more alkaline, part of the calcium in it is immobilized and tetany may be produced.

(e) The Activation of Enzymes

Calcium plays a part in the activation of certain enzymes, notably in the formation of *trypsin* from its inactive precursor *trypsinogen* in the small intestine (see Section 2.3). It also activates the gastric enzyme *rennin*, the action of which is important in the digestion of milk.

10.3 The Main Sources of Calcium in the Diet

The foods which contribute most calcium to the diet are milk and products made from it, such as cheese and dried or condensed milk. Calcium phosphate is a major component of the bones of fish, like those of other creatures; fish like sardines, whitebait and canned salmon, of which the bones can be eaten, are therefore useful sources of calcium.

10.4 Factors Affecting Calcium Absorption

(a) Substances Facilitating Calcium Absorption

The absorption of calcium into the body is greatly affected by the amount of *vitamin D* available (see Unit 14). *Protein* also helps calcium absorption, although to a much lesser degree than vitamin D.

(b) Substances Hindering Calcium Absorption

(i) Phytic acid. This is a phosphorus-containing compound which is widely distributed in cereals. It is present in greater concentration in the outer parts of cereals and in the husk, and wholemeal bread and flour and oatmeal therefore

Table 10.1   The calcium content of certain foods

	mg per 100 g
Good sources of calcium	
Dried skim milk	1 277
Whitebait	860
Cheese: hard (Cheddar)	810
blue (Stilton)	362
Sardines	409
Condensed milk	344
Fresh milk	120
Herring	100
Canned salmon	66
Baking powder	11 300
Moderately good sources of calcium	
Cabbage	65
Turnip	59
Eggs	56
White fish	25
Butter	15
Meat	10
Poor sources of calcium	
Oatmeal	55
Brown flour	24*
White flour	15*
Potato	8
Rice	4
Sugar	0
Cooking fat	0

* Certain countries enforce the addition of calcium, in the form of chalk (calcium carbonate), to the flour used to make bread. In Great Britain, 125 mg of calcium is added per
100 g flour; this makes flour, and bread made from it, fairly rich sources of calcium
(see also Section 10.4(*b*)).

contain more phytic acid than white flour and other more highly refined
cereals. Phytic acid combines with calcium, making it unavailable to the body.
Because of their phytic acid content, Table 10.1 includes oatmeal and flour
in the group of foods which are poor sources of dietary calcium, even though
the figures show that they contain appreciable amounts of calcium. It is
because of the presence of phytic acid that flour, bread and other cereal
products are often enriched by adding calcium to them, usually as a purified
form of calcium carbonate called *prepared chalk*.

Although phytic acid is nutritionally harmful because of its inhibition of
calcium absorption, it is a somewhat unstable compound. It can be split
up and rendered harmless by the action of an enzyme, *phytase*, which is
produced during the fermentation of dough in bread-making. It follows,
therefore, that unfermented cereal products like pancakes or scones reduce

the effective intake of calcium more seriously than bread made with the same flour.

(*ii*) **Oxalic acid.** This substance is present in a number of leafy vegetables and fruit. Like phytic acid, it forms an insoluble compound with calcium, and therefore interferes with its absorption. Rhubarb, spinach and strawberries all contain appreciable amounts of oxalic acid.

(*iii*) **Fat.** The fatty acids released when fat is being digested can combine with calcium to form insoluble soaps. This phenomenon is mainly of practical significance for patients whose condition interferes with their normal ability to absorb fat; under these circumstances they may also suffer from a deficiency of calcium.

10.5 The Calcium Requirements of Different Categories of People

Calcium is primarily needed to form the substance of bones and teeth, and growing children therefore require proportionately more in their diet than adults. Also, as we have already mentioned, nursing mothers who are providing their infants with breast milk rich in calcium themselves need adequate amounts of calcium in their food.

Table 10.2 shows how much calcium people of different ages and conditions are recommended to consume each day in a nutritionally satisfactory diet.

Table 10.2 Recommended daily intake of calcium

	mg per day
Infants (0–1 years old)	600
Children	
1–9 years old	500
9–15 years old	700
15–18 years old	600
Normal adults (men and women)	500
Women in the last 3 months of pregnancy and when breast-feeding their babies	1 200

Although the figures in this table are sensible recommendations, there are two factors which make it necessary for nutritionists to recognize that they are merely the best target values that can be set, rather than rigid physiological necessities for everyone. This means that while some people's well-being might suffer if they obtained less than the amount indicated for them, others—perhaps, indeed, most normal individuals—could probably remain in excellent health on less.

The presence of substances which specifically promote calcium absorption, of which vitamin D is the most important, and *the absence of substances interfering with calcium absorption,* of which phytic acid and oxalic acid are the most significant, will obviously influence the amounts of calcium effectively available to the body (compare Section 10.4). That is to say, two diets could be selected, both calculated to contain the recommended amount of calcium, one of which would actually make a larger contribution of calcium than the other. This is the first factor which obviously modifies the absolute validity of the figures in Table 10.2.

The second factor is that, provided an otherwise reasonably well-balanced diet is available, most people can adjust themselves to levels of calcium intake substantially less than the recommended values. The total amount of calcium taken in by a person can be determined by analysing all the items of food and drink which he consumes, while at the same time the amount of calcium lost from his body (mainly in the faeces but in urine as well) is measured. If more calcium is lost from the system than is gained in the food, the person concerned is obtaining too little and is said to be in *negative balance.* If the amounts consumed and the amounts lost are the same, then the individual is obtaining just enough and is *in balance.* (Growing children, of course, need to be in *positive balance,* that is, retaining more calcium than they lose.) This kind of study is useful, but it does not take into account the subtlety of the physiological mechanisms of the body. It is now recognized that most people (not all) can adapt themselves to changing circumstances. In some communities rickets is never seen and people can be shown to be in calcium balance, yet the daily amount of calcium consumed per head is little more than half the 500 mg recommended for adults by the British Department of Health and Social Security's expert committee. Also, if a diet with a daily calcium content of 500 mg maintains a man in calcium balance, reducing his calcium intake will naturally mean that he will go into negative balance; yet after some weeks, he may adapt himself to the lowered calcium intake and balance will be restored. In spite of this *physiological adaptability* it is prudent to provide the calcium allowances shown in Table 10.2, if the availability of food supplies permits.

10.6   Non-food Sources of Calcium

(a) Water

Water used for drinking and cooking may contain varying amounts of calcium depending upon its origin. Rain water is well known to be 'soft'; it is almost entirely free from all minerals including calcium. On the other hand water from wells in chalk or limestone may contribute significant amounts of calcium to the diet. Although the hardness of water in Great Britain varies widely, from the hard water supplied to London to the very soft water of the peaty hill lochs of Scotland, the *average* daily contribution of calcium from drinking-water has been calculated to be about 75 mg per head of the population.

Calcium derived from water comes partly from the water actually drunk; a further contribution is made by calcium precipitated on to foods during the process of boiling them in water.

(b) The Intentional Addition of Calcium Compounds

Table 10.2 shows that *baking powder*, which is used for culinary rather than nutritional reasons, can make a small but significant contribution of calcium to the diet. Also, as we have said, purified *chalk* is added by government regulation to the bread flour used in Great Britain and certain other countries.

10.7 Phosphorus

Phosphorus occurs in the body and in foods as phosphate ions, which contain both phosphorus and oxygen; elemental phosphorus, which is highly poisonous and very inflammable, is never found in nature.

The body of an adult man contains about 900 g of phosphorus, most of which is in the bones. Phosphorus plays an essential part in the basic biochemical mechanism by which energy is obtained for the processes of life. It is an essential component of the blood and a constituent of certain of the enzymes and hormones which control the working of the body. Yet in spite of these various physiological functions phosphorus is of little or no practical interest to nutritionists, since, being essential to almost all the processes of living, it is present in all living things and is thus found in all natural foodstuffs. The amounts present in some of the commoner foods are shown in Table 10.3.

Because phosphorus is so readily available dietary deficiency is never

Table 10.3   The phosphorus content of certain foods

	mg per 100 g
Meat and fish	
Calf's brains	355
Beef, lamb, pork	250–300
Fish	
Cod, haddock, herring	200–300
Dairy produce	
Cheese	550
Eggs	220
Milk	95
Green vegetables	
Spinach	95
Cabbage	65
Lettuce	30

diagnosed, and no recommended minimum intake has been calculated. On the other hand, the body maintains its equilibrium so efficiently that symptoms of an excess of dietary phosphorus have not been observed either. Early in the present century when it was first discovered that phosphorus played a part in muscle function, it was thought that the provision of additional phosphate, for example, in the form of a drink, would make the person consuming it more muscular. This was the origin of the soft drinks sometimes called 'phosphates'. Unfortunately, the basic idea proved to be erroneous.

Interest in dietary phosphorus has had an unlucky history. For example, the discovery that brain tissue contains a comparatively high concentration of phosphorus, as Table 10.3 shows, led to the notion that foods rich in phosphorus were 'good for the brain', especially fish, which oddly enough attracted public attention rather than cheese, as might have been expected. It is regrettable that this idea is also mistaken.

Unit Eleven
Iron and Anaemia

11.1 Introduction

Iron is an essential nutrient, and a common substance seen all around us in our daily life. Yet in rich industrial and poor developing countries alike, dietary deficiency of iron is the cause of widespread ill-health, inefficiency and unhappiness. Not long ago, large sums of money used to change hands, and fortunes were made, from the sale of 'tonics', the active ingredient of which was usually an iron compound. When a consumer, who was usually a woman, felt better after taking the tonic, the reason often was that she had previously been subsisting on a nutritionally deficient diet lacking in iron which the 'tonic' was providing, generally at an inflated cost.

11.2 The Function of Iron-containing Compounds in the Body

(a) Haemoglobin

Iron is a component of the complex protein, haemoglobin, the pigment of red blood cells. The function of haemoglobin is to carry oxygen from the lungs to the tissues of the body where it is needed for the processes of metabolism. When there is a shortage of iron, sufficient haemoglobin is not produced, the oxygen-carrying capacity of the blood is reduced and the efficiency of almost all the body's processes is impaired, a condition called *anaemia*.

(b) Myoglobin

Whereas haemoglobin is a constituent of red blood cells, myoglobin, a similar type of compound, is found in red muscles, which are called upon to undertake particularly strenuous activity; it has the same oxygen-transporting function as haemoglobin.

(c) Cytochromes

There are several complex protein pigments called cytochromes, which have somewhat similar molecular structure; all of them contain iron as an essential component. They are distributed widely in the cells of the body where they function as respiratory enzymes.

11.3 The Absorption and Excretion of Iron

(a) Iron Absorption

The mechanism which controls the absorption of iron into the body is not yet properly understood. The body of a full-grown man contains about 4 g of iron altogether. Most of this, about 2.5 g, is present as an essential component of the haemoglobin which gives blood its red colour. The rest is distributed as myoglobin, cytochrome and certain other enzymes. Some is in the marrow of the long bones where new red blood cells are constantly being elaborated to replace the old ones, which disintegrate after four months or so. When iron is being transported from one part of the body to another it does so as a compound with a protein molecule called *transferrin*. When it is stored as reserve in the bone marrow, the spleen, the kidneys and the liver, it is also held in combination with protein as *ferritin*. The interesting feature about the absorption of iron from the diet is that, almost regardless of how much iron comes into the digestive system in the food eaten, the body only absorbs exactly the amount it needs at that time.

Under normal circumstances, a man's body loses about 1 mg of iron a day. It is generally recommended that a good diet should provide 10 mg of iron a day to allow for possible extra losses which are described in Section 11.3(*b*). But if he consumes the recommended 10 mg of iron, or even the 14 mg which is the average intake from a conventional western diet, his body will only absorb the 1 mg needed to replace what he has lost. The rest will not enter his body at all, but is disposed of in his faeces. On the other hand, if the man's body is deficient in iron, either because he has lost blood or because his diet had previously been lacking in iron, the amount absorbed will be greater than this.

There are a number of factors which influence the absorption of iron.

(*i*) **The chemical state of the iron.** Iron is a nutrient and the dietary needs of iron are usually best obtained as components of natural foods; but the quickest and most effective way to treat the malnutrition arising from a lack of iron in the diet is to consume iron itself, but *iron in the ionized condition* (that is, not as part of an organic compound) and preferably as *divalent* (sometimes called *ferrous*) iron (Fe^{2+}).

It is a matter of common observation that iron is quite a reactive element. For example, an iron bar exposed to the atmosphere reacts with oxygen: part of the iron is converted into rust. However, iron can react, for example with oxygen from the air or with hydrochloric acid, in more than one way. It may pass into the *divalent* state and form iron(II) oxide or iron(II) chloride (FeO, $FeCl_2$), or, depending on the conditions, pass into the *trivalent* state, yielding iron(III) oxide or iron(III) chloride (Fe_2O_3, $FeCl_3$). Although it is not fully understood how iron is absorbed through the intestines, the available evidence suggests that it is probably mainly in the divalent state, and that trivalent iron is not absorbed. There is some doubt as to the extent of absorption of iron in organic combination, for example as haemoglobin in the blood in meat or black pudding, or as cytochrome in the meat itself. What is clear, however, is that the body has a remarkable ability to regulate the absorption of iron from the diet.

When the haemoglobin concentration of the blood is at a satisfactory level, little or no iron is absorbed: most of it passes unabsorbed through the intestines and leaves the body in the faeces.

When the body requires iron and the concentration of haemoglobin in the blood is low, iron derived from the diet is absorbed through the intestines into the bloodstream.

That is to say, the body absorbs iron when, and *only* when, iron is required.

(*ii*) **The presence of substances facilitating iron absorption.** *Vitamin C* (ascorbic acid, discussed in Unit 17) increases the absorption of iron, probably because ascorbic acid is a strong reducing agent, and tends to convert iron into the divalent state. *Protein* in the diet is also thought to assist the absorption of iron to some extent, possibly because of the presence of the sulphur-containing amino acids (see Section 5.2) which have a certain amount of reducing action.

(*iii*) **Phytic acid.** This compound interferes with iron absorption in the same way as with the absorption of calcium or zinc, that is by forming an insoluble compound. Since phytic acid occurs in the outer husks of cereals, it may cause a serious lack of iron among people who eat as their staple diet foods like chapattis, made from wholemeal cereals. None of the high concentration of phytic acid is destroyed by fermentation because chapattis are made without yeast.

(*b*) **Loss of Iron from the Body**

Most nutrients are absorbed into the system from the diet and then, if more has been consumed than the body needs, the excess is excreted. The situation with iron is different. We have already seen how, if the body's requirements are satisfied, the iron in the diet is not absorbed at all but passes straight through the digestive tract. Neither is any significant amount of iron that is already in the body excreted. When, for example, the red cells of the blood die and disintegrate the iron component of their haemoglobin is not excreted but is stored (as ferritin) in the bone marrow, the liver and the tissues, and is thus available for re-use.

Although iron is not excreted in any significant amount, it can be lost from the body in several ways. *It is because such losses may occur that it is important, if a diet is to be nutritionally satisfactory, that it should provide an adequate amount of iron.* The fact that this is not always so is demonstrated by the large numbers of people who suffer from *iron-deficiency anaemia.*

(*i*) Only small quantities, amounting to about 1 mg a day for an adult man, are lost in *sweat,* in *bile* passing into the faeces and in *dead skin* naturally eroded during the wear and tear of daily life.

(*ii*) Iron is lost from the body through *bleeding.* Considerable amounts may need to be replaced following a wound or injury.

(*iii*) Small repeated losses of blood can deplete the iron supplies of the body; such losses may arise from *haemorrhoids* or more serious conditions such as bleeding from *gastric* or *duodenal ulcers.*

(*iv*) Women of reproductive age have an increased need for iron to replace their monthly losses due to *menstruation*. The loss of blood in *childbirth* also imposes substantial demands on the body's stores of iron which must be replaced.

11.4   The Main Sources of Iron in the Diet

Owing to the curious fact that people only absorb iron when they need it, it is difficult to state with any certainty what proportion of the amount of iron in a particular foodstuff, as determined by analysis, is available to the body. Nor is it easy to be sure to what extent iron present in other forms is converted during digestion to the divalent state, and thus made available for absorption. What is certain, however, is that if a diet containing little iron is fed for a considerable time, nutritional deficiency will become apparent as anaemia.

Table 11.1 shows clearly that milk and milk products contain little iron. Indeed, when research workers wish to produce anaemia experimentally in rats they do it by feeding them on a diet mainly composed of milk powder. Babies born of well-nourished mothers have adequate stores of iron in their livers to tide them over the period during which milk is their sole source of nourishment. But now that milk is recognized as being notoriously lacking in iron, it has become usual to provide infants with supplementary feeds of sieved vegetables or meat as soon as they are a few weeks old.

11.5   The Iron Requirements of Different Categories of People

In view of the fact that the main nutritional function of iron is as an essential component of the haemoglobin of the red blood cells, it is clear that under normal circumstances the people with the greatest need for iron are likely to be *growing children, women of menstruating age* and *women at childbirth*.

The levels of recommended iron intake for groups of average people under ordinary circumstances are given in Table 11.2.

11.6   The Harmful Effect of too much Iron

Under ordinary circumstances and when eating the customary types of food it is not possible for people to consume a harmfully large amount of iron since, as we have said, the body does not absorb iron it does not need. The quantity of iron consumed may often be larger than the amounts shown in Table 11.1 indicate, if food is cooked in iron vessels or picks up iron from kitchen utensils and equipment, as may easily happen. This supplementary iron may be of nutritional value if the diet does not otherwise provide an adequate allowance.

Certain Bantu communities in South Africa who cook their maize and other foods in iron pots may eat a diet containing as much as 100 mg of iron a day. Sometimes in these circumstances the digestive tract eventually fails to reject this large amount of unwanted iron, some of which in consequence is able to enter the system and may lead in time to cirrhosis of the liver. A condition in which excess iron accumulates in the tissues is called *siderosis*.

Table 11.1   The iron content of certain foods

Good sources of iron	mg per 100 g		mg per 100 g
Black pudding (blood		Parsley	8·0
sausage)	20·0	Turnip tops	3·1
Ox kidney	15·0	Cabbage	1·0
Pig's liver	13·0	Potatoes	0·7
Sheep's kidney	11·7		
Sheep's liver	10·9	Dried apricots	4·1
Corned beef	9·8	Prunes	2·9
Calf's liver	8·8	Dates	1·6
Chicken liver	7·9	Blackcurrants	1·3
Ox liver	6·5	Blackberries	0·8
		Melon	0·4
Curry powder	75·0	Oatmeal	4·1
Cocoa powder	14·3	Wholemeal flour	2·2
Black treacle (molasses)	9·2	White flour	0·9*
Cockles	26·0	Poor sources of iron	
Winkles	15·0	Cheese	0·6
Whelks	6·2	Rice	0·4
Oysters	6·0	Suet	0·4
		Rhubarb	0·4
Moderately good sources of iron		Grapes	0·3
Beef	4·0	Oranges	0·3
Lamb	2·0	Apples	0·3
Chicken	1·5	Butter	0·2
Pork	1·0	Dripping	0·2
		Lard	0·1
Canned sardines	4·0	Milk	0·1
Eggs	2·5		
Herring	1·5		
Salmon	1·3		
Haddock	1·0		

* Because of the danger of iron deficiency as a cause of widespread ill-health and disability, the enrichment of flour from which bread is made (and sometimes of other foods as well) is often required by law. In Great Britain, iron salts are added to white flour intended for bread-making so that it shall provide 1·65 mg of iron per 100 g. In the United States, the iron content of so-called 'enriched' breadmaking flour is brought up to 2·9 mg per 100 g.

An alternative form of siderosis which is not due to nutrition may occur following a disease called *haemolytic anaemia*, a condition in which the blood cells break down. Sometimes when these patients are treated by blood transfusion, the transfused blood may also be destroyed and the iron is then released from its haemoglobin. Since each 500 ml of blood contain 200 mg of iron, the tissues may become overloaded with iron and the symptoms of siderosis consequently appear.

Table 11.2   Recommended daily intake of iron

	mg per day
Children	
0–1 year old	6
1–3 years old	7
3–7 years old	8
7–9 years old	10
9–12 years old	13
12–15 years old	14
15–18 years old	15
Men (all ages)	10
Women	
18–55 years old	12
55 and over	10
pregnant and nursing	15

11.7   Anaemia

Anaemia, that is, a lowered level of haemoglobin in the blood, may be due to a variety of causes of which malnutrition is only one. Even when it is caused by nutritional deficiency it may be due to a lack of nutrients other than iron. Nevertheless, a shortage of iron in the diet is by far the most common cause of anaemia in every part of the world and nutritional anaemia due to lack of iron is among the most common of all kinds of malnutrition. Within a population, infants and young children and women, particularly those of child-bearing age, are the commonest sufferers.

In an anaemic person, the blood's power to carry oxygen from the lungs to the rest of the body is reduced because of the lack of haemoglobin. So many metabolic processes depend upon having sufficient oxygen available that the symptoms of anaemia reflect the effects of oxygen shortage in a wide variety of ways: they may include lassitude, breathlessness following exertion, giddiness, dim vision, headache, difficulty in sleeping, poor appetite and dyspepsia, and a tingling 'pins and needles' sensation in the fingers and toes.

(a) Detection of an Inadequate Intake of Iron

A nutritionist can assess the adequacy of the iron intake of a particular community or of its members by first estimating the iron content of the diet being eaten. This may be done by recording the weight of every item eaten or drunk and calculating the total amount of iron in them, using tables of food composition. A general estimate of the iron intake can be obtained in this way. The total actually consumed may, however, be quite different if, for example, the food has been in contact with metal surfaces or has been cooked in iron vessels. If a more accurate knowledge of iron intake is required, samples of the actual foods eaten must be analysed. When the total iron consumed each day is compared with the recommended iron intake as given in Table 11.2, an idea of the adequacy or inadequacy of the diet can be obtained.

(b) Measurement of the Haemoglobin Content of the Blood

A more direct way of measuring whether sufficient iron has been supplied by a diet is to measure the haemoglobin levels of the people who have eaten it. There are a number of methods for determining the haemoglobin content of a small sample of blood, usually a drop taken from a finger-prick or the lobe of the ear. A diagnosis of dietary iron deficiency can, however, only be made safely if a really accurate analytical method is used, and if it is also certain that the diet contains adequate amount of the factors necessary for haemoglobin formation, such as cyanocobalamin and folic acid (see Sections 16.5 and 16.6).

Table 11.3 shows the minimum values accepted by an expert committee of the World Health Organization for haemoglobin values for people receiving *just sufficient* dietary iron. Should values lower than these be found, the people concerned can be taken as suffering from some degree of anaemia.

Table 11.3   Haemoglobin levels below which anaemia can be diagnosed

	g haemoglobin per 100 ml of blood
Children	
6 months to 4 years	10·8
5–9 years	11·5
10–14 years	12·5
Men	14·0
Women	12·0
Women during pregnancy	10·0

Unit Twelve
Iodine and Fluorine

12.1 Iodine

Iodine is an essential nutrient, although the amount an individual needs each day is very small, probably between 0.05 and 0.30 mg; the exact quantity is not precisely known. The main function of iodine is as a component of the compound thyroxine and other related substances manufactured by the thyroid gland in the neck, which control the metabolic rate at which the body's biochemical mechanism operates (see Section 7.1(e)).

The total amount of iodine in a man's body is between 20 and 50 mg; about a third of this is concentrated in the thyroid gland.

(a) The Main Sources of Iodine in the Diet

The pure element iodine takes the form of shiny purplish-black flakes with a metallic appearance; but these are unknown in nature, and iodine is always found as iodide or iodate ions. It occurs in trace concentrations in sea water and is widely but unevenly distributed in soil. Where the soil is relatively rich in iodine, the plants which grow on it and the animals which feed on these plants contain corresponding proportions of iodine in their tissues. But in some areas of high land, in Switzerland, in parts of India remote from the sea, in Africa, in extensive areas of America and in Derbyshire, the level of iodine is low, and large numbers of people receive insufficient iodine in their diet and suffer accordingly.

Because the iodine content of foods is so much affected by the soil chemistry in the geographical areas from which they are derived, we cannot write down a table of food items showing just how much iodine each contributes to the diet. The best we can do is to say that it can be expected that significant amounts of iodine may be obtained from *sea fish*, *vegetables*, *milk* and *cereals*. Drinking-water does not contribute much iodine to the daily intake, but the analysis of water to determine its iodine content is useful since it indicates whether or not the ground from which the water comes is likely to grow crops providing enough iodine. Although sea water only contains traces of iodine, *sea weed* has the ability to concentrate these small amounts in its cells, and therefore is one of the best raw materials for the manufacture of iodine.

(b) The Iodization of Salt

Because of the uneven distribution of iodine in different territories and different soils, so that foods from different places contain different amounts, it is unusually difficult to recommend a diet guaranteed to provide the amount of iodine needed. Although sea fish are a reliable source of iodine, communities living far from a source of supply or where fish is difficult and expensive to obtain may find it hard to ensure themselves a steady intake. In parts of the world where iodine deficiency is common, this may well be because it is virtually impossible to design a diet made up of local foods which will provide enough iodine. Under these circumstances, a nutritionally adequate supply of iodine can conveniently be provided by adding iodine in the form of *potassium iodide* to all salt used for culinary purposes, a measure which protects the whole community from deficiency. Iodized salt is commonly prepared by incorporating 25 parts of potassium iodide per million parts of salt (sodium chloride).

(c) Goitre

Goitre has various causes; it always takes the form of an enlargement of the thyroid gland which appears as a swelling of the neck, either on one side or both. The swelling may be small and inconspicuous or very large and disfiguring (see Fig. 12.1).

Fig. 12.1 A case of goitre

Although the commonest cause of goitre is known to be nutritional deficiency of iodine and although supplementary iodine can be provided in salt quite easily and cheaply, it has been estimated that some 200 million people suffer from goitre caused by iodine deficiency, and that this number is actually increasing. This emphasizes several important nutritional principles.

(*i*) In real life, nutrition is seldom a straightforward matter. Apparently simple biochemical principles, for example that obesity is due to a diet of too high an energy value and can therefore be prevented by eating less, or that goitre is always due to a lack of iodine and can be prevented by adding it to the diet, are seldom as self-evident as they sound.

(*ii*) The composition of food is always influenced by the land on which it grows; this is particularly true in the case of iodine. Mountain country in Europe, Asia, Africa and the Americas alike, together with alluvial plains in North America and New Zealand, and particular districts such as Derbyshire are recognized to be notorious areas where goitre is common unless preventive measures are taken.

(*iii*) Although we have said that the primary cause of goitre is iodine deficiency, this is an oversimplification. Not only must the diet contain iodine which acts to *prevent* goitre, it must also not contain certain compounds which have the property of actively *encouraging* goitre. These substances are called *goitrogens*.

(*d*) Foods containing Goitrogens

Several substances occurring naturally in foods are known to increase people's tendency to develop goitre. These substances are all sulphur-containing compounds, and probably act by interfering with the uptake of iodine by the thyroid gland. Goitrogens are most commonly found in *green vegetables* like cabbage, cauliflower, Brussels sprouts, broccoli and kale, in *root vegetables* of the same botanical family, the *Cruciferae*, including radishes and turnips, in *onions, garlic* and *horseradish*, and in *cassava* (the plant from which tapioca is made), which is a staple food in parts of Africa. In addition, some goitrogens are found in the *milk* from cows fed on kale or roots, or which have access to weeds like charlock, shepherd's purse and hedge mustard (which are also *Cruciferae*). The subtle way in which the supply of iodine in the diet needs to be assessed in relation to the land, the weather and the season of the year, all of which influence the amount of goitrogens in food, is shown by studies carried out in Tasmania and Australia. It has been found that the incidence of seasonal epidemics of thyroid enlargement can be correlated with the concentration of goitrogens in the milk of cows feeding on pastures where cruciferous weeds grow at certain times of the year.

Very many useful and nourishing foods contain some components which could be harmful (compare Section 21.5(*a*)). The fact that certain foods contain goitrogens does not imply that they should be avoided altogether. Success in nutrition is attained by the just assessment of the value of the foods which make up the diet, in sensible balance with the drawbacks all foods possess.

12.2   Fluorine

The four elements fluorine, chlorine, bromine and iodine possess certain chemical similarities, and are, in fact, all classified by chemists as *halogens*. *Chlorine*, which is a component of salt (sodium chloride) and of the hydrochloric acid in the stomach, is important in several metabolic processes. *Iodine*, as we have just described, is concerned with the control of the rate at which the body's metabolism functions, through the effect of thyroxine produced by the thyroid gland. Only *bromine* appears to have no particular biochemical function, although bromides have for a long time been used as drugs to suppress the activity of the higher centres of the brain, as in the treatment of epilepsy. *Fluorine* is a nutrient substance, of which approximately 1–2 mg are required daily by a normal adult; this quantity is contained in any ordinary diet, so that the element has little practical significance for a nutritionist, unless he is responsible for feeding children (see Section 12.2(*b*)).

(a) The Nutritional Function of Fluorine

Fluorine is readily absorbed into the body and is found widely distributed in the tissues. However it accumulates particularly in the bones and teeth, in the thyroid gland and in the skin.

(b) The Biological Functions of Fluorine

So far as is known, the precise amount of fluorine in the diet is only significant for children. The deposit of fluorine in the enamel surface of developing teeth protects them from decay (cf. Section 3.2(b)). It is not fully understood whether this beneficial action is due to a greater resistance of the enamel itself to the attacks of the bacteria which cause decay or whether the fluorine discourages the activity of the bacteria and thus reduces the virulence of their attack.

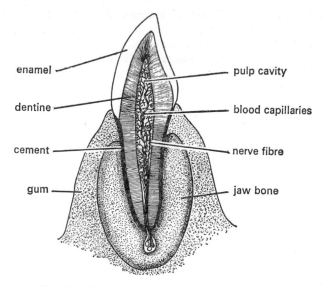

Fig. 12.2 Vertical section through an incisor tooth

(c) The Main Sources of Fluorine in the Diet

Some fluorine is contributed to the diet by sea fish, which contain 5–10 ppm of the element, and by tea (although it is not strictly a food): certain China teas in the dry form contain up to 100 ppm of fluorine. The main source of dietary fluorine, however, is not food at all: it is *drinking-water*. The amount of fluorine in natural water supplies varies widely, depending on the composition of the rocks from which the water comes or over which it flows. The concentration may vary from no fluorine at all up to 10 ppm or even more.

(*d*) **The Daily Requirement of Fluorine**

As we have said, it cannot be claimed that *adults* require specific amounts of fluorine to maintain their health. In *children* it is found that their teeth develop most satisfactorily and are most resistant to decay when the water they drink and which is used in cooking their food contains 1 ppm of fluorine, either naturally or added artificially by the water authorities.

(*e*) **The Effect of Consuming Too Much Fluorine**

In certain districts, the concentration of fluorine in drinking-water considerably exceeds the optimum level of 1 ppm because of the large amounts of fluorine in the local soil and rocks. In places where the fluorine concentration reaches 3–5 ppm, although teeth retain their resistance to decay, they acquire a greyish mottled appearance; there appears to be no other adverse result of taking fluorine in these quantities. Exceptionally, in parts of North India, China, Argentina and the Transvaal, the natural waters contain as much as 14 ppm of fluorine, or even more. In these districts, and also in places contaminated by fumes from aluminium smelting or certain other industrial processes, serious symptoms of excess fluorine consumption (*fluorosis*) may appear. These include changes in the bone structure (so that it becomes unnaturally dense), stiffening of the spine and loss of appetite.

Unit Thirteen
Vitamin A (Retinol)

13.1 Accessory Food Factors

It is not enough for the foods composing the diet to provide the factors we have so far considered, that is:

(a) energy value sufficient to satisfy hunger and provide what is needed for work and warmth;

(b) enough protein for growth, maintenance and repair of the body's tissues;

(c) fats for the various functions described in Section 4.2;

(d) the range of mineral nutrients, each performing its own particular function.

As long ago as 1753, a Scottish naval surgeon called James Lind demonstrated that orange juice, which contains little or none of the four well-known groups of nutrients, nevertheless prevented the disease of scurvy, from which thousands of sailors were then suffering and dying in spite of rations which were both ample and wholesome according to the understanding of the times. Today it is recognized that the body requires quite a large number of *accessory food factors*, even if sometimes in minute quantities only, in addition to the carbohydrate, protein, fat and minerals which constitute the main substance of foods. The general term used for these accessory substances is *vitamins*; all are organic compounds, but their molecular structures are very different. When they were first found to exist they were designated by letters of the alphabet, as vitamin A, vitamin B and so on, as their discoverers had little knowledge of their chemical nature. Sometimes it was found that a nutritional effect thought to be due to a single substance was actually a combination of effects produced by several associated compounds; these were then given names like vitamin B_1, vitamin B_2 and so on.

In due course, the chemistry of the various vitamins was elucidated, and today many of them can be synthesized in the laboratory, and even manufactured in quantity. The exact biochemical function of several of them is now also understood. This has made it possible to describe some vitamins by a more appropriate name, usually illustrative of its chemical composition. Thus, for example, the name of *thiamine* (vitamin B_1) implies the presence of sulphur and nitrogen in its molecule, and that of *cyanocobalamin* (vitamin B_{12}) refers to its content of cobalt. On the other hand, the compound originally called vitamin C is now known as *ascorbic acid*, a name which indicates its function of curing the *scorbutic* symptoms of scurvy.

13.2   The Chemistry of Vitamin A

(a) **Vitamin A is soluble in fat and insoluble in water.** Because this is so it is either found associated with fats, that is, in butter fat or in the fatty part of the liver of animals, especially fat from the livers of certain fish, like cod-liver oil, halibut-liver oil and shark-liver oil. Vitamin A activity is also associated with the small but important amount of fatty material present in green vegetables and yellow roots like carrots and sweet potatoes.

(b) **Vitamin A is stable under the normal conditions of heat encountered in cooking.** Furthermore, because it is not soluble in water it is not lost in any cooking water which may be strained off and discarded.

(c) **Vitamin A can be destroyed by oxygen.** If, for example, oil or fat in which it is present is incorporated in a mixture with flour or other ingredients which exposes a large surface area to the air its activity will be lost. Destruction of vitamin A in this way is greatly accelerated if it is also exposed to bright light.

(d) **The structure and activity of vitamin A.** The molecule of vitamin A consists of carbon and hydrogen atoms linked together with a single hydroxyl (—OH) group into a fairly complex structure, which can be elucidated by the recognized methods of organic chemistry. Once the structure of this compound— *retinol*—had been identified, its biological activity could be studied by adding varying amounts to the diet of young rats, and observing the way in which their growth was affected. This kind of experiment was used to establish the internationally used unit of vitamin A activity as follows:

$$\text{unit of vitamin A activity} = 1 \text{ retinol equivalent}$$
$$= 1 \text{ microgram* of retinol}$$

At one time vitamin A activity was expressed in international units (IU):

$$1 \text{ retinol equivalent} = 3 \text{ IU.}$$

This method of assessing vitamin activity enables the vitamin A value of different foods to be conveniently compared without analysing them chemically, so that nutritionists can determine whether or not a certain diet has a satisfactory content of vitamin A. The *precise* vitamin A content of any particular food may, however, be more difficult to determine than biochemists thought at first, for it is now recognized that the long chain of carbon atoms in the vitamin A molecule can take up several different shapes in different circumstances.

The significance of these various forms of the vitamin is that, while all of them can be included in the term 'vitamin A', not all of them have the same

---

* 1 microgram (written 1 μg) = 1 millionth (10^{-6}) of a gram
                              = 1 thousandth of a milligram

physiological activity, and indeed one form has been found to be somewhat more active than the rest. The lesson for the practising nutritionist is that, while he can have a good idea of the general level of vitamin A activity in a mixture of foods constituting a diet, the *exact* physiological efficiency may not be quite so certain, since it depends on the particular chemical configuration of whatever vitamin A compounds they may contain.

(*e*) β-Carotene. The chemical compound retinol is only found in animal products. But although vegetable foods like carrots, green leafy vegetables, palm oil, sweet potatoes and yellow maize do not contain vitamin A itself, they do contain yellow pigments called *carotenoids*, some of which are converted into vitamin A during the process of absorption through the small intestine. There are a great many carotenoids in nature; the molecular structure of the most important, β-*carotene*, closely resembles two retinol molecules joined together. But although β-carotene is converted into the active vitamin during its absorption by the body the conversion is less efficient than its chemical structure might suggest. The vitamin A activities of retinol, β-carotene and other allied carotenoid pigments are related as follows:

1 'retinol equivalent' of vitamin A activity is produced by:
1 μg of retinol,
6 μg of β-carotene, and
12 μg of other biologically active carotenoids.

13.3 The Main Sources of Vitamin A Activity in the Diet

Vitamin A activity is derived mainly from retinol itself in animal foods and solely from carotenoids in vegetable foods. The main dietary sources are shown in Table 13.1. Again, it must be remembered that the values shown can only be accepted as roughly representative of the kind of food to which they are assigned; the vitamin contents of individual samples may be as high as several times the values given, or only a small fraction of these values. This arises because the amount of vitamin A in the liver of a fish or an animal, accumulated during the creature's lifetime, will be affected by the type of diet it ate when it was alive. Similarly, the amount of β-carotene in vegetable foods, while characteristic of the type and strain of plant, will also be influenced by the weather and the cultural conditions under which it has been grown.

13.4 The Daily Requirement of Vitamin A

Because vitamin A is fat-soluble and is stored in considerable amounts in the liver (demonstrated by the very high concentrations in the livers of meat animals and fish), a 'daily requirement' of the vitamin cannot really be fixed. But although it would be feasible to provide a person with the amount of vitamin A needed for health by giving him periodic substantial doses of fish-liver oil or palm oil, it is better nutritional practice to ensure that his diet consistently provides him with a steady daily supply. It is on this basis that the recommendations in Table 13.2 have been worked out.

Table 13.1   The vitamin A activity of certain foods

	retinol equivalents (μg per 100 g)
Very rich sources of vitamin A activity	
Halibut-liver oil	10 000 000
Shark-liver oil	100 000
Cod-liver oil	70 000
Red palm oil	20 000
Good sources of vitamin A activity	
Sheep's liver	17 000
Ox liver	15 000
Calf's liver	7 000
Chicken's liver	4 000
Pig's liver	3 000
Sweet potatoes	3 000
Kale	3 000
Turnip greens	2 500
Carrots	2 000
Spinach	1 000
Butter	995
Margarine*	900
Useful sources of vitamin A activity	
Cheese (Cheddar)	420
Eggs	300
Tomatoes	117
Salmon	66
Herring	45
Sardines	38
Milk	44

Foods contributing little or no vitamin A activity
Bread, flour and other cereals (except yellow maize)
Bacon, pork, beef, mutton
White fish
Potatoes
Lard, suet and cooking fat
Sugar, syrup and jam (except apricot jam)

* Vitamin A is usually incorporated in table margarine but is not always put into margarine intended for manufacturing purposes.

Table 13.2   Recommended daily intake of vitamin A activity

	µg retinol equivalent
Boys and girls	
0–1 year	450
1–7 years	300
7–9 years	400
9–12 years	575
12–15 years	725
15–18 years	750
Men (all ages and degrees of activity)	750
Women	
all ages and degrees of activity	750
pregnant	750
nursing	1 200

The intake levels shown in Table 13.2 can readily be maintained by a judicious choice of foods like butter and milk, green vegetables and carrots, all common in western diets. Generally a surplus of vitamin A activity will then be available to maintain reasonable stores in the liver. On the other hand, when a deficiency of vitamin A has developed, for example in a poor community living in a tropical country, it is effectively treated by replenishing the body's stores by giving fish-liver oil or some other concentrated source of vitamin A, before attempting to provide a dietary pattern which can supply an adequate daily supply of the vitamin.

13.5   Deficiency of Vitamin A

A man fed on bread as a source of energy, together with, say, dripping, to make it palatable, and meat to add protein, with an apple a day as well, would in due course fall ill. Such a diet would be lacking in vitamin A. If he had previously eaten a diet rich in vitamin A, the stored vitamin in his liver would protect him from symptoms of the deficiency for up to a year or so; but if the shortage continues, the following symptoms might appear:

(a) Xerophthalmia

This condition is a failure of the normal moistness of the eyes, which become lustreless and later grey and opaque. It is the most reliable indication of lack of vitamin A.

(b) Night-blindness

Vitamin A is directly concerned with the biochemical mechanism which enables the eyes of a healthy person to become quickly adjusted to a dim light after having previously been exposed to bright light. When the body is short of vitamin A, this adaptation becomes very slow, and the power to adapt may even be lost altogether. It is because this is a function of the *retina*, the light-sensitive organ at the back of the eye, that vitamin A has been re-named *retinol*.

(c) Keratomalacia

This is a serious disease which is a common cause of blindness in many parts of Asia and Africa, and which can even be fatal. Xerophthalmia, described above, is only one stage of vitamin A deficiency. If it persists, the eyes become infected and ulcerated and the sight is lost if the ulcer penetrates into the eye through the outer cornea.

Keratomalacia most commonly occurs in children living in dirt and poverty. Severe deficiency of vitamin A is sometimes, however, found in prosperous communities when otherwise satisfactory diets are provided. It was found among Danish children during the First World War, when much of the nation's dairy produce was being exported; the existence of vitamin A was still generally unknown, and no vitamin supplements were therefore given. In Singapore, an increase in keratomalacia among children was thought to be due to the use of dried-milk formulae and poor-quality condensed milk lacking in vitamin A in place of liquid milk.

(d) Follicular Keratosis

This is a general effect of a diet lacking in vitamin A; it is a particular kind of roughening of the skin, which tends to block up the sweat glands and the tear glands as well. It is this blockage which produces xerophthalmia leading on, if the vitamin A deficiency is prolonged, to the disaster of keratomalacia.

13.6   The Harmful Effect of too much Vitamin A

Because vitamin A is not soluble in water and cannot be broken down by the body into a form in which it can be excreted, any excessive amount consumed remains in the tissues. Although, as we have said, considerable amounts can be stored, toxic symptoms will occur if a large excess is taken over a prolonged period. These may include a loss of appetite, a dry itching skin, a coarseness of the hair and painful swellings on the long bones of the arms and legs.

Vitamin A poisoning is most commonly caused by mothers who have been instructed to give babies or young children one or two *drops* a day of halibut-liver oil, sufficient to provide, say, 500 µg retinol equivalents, deciding instead to give them one or two *spoonfuls*. This could amount to 10 g, and could contain 1 000 000 µg retinol equivalents (see Table 13.1). If such a dose is continued for any length of time toxic symptoms will appear.

Hypervitaminosis A (the condition due to too much vitamin A) has also occasionally been reported in Arctic explorers. The symptoms, including drowsiness, headache, vomiting and itching and peeling of the skin followed the unwise consumption of polar-bear liver. This is now known to contain vitamin A at enormously high concentrations, up to 600 000 μg retinol equivalent per 100 g.

Unit Fourteen
Vitamin D (Cholecalciferol)

14.1 The Chemistry of Vitamin D

Vitamin D, like vitamin A, is soluble in fat and insoluble in water. Like vitamin A and other *fat-soluble vitamins*, some of which are discussed in Unit 15, vitamin D occurs in association with fats. Again like vitamin A, it was early discovered in cod-liver oil. In due course, it was extracted from cod-liver oil and purified, and found to be one of the group of compounds called *sterols* (see Section 4.3(*b*)). Its most important function is to facilitate absorption of calcium into the body; deficiency of vitamin D produces the diseases of rickets in children and osteomalacia in adults.

(*a*) Vitamin D_3 (Cholecalciferol)

This is the form of vitamin D which occurs in cod-liver oil and other foods and the form in which it is most effective for children. It is also effective for growing chickens, which have a special need for it.

(*b*) Vitamin D_2 (Calciferol)

Ergosterol is a sterol which is present in fungi and in yeast. When ergosterol is irradiated with ultraviolet light, its molecular structure is modified so as to produce the compound calciferol. Calciferol has powerful vitamin D activity and has been called *vitamin D_2*. Since ergosterol is freely available, it is used as the raw material for the large-scale manufacture of calciferol. Although calciferol is as effective as vitamin D_3 in preventing rickets in rats, it is not quite as potent in chickens or children. This is why, just as vitamin A activity is measured in terms of µg of 'retinol equivalent', thus taking into account the different chemical forms of vitamin A active substances, so also vitamin D is measured in terms of cholecalciferol.

(*c*) Biologically Active Vitamin D

It could be said that a nutritionist today need only be concerned with either calciferol, produced artificially by irradiating ergosterol, or the naturally occurring cholecalciferol, which is probably derived from cholesterol (discussed in Sections 4.3(*b*) and 4.4); nevertheless it may eventually prove that this is not the end of the story.

Although both calciferol and, somewhat more potently, cholecalciferol can facilitate calcium absorption and thus protect normal infants from rickets, on rare occasions rickets is observed which is resistant to the administration of either of these two vitamins. However, a third substance, with a molecular structure slightly different from either, is found to put things right in such cases. This compound, resembling cholecalciferol with one extra oxygen atom in its molecule, may be the form in which vitamin D actually performs its function in the body. Nutritionists, therefore, while able now to make use of the two forms of the vitamin so far available, can usefully bear in mind the possibility of having to adjust their ideas in the future.

14.2   The Production of Vitamin D by Irradiation of the Skin

Vitamin D is an essential component of the diets of infants, young children and expectant mothers during the latter part of pregnancy *only* in places where there is little sunshine or where mothers and children protect themselves from sunshine either with clothes or by staying indoors. Irradiation of the skin by ultraviolet light, either in sunshine or produced by an 'ultraviolet lamp', causes the formation of vitamin D from the natural sterols always present in the skin. This is the reason why rickets occurs mainly in cool cloudy climates or in places where smoke or other air pollution prevents the ultraviolet rays from reaching the body. However, it is known even in sunny climates when custom dictates that much of the body is kept covered as, for example, among girls kept in *purdah* in India, or among certain Muslim communities.

Ordinary window glass is not transparent to ultraviolet light; this means that sunlight shining through a closed window does not produce vitamin D in the skin.

14.3   The Daily Requirement of Vitamin D

It is not known for certain whether or not adults need to obtain any vitamin D at all in their food. In view of the element of doubt that exists, however, it is prudent to ensure that a certain amount is included in the daily diet; Table 14.1 lists recommended allowances for various categories of people.

Table 14.1   The daily requirement of vitamin D

	µg cholecalciferol*
Children	
0–5 years	10·0
6–18 years	2·5
Men	2·5
Women	2·5
during pregnancy	10·0
during lactation	10·0

* Vitamin D activity was measured at one time in 'international units'. Now that the chemistry of the vitamin is better understood and the activity of its different forms recognized, activity is measured in terms of µg cholecalciferol (see Section 14.1(b)):
1 international unit = 0·025 µg cholecalciferol

14.4   The Main Sources of Vitamin D in the Diet

Vitamin D is only found in fatty fish like herrings, salmon and sardines, in dairy produce including milk, cheese, butter and eggs, and also in a few unexpected commodities including cacao shells. Enrichment with synthetic vitamin D—either calciferol or cholecalciferol—is also used to improve the nutritional value of certain foods like infant-feeding formulae and margarine. The vitamin D activities of characteristic samples of the principal foods in which it occurs are shown in Table 14.2.

Table 14.2   The vitamin D content of certain foods

	µg cholecalciferol per 100 g
Fish and fish oils	
Tunny-liver oil	up to 600 000
Halibut-liver oil	up to 10 000
Swordfish-liver oil	25 000
Cod-liver oil	200–750
Herrings, kippers, sardines	5–45
Salmon	4–30
Dairy produce	
Egg yolk	3–10
Margarine (as commonly vitaminized)	2–9
Butter	0·2–2*
Eggs	1–1·5
Cheese	0·3–0·4
Milk	0·02–0·10

* The vitamin D content of butter depends very much on the way the cow is fed and on the time of year.

Clearly, in view of the comparatively limited selection of foods containing vitamin D and the quite large requirements of infants for the vitamin, young babies need either an appropriate daily dose of fish-liver oil or the enrichment of their feed formula with synthetic vitamin. Children up to five years old have similar requirements, but they can, of course, be given egg yolk, butter and enriched margarine together with milk and cheese to ensure an adequate intake of vitamin D. The same consideration also applies to expectant and nursing mothers, who can also usefully obtain part of their requirement as a vitamin D concentrate.

14.5   Deficiency of Vitamin D

(a) Rickets

The symptoms of this deforming disease of children are discussed in Section 10.1. It appears in children who are not given enough *calcium* in their diet;

but children receiving inadequate supplies of *vitamin D* also develop rickets, even if their calcium intake is satisfactory, since without the necessary amounts of the vitamin they are unable to absorb the calcium into their bodies for the development of their bones and teeth.

Until the early years of this century rickets was common among poorly fed children in industrial cities in Great Britain and northern Europe. It is also seen in parts of India and other tropical countries where the custom is to keep babies indoors and to avoid exposing their skins to sunlight.

(b) Osteomalacia

This rare disease is the adult counterpart of rickets in children. However, whereas the bones of a child with rickets do not become completely rigid because he does not receive enough calcium for the build-up of a sound bone structure, the bones of an adult with osteomalacia actually *lose* calcium, and their normal hard substance is replaced with softer tissue.

Osteomalacia is most common among women who have lived for a long period on a poor diet lacking in calcium, and may appear when they become pregnant and the development of the foetus creates an increased need for calcium. The treatment of osteomalacia is similar to that of rickets. Initially, large doses of up to 1 200 mg of calcium daily may be useful. For full restoration to health, however, the patient needs a good diet containing plenty of milk and milk products to supply calcium, and eggs to provide vitamin D. Unfortunately people who suffer from osteomalacia are usually poor, so that although their condition is curable, they may not be able to afford the cure.

14.6   The Harmful Effect of too much Vitamin D

Since vitamin D, like vitamin A, is insoluble in water, any large excess which may be absorbed cannot be readily disposed of in urine. It is, therefore, important to bear in mind that *excessive amounts of vitamin D are poisonous.*

As Table 14.2 shows, halibut-liver oil and certain other fish-liver oils contain enormously high concentrations of vitamin D. These are sometimes dispensed to a mother with the instruction that she should give her baby, say 1 *drop* a day in its feed. If she has been accustomed, perhaps with an earlier baby, to administer 1 *teaspoonful* of the far less concentrated cod-liver oil, she may well make the mistake of giving the infant fifty times too much.

A baby receiving such a high dosage of vitamin D will develop toxic symptoms which can include loss of appetite and vomiting, intense thirst, alternating constipation and diarrhoea, loss of weight and irritability. If the excess dosage is continued, the child may go into a coma and eventually die.

Vitamin E and Vitamin K

15.1 Vitamin E

When rats are fed on a highly purified diet of adequate energy value, containing enough protein, minerals and vitamins but totally lacking in vegetable fats, they appear to grow and thrive tolerably well but they fail to reproduce. The males become sterile, and if the females do become pregnant they tend to suffer spontaneous abortions and lose their young. These effects can be prevented by supplementing the diet either with one of several vegetable oils or fats, or with a concentrate made from them. Eventually a series of closely related substances collectively called *vitamin E* were identified as the preventive compounds; about seven or eight have now been recognized and they have been re-named *tocopherols*. The only difference between their molecular structures lies in the replacement of hydrogen atoms by methyl ($-CH_3$) groups in some of them. Tocopherols are fat-soluble vitamins like vitamins A and D; they are insoluble in water.

Since the discovery in 1923 of the existence of vitamin E, its chemistry and biochemical function have been extensively studied. It is an essential nutrient for dogs, guinea pigs, rabbits, certain monkeys and young pigs, and is particularly important in the diets of chickens and turkeys. However, there has been until recently no convincing evidence that the vitamin is of any nutritional value for human beings.

(a) The Main Sources of Vitamin E in the Diet

Most foods contain at least traces of vitamin E. The richest sources of the vitamin are *eggs* and *oils derived from cereals*, like wheat-germ oil, maize oil and cottonseed oil. Animal fats, meat, fruit and vegetables contain little vitamin E.

(b) The Antioxidant Activity of Vitamin E

One of the changes occurring when fats 'turn rancid' is that oxygen from the air reacts with the unsaturated part of the fatty-acid chain of carbon atoms (see Section 4.3(a)). This *oxidation* reaction produces *peroxide* and *hydroperoxide* compounds, which give rise to the rancid flavour. Chemists investigating the molecular structure of the tocopherols discovered that, as well as any biochemical activity they may have, they are also powerful antioxidants; that is, they protect fats containing unsaturated fatty acids from oxidation and consequent rancidity.

(i) The technical usefulness of antioxidant activity. It is now recognized that the presence of vitamin E *as a natural component* of vegetable fats protects

them, at least for a time, against rancidity. There therefore seems no reason to object to the use of vitamin E in limited quantities *as an additive* to protect foods against the onset of oxidation and rancidity: the vitamin is in any case a natural food constituent and while certainly harmless, may actually be a useful component of the diet.

(*ii*) **The possible nutritional benefit of antioxidant properties.** The nutritional significance of polyunsaturated fatty acids was described in Sections 4.4 and 4.5. The presence of vitamin E could therefore be beneficial, not necessarily on account of some vitamin activity of its own, but by virtue of its ability to prevent the oxidation of polyunsaturated fatty acids actually within the living body, with the consequent destruction of *their* special ability to control the cholesterol level of the blood. In this way vitamin E may play some part in reducing susceptibility to coronary heart attacks.

The possibility has also been suggested that polyunsaturated fatty acids have a role in brain development during early life, and that the antioxidant properties of vitamin E may perhaps be important in preserving the acids from oxidation for this purpose.

Clearly a great deal has been learnt about the nutritional function of vitamin E in various animals and the molecular structure and antioxidant properties of the tocopherols, but it is still uncertain whether or not the vitamin has any part at all in human nutrition. However, while the possibility exists that some role of vitamin E in man may still be elucidated, prudent nutritionists will do well to bear its existence in mind.

15.2 Vitamin K

(*a*) The Discovery of Vitamin K

Like vitamin E, vitamin K is a fat-soluble vitamin about which a great deal is known, but about which there is still uncertainty as to whether it is really of any usefulness as a component of human diets. Its existence was discovered when it was found that chickens fed on a specially purified diet developed symptoms of bleeding, which were prevented when either lucerne (a clover-like plant) or decayed fish-meal was added to their food. The substance giving these materials their protective activity was named 'vitamin K' and its molecular structure identified: again, it was found that there were several quite similar compounds having vitamin K activity.

(*b*) The Main Sources of Vitamin K in the Diet

Vitamin K is widely distributed in a number of foodstuffs, including green vegetables, fish-liver oils and foods which have undergone bacterial decay. One of the reasons why it has not been possible to determine whether human beings require vitamin K in their food or whether they produce it within their own bodies is because the vitamin is constantly being synthesized by the bacteria naturally present in the large intestine.

(c) The Physiological Function of Vitamin K

Vitamin K is known to play a part in the mechanism of blood-clotting; this is why chickens made deficient in vitamin K suffer from bleeding. Bleeding sometimes occurs in newborn babies, but it is not fully understood whether this is connected with the fact that the gut of an infant lacks micro-organisms to synthesize the vitamin. But babies never have intestinal bacteria at birth; since bleeding in the newborn is uncommon, the condition is probably due to some other cause. The affected infants can however be successfully treated with carefully controlled doses of synthetic vitamin K. This hardly comes within the scope of nutrition and vitamin K, like vitamin E, must be considered as a substance of which nutritionists should be aware although they need not take any practical action about it.

Unit Sixteen
The B-group Vitamins

16.1 Thiamine (Vitamin B_1)

Although thousands of people have died from beri-beri, mainly in Asia and Africa, it is important to remember that it is almost entirely a man-made disease and hardly existed before the days of modern industrialization. Beri-beri is primarily due to a dietary deficiency of a compound once called vitamin B_1, which is today known as *thiamine* (some writers use the term *aneurine*). This deficiency was unknown before the development of modern milling technology which produced white rice (so-called 'polished' rice) at a lower cost than that of home-pounded rice. Similarly, beri-beri only became a public-health problem in many African countries when white flour refined by modern milling techniques became popular because of its cheapness and palatability.

Beri-beri came to notice as a serious epidemic disease in the Japanese navy in 1879 when there were nearly two thousand cases among five thousand men, the main part of whose rations was white rice. It appeared later in China, Malaya, Indonesia, Singapore, parts of India and in the Philippines and still occurs in these countries.

(a) Beri-beri

The symptoms of beri-beri vary, depending on the kind of diet eaten by the patient and the degree of thiamine shortage in it. In *wet beri-beri* the tissues, especially those of the legs, become 'waterlogged' (a condition called *oedema* or dropsy) and the patient is subject to palpitations, breathlessness and muscular pains; if thiamine is not given to relieve his symptoms he may die from extreme breathlessness and failure of the circulation. In the condition called *dry beri-beri* there is wastage and emaciation of the tissues instead of oedema, and the patient suffers from extreme weakness.

In both wet and dry beri-beri the victim may die from a sudden onset of oedema or an attack of diarrhoea. In populations where the diet largely consists of white polished rice, where mothers consequently do not receive adequate thiamine and infants are often weaned on to thin rice gruel, these infants too may develop beri-beri and die suddenly from heart failure.

(b) The Main Sources of Thiamine in the Diet

As we have said, beri-beri is often observed among people who eat a diet consisting mainly of white rice. Now that we know that the disease is caused by thiamine deficiency, the question arises as to why modern milling techniques are capable of producing a material so completely lacking in the vitamin. The reason lies in the structure of the cereal grain shown in Fig. 16.1 (grains of rice, wheat and other cereals have a similar structure).

The thiamine content of a grain of rice is held almost entirely in two parts of the grain: in its *outer layers* (the *bran*), and in the *scutellum*, the thin flat layer which separates the *endosperm* (the starchy part of the grain) from the embryo or 'germ'. After the milling process, little but the endosperm is left; the outer layers of the grain and the embryo are lost.

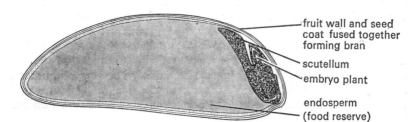

fruit wall and seed coat fused together forming bran

scutellum

embryo plant

endosperm (food reserve)

Fig. 16.1 Longitudinal section of a cereal grain

The distribution of thiamine in a variety of different foods is shown in Table 16.1.

(c) The Properties of Thiamine

Thiamine is readily soluble in water, so that when foods containing the free vitamin are cooked in water, a proportion of it may be lost. It is tolerably resistant to heat in acid solution and may survive temperatures up to 120 °C for short periods; however, it is rapidly destroyed by heat in alkaline or neutral conditions.

(d) The Daily Requirement of Thiamine in the Diet

In Section 6.1 we mentioned how the long chains of six-carbon-atom glucose units making up the starch molecule are first unlinked and then oxidized to carbon dioxide and water in order to release energy for the body's needs, and how this process consists of a series of step-by-step changes, so that the energy becomes available in a controlled manner. Each step in this sequence requires the presence of its own specific enzyme. The importance of thiamine in the process lies in the fact that it forms part of the particular enzyme concerned with the breakdown of a three-carbon-atom intermediate compound, pyruvic acid. If thiamine is lacking, the whole process of releasing energy from carbohydrates is impaired.

Table 16.1   The thiamine content of certain foods

	mg per 100 g
Good sources of thiamine	
Dried brewers' yeast	20·0
Wheat germ	1·6
Peanuts	1·0
Lean pork	0·9
Kidney	0·6
Whole-wheat flour	0·5
Moderately good sources of thiamine	
Meat (beef, lamb)	0·2
Chestnuts	0·2
Walnuts	0·2
Fish	0·1
Eggs	0·1
Potatoes	0·1
Green vegetables	0·05
Apples	0·04
Poor sources of thiamine	
White flour	0·06*
White rice	0·03
Jam	0
Sugar	0

* In some countries, including Great Britain, thiamine is added to white flour to bring the content up to 0·24 mg per 100 g; in these circumstances white flour can be classed as a moderately good source of thiamine.

It follows from this that:

(i) the more starch or other carbohydrate the diet contains the more thiamine is needed;
(ii) eating foods rich in carbohydrate but containing little or no thiamine, like white rice or sugar, produces a serious thiamine deficiency which must be made good by other foods in the diet;
(iii) although fat has more than twice the energy value of carbohydrate, eating fatty foods lacking in thiamine like cooking fats or suet does not give rise to thiamine deficiency, because thiamine is primarily concerned with the metabolism of carbohydrate, not fat.

Even though the relative proportions of carbohydrate and fat in the diet affect the precise amount of thiamine required, for practical purposes the figures given in Table 16.2 can be taken to represent adequate thiamine intakes for different types of people, regardless of the precise composition of their diet.

An adult man stores about 25 mg of thiamine in the various tissues of his body, so that even on a diet totally lacking in thiamine—unlikely to be

Table 16.2   Recommended daily allowances of thiamine

	energy intake (kJ)	thiamine (mg per day)
Boys and girls		
0 up to 1 year	3 300	0·3
1 up to 2 years	5 000	0·5
2 up to 3 years	5 900	0·6
3 up to 5 years	6 700	0·6
5 up to 7 years	7 500	0·7
7 up to 9 years	8 800	0·8
Boys		
9 up to 12 years	10 500	1·0
12 up to 15 years	11 700	1·1
15 up to 18 years	12 600	1·2
Girls		
9 up to 18 years	9 600	0·9
Men		
18 up to 35 years sedentary	11 300	1·1
moderately active	12 600	1·2
very active	15 100	1·4
35 up to 65 years sedentary	10 900	1·0
moderately active	12 100	1·2
very active	15 100	1·4
65 up to 75 years	9 800	0·9
75 and over	8 800	0·8
Women		
18 up to 55 years normally active	9 200	0·9
very active	10 500	1·0
55 up to 75 years	8 600	0·8
75 and over	8 000	0·7
pregnant (3–9 months)	10 800	1·0
nursing	11 300	1·1

encountered in practice—the full needs of 1 mg or so a day would be available from these stored supplies for a period of a few weeks at least. Experiments have shown that people receiving about 0.3 mg of thiamine a day show no symptoms of deficiency that could be recognized as due to an inability to break down pyruvic acid within three months. Malnutrition due to thiamine deficiency is most likely in people who have received less of the vitamin than they need over a prolonged period.

(e) **Symptoms of Thiamine Deficiency**
The symptoms of beri-beri, arising from severe and prolonged thiamine deficiency, are described in Section 16.1(a). In experiments where people were given diets lacking in thiamine the early symptoms of deficiency were rather general, and included lack of appetite, apathy and depression.

Alcoholics who, besides suffering from symptoms directly due to their excessive drinking, often eat a very unsatisfactory and inadequate diet, sometimes also develop *alcoholic neuritis* which is partly due to an insufficient intake of thiamine.

(f) Antivitamin B_1 in Raw Fish

Raw fish, which is sometimes eaten in Scandinavian countries and elsewhere, contains *thiaminase*, an enzyme capable of destroying the vitamin activity of thiamine. Where raw fish is a regular item of the diet it may reduce the availability of thiamine present in other foods by about 50 per cent.

(g) Excessive Intake of Thiamine

If more thiamine is eaten than the body requires the excess will do no harm, since the vitamin is readily excreted through the kidneys and leaves the body in the urine. It also follows, therefore, that there is no benefit to be gained by taking extra thiamine, for example by swallowing vitamin tablets, providing the diet already contains adequate thiamine.

16.2 Riboflavine (part of the so-called Vitamin B_2)

If people, or experimental rats, pigeons or chickens, are given a diet which is mainly composed of polished rice, the first symptoms to appear will be due to thiamine deficiency. If purified thiamine is added to such a diet, the people eating it will not develop beri-beri nor will the rats die of 'polyneuritis' as they did before, but the people will not be well, nor will the rats grow normally. The diet is still nutritionally deficient, even though it contains plenty of thiamine. It lacks, among other substances, an essential vitamin once called vitamin B_2, but later named *riboflavine*.

(a) The Properties of Riboflavine

Riboflavine is a bright yellow compound (the Latin word *flavus* means *yellow*). Compounds early identified in milk under the name of *lactoflavine*, in liver as *hepatoflavine*, in eggs as *ovoflavine* and in kidney as *renoflavine* were soon found to be identical with riboflavine.

Riboflavine is quite stable to heat, except under alkaline conditions; if cooking is being done in the presence of an excess of soda, for example, the vitamin is destroyed by heat.

Riboflavine is susceptible to light, so that if milk is left outside in strong sunlight its riboflavine content will gradually be destroyed.

(b) The Main Sources of Riboflavine in the Diet

Good sources of riboflavine are liver, kidney, and meat extracts like Bovril, cheese, eggs and lean meat. Yeast and yeast extract contain comparatively large amounts. It is interesting that while yeast contains thiamine, the vitamin is held so closely within the yeast cells that there is little or none in beer. On the other hand, yeast releases a good deal of its riboflavine content during brewing, so that beer is as good a dietary source of riboflavine as milk. The distribution of riboflavine in a number of foodstuffs is shown in Table 16.3.

Table 16.3   The riboflavine content of certain foods

	mg per 100 g
Good sources of riboflavine	
Dried brewers' yeast	15·6
Yeast extract (e.g. Marmite)	5·0
Liver	3·0
Kidney	2·0
Meat extract (e.g. Bovril, Oxo	2·0
Wheat germ	1·0
Cocoa powder	0·5
Cheese	0·5
Eggs	0·4
Beef (lean)	0·2
Lamb (lean)	0·2
Pork (lean)	0·2
Chocolate	0·2
Beans (dried, uncooked)	0·1
Moderately good sources of riboflavine	
Spinach	0·20
Dried apricots	0·20
Milk	0·15
Oatmeal	0·10
Fish	0·10
Cauliflower	0·10
Brown bread	0·07
Cabbage	0·05
Carrots	0·05
Beer	0·05
Potatoes	0·04
White flour	0·04
Poor sources of riboflavine	
Maize meal	0·03
Polished rice	0·03
White bread	0·02
Fruit	0·02
Tea (as drunk)	0·01
Jam	0
Syrup	0
Sugar	0

(c) **The Daily Requirement of Riboflavine**

The function of riboflavine is somewhat similar to that of thiamine in that it too is a part of one of the enzymes concerned with making the energy of carbohydrates available to the body. Unlike thiamine, however, there is little relationship between the energy requirement of an individual and the amount of riboflavine needed for good nutrition. Table 16.4 shows the recommended allowances of riboflavine for different types of people.

Table 16.4   Recommended allowances of riboflavine

	mg per day
Boys and girls	
0 up to 1 year	0·4
1 up to 2 years	0·6
2 up to 3 years	0·7
3 up to 5 years	0·8
5 up to 7 years	0·9
7 up to 9 years	1·0
9 up to 12 years	1·2
12 up to 15 years	1·4
Boys 15 up to 18 years	1·7
Girls 15 up to 18 years	1·4
Men of any age and any level of physical activity	1·7
Women	
of any age and any level of physical activity	1·3
pregnant	1·6
nursing	1·8

(d) **Symptoms of Riboflavine Deficiency**

Although several different species of experimental animals ranging from rats and monkeys to chickens develop a variety of recognizable symptoms when fed on diets lacking in riboflavine, there is little unequivocal evidence that any particular symptom or disability in man is due to a shortage of this vitamin. Young rats fail to grow satisfactorily when their diet contains inadequate riboflavine, and adult rats sometimes develop peculiar eye symptoms. Hens kept short of riboflavine lay eggs also lacking in riboflavine which fail to hatch properly. But while all this implies that riboflavine has something to do with the health of these creatures, there is no conclusive proof that it plays a particular role in the healthy functioning of people. However, there is perhaps an indication that it is prudent to ensure that the amounts suggested in Table 16.4 are included in people's diets. In the main, the table has been compiled having consideration of the amounts naturally provided by what is thought to be a good mixed diet, and the amounts found to maintain a normal concentration of riboflavine in the tissues.

It has been claimed that riboflavine deficiency in people produces a particular type of cracking and fissuring of the skin at the corners of the mouth, soreness of the tongue and the development of a special kind of bloodshot appearance of the white of the eyes. There is, however, no clear indication that lack of riboflavine is solely to blame, since all these signs and symptoms are relatively common and all can be due to other causes. Furthermore, when it can be calculated or established by analysis that a person's diet is deficient in riboflavine, it will almost always be found to be lacking in other nutrients as well.

The lesson for the nutritionist therefore is that it is useful to know about riboflavine and prudent to ensure that foods containing it are provided in the diet, yet at the same time it is wise not to attribute too high a value to its presence until such time as unambiguous evidence of its importance in human nutrition may be discovered.

(e) Excessive Intake of Riboflavine

As always happens when the precise role of a vitamin is uncertain, various claims have been made about the beneficial effect of large doses of riboflavine administered for all sorts of reasons. None of these suggested virtues of excess riboflavine have been substantiated, but on the other hand no harm has ever been demonstrated to result from the consumption of the vitamin in these large quantities.

16.3   Niacin

Niacin is another of the water-soluble vitamins which occur together in yeast and certain other foods and which make up what was once called the 'vitamin B complex'. Unlike other vitamins, however, which were found to have molecular structures previously unknown to science, niacin activity is due to two quite simple chemical substances which have been known since 1867, *nicotinic acid* and *nicotinamide*.

(a) The Function of Niacin in the Body

Niacin, like both thiamine and riboflavine, constitutes part of one of the enzyme systems which control the release of energy from carbohydrates. The classification of all three of these substances, thiamine, riboflavine and niacin, as vitamins which must be provided in the diet implies that none of them can be synthesized in the body (as most enzymes are synthesized). This, however, is not strictly true for niacin.

(*i*) Some niacin may be synthesized within the body by the micro-organisms present in the large intestine. It is, however, difficult to determine how much of the vitamin is produced in any particular individual and we cannot easily compare the niacin-synthesizing abilities of different people.

(*ii*) The amino acid *tryptophan* (see Section 5.2) has some niacin activity: we can say that roughly 60 mg of tryptophan has the same vitamin activity as 1 mg of niacin. It follows therefore that less niacin is required by people who eat plenty of good-quality proteins—such as those in eggs and milk—containing comparatively large amounts of tryptophan. On the other hand, more niacin is needed by people living on diets composed largely of food-stuffs in which the protein is lacking in tryptophan. *Pellagra* (see Section 16.3(*d*)), the disease due to niacin deficiency, is commonest in those parts of the world where people's staple food is maize, the protein of which is notoriously lacking in tryptophan.

(b) The Main Sources of Niacin in the Diet

The richest sources of niacin are extracts of meat and yeast, although it is also present in comparatively high concentration in liver, kidney and lean meat, wholemeal flour and cereal by-products like bran. In general, however, niacin is quite widely distributed so that it is unlikely to be lacking in the normal kind of mixed diet eaten in western industrial countries. Characteristic niacin levels in a variety of foods are listed in Table 16.5.

Table 16.5 The niacin content of certain foods

	mg per 100 g
Good sources of niacin	
Meat extract (e.g. Bovril, Oxo)	70
Yeast extract (e.g. Marmite, Yeastvite)	60
Wheat bran	30
Liver	12
Kidney	12
Meat (beef, mutton, pork)	5
Wheat germ	5
Wholemeal flour	5
Brown rice	4
Fish	4
Moderately good sources of niacin	
Peas and beans	2·0
White flour	1·0
Polished rice	1·0
Oatmeal	1·0
Dried fruit	1·0
Chocolate	1·0
Poor sources of niacin	
Maize meal	0·8
Potatoes	0·8
Green vegetables	0·8
Fruit	0·7
Milk	0·1
Eggs	0·1
Cheese	0·03

(c) The Daily Requirement of Niacin

Table 16.6 lists the recommended allowances of niacin for a nutritionally satisfactory diet, but in using these figures for practical purposes two points must be remembered:

(*i*) The amount of niacin required will be affected by the amount of protein in the diet, and also by the quality of the protein in terms of its tryptophan content.

(*ii*) Some niacin appears to be synthesized actually within the large intestine; thus, while it is impossible to say how much niacin is manufactured in the intestine of any particular person, ample supplies of niacin are especially important for malnourished people, who often suffer from diarrhoea and other gastro-intestinal disturbances.

Table 16.6   Recommended daily allowances of niacin

	mg nicotinic acid equivalent (1 mg niacin or 60 mg tryptophan)
Boys and girls	
0 up to 1 year	5
1 up to 2 years	7
2 up to 3 years	8
3 up to 5 years	9
5 up to 7 years	10
7 up to 9 years	11
Boys	
9 up to 12 years	14
12 up to 15 years	16
15 up to 18 years	19
Girls	
9 up to 12 years	13
12 up to 18 years	16
Men (all degrees of activity)	18
Women	
all degrees of activity	15
pregnant (last 6 months)	18
nursing	21

(d) Symptoms of Niacin Deficiency

Serious and prolonged lack of niacin in the diet eventually produces the unpleasant deficiency disease *pellagra*. The symptoms of pellagra include a characteristic skin discoloration, rather resembling severe sunburn, affecting the parts of the cheeks, the neck and the backs of the hands normally exposed to the sun; the mouth may become sore and ulcerated at the corners, and the tongue may have a 'raw beef' appearance. There may be nausea and diarrhoea, or sometimes constipation, and nervous symptoms which may also appear include depression, anxiety, irritability, lack of concentration and even, in extreme cases, delirium.

(e) Excessive Intake of Niacin

There is no possibility of any excess niacin derived from a diet rich in meat or liver, or containing large amounts of yeast or meat extract, proving harmful to the body. As with other water-soluble vitamins, any niacin not required by the body is excreted in the urine.

Niacin can, however, be readily obtained as the synthetic products nicotinic acid and nicotinamide, and nicotinic acid, even when taken in the quantities recommended in Table 16.6, can cause flushing which, although transient and harmless, is found unpleasant by some people.

When taken in very large doses of from 1 to 4 g at a time, niacin no longer acts as a vitamin and can more properly be considered as a drug. As such it is of some use in medicine in controlling the concentration of free fatty acids in the blood plasma. In doses of this magnitude, however, niacin may eventually cause lack of appetite, nausea, vomiting and some disturbance of liver function.

16.4   Pyridoxine (Vitamin B_6)

Pyridoxine, a fairly simple compound which is also called vitamin B_6, is a further member of the vitamin B complex, and is generally associated with other B-group vitamins in foods. Like niacin, it can occur in several forms, including compounds called *pyridoxine* and *pyridoxamine*. Again, it resembles the other B vitamins in that it is water-soluble.

(a) The Function of Pyridoxine

Pyridoxine, like other members of the vitamin B complex, functions as part of an enzyme, in this case one which is concerned with the reconstitution of the amino acids derived from food proteins into the proteins of the body's own tissues.

(b) Distribution of Pyridoxine in Foods

There are few reliable estimates of the precise amounts of pyridoxine in different foods, but it seems clear that the vitamin is widely distributed. Good sources of pyridoxine include meat, especially liver, green vegetables, bran, wheat germ and wholemeal flour.

(c) Symptoms of Pyridoxine Deficiency

There is a great deal of experimental evidence indicating that pyridoxine is necessary in the diet for the health and well-being of various kinds of laboratory animals. Although it is clear that it is needed by people, symptoms of malnutrition due solely to a shortage of pyridoxine are uncommon. Among poor communities eating a diet deficient in several ways, some of the symptoms found among them may be due to pyridoxine shortage while others will be caused by lack of other vitamins, of protein, or even simply of enough to eat. Where they can be isolated, the following symptoms of pyridoxine deficiency have been identified:

(*i*) On very rare occasions, irritability in infants, which may even extend to convulsions, has been attributed to insufficient pyridoxine.

(*ii*) A particular kind of anaemia has been found to be associated with a pyridoxine-deficient diet, and to be cured when pyridoxine is given.

(*iii*) Insomnia, soreness of the corners of the mouth and tongue and a particular kind of dermatitis have all been reported in people eating poor diets lacking in pyridoxine.

16.5   Cyanocobalamin (Vitamin B$_{12}$)

Vitamin B$_{12}$, the chemical name for which is cyanocobalamin, is particularly interesting for several reasons.

(*i*) Although it is essential for health, the amount required is exceedingly small, even when compared with other vitamins. The daily requirement for a man is certainly less than 1 µg (one-millionth of a gram).

(*ii*) The vitamin is widely distributed in animal foods, and deficiency symptoms in previously healthy people are therefore very uncommon. Indeed, the strictest vegetarians, called Vegans, who refuse not only meat but dairy products and eggs as well, are almost the only people in whom cyanocobalamin deficiency has been observed.

(*iii*) The disease of *pernicious anaemia*, although not caused by nutritional deficiency, can be treated by giving cyanocobalamin, usually by injection, although administration by mouth is satisfactory if sufficiently large dosages are used.

(*a*) The Chemistry of Cyanocobalamin

Like other B-group vitamins, cyanocobalamin is water-soluble. When isolated in its pure form it is a red compound, but the amount naturally present in foods is so little that they are not coloured by it. Its molecule is large and complicated, and contains an atom of cobalt, as indicated by its name.

(*b*) The Distribution of Cyanocobalamin in Foods

Meat, fish, dairy products and eggs are all good sources of cyanocobalamin.

16.6   Folic Acid (Pteroylglutamic Acid)

Folic acid, like cyanocobalamin, is a substance present in food which is effective in remedying a particular type of anaemia. Again like cyanocobalamin, the amount of dietary folic acid needed for health is insufficient only when a very inadequate and impoverished diet is eaten for a prolonged period. Deficiency was first reported in pregnant women subsisting on a very poor diet.

As implied by the chemical name for folic acid, *pteroylglutamic acid*, its molecular structure comprises a molecule of one of the compounds called *pterins* (discovered in 1885 as pigments in the wings of butterflies) linked with a molecule of the amino acid *glutamic acid*.

The exact amount of folic acid needed each day for health is not known. A daily intake of 200 μg has been recommended for a normal adult, with 400 μg to protect a woman during pregnancy. The distribution of folic acid in certain foods is shown in Table 16.7.

Table 16.7   The folic acid content of certain foods

	μg per 100 g
Good sources of folic acid	
Liver	300
Oysters	250
Spinach	80
Broccoli tops	50
Fish	50
Moderately good sources of folic acid	
Peas and beans	30
Cabbage and lettuce	20
Wholemeal bread	20
Rice (uncooked)	10
Bananas	10
Beef	8
Eggs	8
Poor sources of folic acid	
Mutton, pork	3
Chicken	3
Fruit	3
Milk	0·3

16.7   Other Compounds of the Vitamin B Complex

From the preceding sections of this Unit, it will be clear that the beneficial effect of incorporating substances like yeast or rice polishings in a purified diet is not, as originally thought, due to a single 'vitamin B', but to the combined activities of nearly a dozen vitamins. Some of these, like thiamine, riboflavine and niacin, are of direct importance in human diets. Unless there is enough of them in their diet, children will fail to thrive and adults will suffer from various forms of malnutrition and, if the lack is very severe or prolonged, may die of a deficiency disease like beri-beri or pellagra.

As well as these three compounds, cyanocobalamin and folic acid, other B-group vitamins have been discovered as a result of experiments on animals. Even though these substances may not so far have been demonstrated to be essential in man, it is clearly sensible to be aware of their existence and of the foods which contain them; it is possible that their function may one day acquire practical importance through circumstances at present unforeseen, perhaps the introduction of new methods of cooking or food processing or some drastic change in the availability of staple foods.

(a) Pantothenic Acid

This vitamin is very widely distributed, being found in almost all foodstuffs. Like other B-group vitamins, it functions as a part of one of the body's important enzymes. Although experimental animals, notably chicks and rats, benefit when pantothenic acid is added to purified diets, human deficiency has not been observed. This is probably because almost any practical diet would contribute enough of the vitamin, or, if a deficient diet were eaten, because symptoms of a lack of one of the other vitamins would appear first. Liver, kidney, yeast, egg yolk and fresh vegetables are all rich sources of pantothenic acid.

(b) Biotin

Biotin is another widely distributed vitamin, active in extremely small amounts. Human deficiency, shown by a particular form of dermatitis, occurs almost exclusively in a few eccentric individuals who eat large numbers—several dozen a week—of raw eggs. The reason for this is that raw egg white contains an antivitamin, *avidin*, which makes biotin unavailable to the body; it is destroyed when the eggs are cooked.

(c) *para*-Aminobenzoic Acid and Inositol

Deficiency of either of these vitamins produces various symptoms in experimental animals. Again, both are widely distributed in foods, and in neither case has any symptom of deficiency been demonstrated in man.

Unit Seventeen
Vitamin C (Ascorbic Acid)

17.1 Introduction

Ascorbic acid, also called vitamin C, is a vitamin which requires particular attention from the practising nutritionist. Unlike some of the B-group vitamins which are known to exist and play a part in the biochemistry of the body but of which a dietary shortage hardly ever seems to occur, ascorbic acid is quite often found to be deficient in people's diets, and their health may suffer when this is so. The reasons why ascorbic acid is lacking more often than perhaps any other nutrient are as follows:

(a) It is only present in any significant amount in a restricted range of foods, that is, in fresh fruit and vegetables.

(b) It is readily soluble in water and may be washed out of food in cooking-water.

(c) It is quite susceptible to heat and may be destroyed when vegetables are cooked or when they are kept hot for a period of time.

(d) It gradually decomposes when vegetables are stored or when they become stale and wilted.

(e) There is considerable variation in the amount of ascorbic acid in different varieties of the same fruits and vegetables, so that a deficiency can arise even when some care is taken in choosing a satisfactory diet.

(f) Under some circumstances it is lost during processing, for example, when potatoes are dehydrated.

(g) It is not stored by the body to any significant extent, so that a steady and adequate supply is necessary for complete health.

17.2 The Chemistry of Ascorbic Acid

Ascorbic acid is a substance which has what chemists call 'reducing properties', that is, it is readily oxidized; but on oxidation its vitamin activity is lost. As we have said, the vitamin is unstable to heat, especially in the presence of oxygen of the air. This instability is enhanced by exposure to light and by the presence of traces of metals, particularly copper; it is especially marked in alkaline conditions. (This is why adding soda during the cooking of green vegetables, although it preserves their colour, is nutritionally very undesirable: the alkali destroys nearly all their ascorbic acid content.) On the other hand, the vitamin is quite stable under acid conditions, as in many fruits.

17.3   The Main Sources of Ascorbic Acid in the Diet

Table 17.1 shows that ascorbic acid is, with few exceptions, only found in fruit and vegetables. Furthermore, the amounts of the vitamin even in these may vary or may be lost altogether; they are only significant when the foods are fresh or have been carefully preserved or stored in the fresh form. Dried peas and beans and dried fruit do not contain any ascorbic acid.

Table 17.1   The ascorbic acid content of certain foods

	mg per 100 g of uncooked food
Rich sources of ascorbic acid	
Blackcurrants	200
Brussels sprouts	100
Cauliflower	70
Cabbage	60
Spinach	60
Strawberries	60
Oranges, lemons	50
Pineapple	40
Grapefruit	40
Moderately good sources of ascorbic acid	
Liver	30
Green peas	25
Tomatoes	20
Lettuce	15
Bananas	10
Carrots	6
Apples	5
Plums	3
Potatoes:	
new	30
Oct.–Nov.	20
Dec.	15
Jan.–Feb.	10
March	8
Poor sources of ascorbic acid	
Milk	
Eggs	
Fresh meat	
Foods containing no ascorbic acid	
Bread, flour and all cereal foods	
Baked beans , haricot beans, dried and 'processed' peas	
Fats of all sorts	
Sugar, syrup	

17.4   Scurvy

Scurvy is a disagreeable and painful condition which arises when a diet lacking in sufficient ascorbic acid is eaten for some time; if not relieved it is fatal. Before potatoes were adopted as a staple food in Great Britain and other northern European countries, cases of scurvy were common each year in the late winter and spring. Before the nature of ascorbic acid was understood, scurvy was a serious disease among the crews of sailing ships making long voyages, for example, round the Horn from California to Boston, and among explorers in the polar regions who lived on carried rations made up of durable foods like flour, biscuits and salted meat.

There are several symptoms of ascorbic acid deficiency, leading eventually to scurvy:

(a) Listlessness and a feeling of weakness are the first indications of ascorbic acid deficiency, other than a fall in its concentration in the blood, detectable only by chemical analysis.

(b) Swelling and bleeding of the gums, particularly if they have been previously infected, so that minor injury or little more than a touch will cause them to bleed.

(c) Bleeding under the skin, particularly around the points where the hairs grow on the legs and ankles, is apparent as purple patches.

(d) The function of ascorbic acid particularly concerns the 'cement' which holds together the cells of the body tissues. When lack of ascorbic acid is prolonged this function is damaged and wounds consequently heal very slowly or fail to heal at all. When scurvy is severe, one of its most distressing symptoms is that old wounds, healed and forgotten long before, break open and bleed again.

Scurvy in Babies

Human breast milk usually contains enough ascorbic acid for the baby's needs. Fresh cows' milk also contains a small amount, but this may be easily lost when the milk is heated or if it is left on the doorstep in the sunlight; processing milk to make milk powder or condensed milk also destroys the vitamin. It follows therefore that young bottle-fed babies receive little or no ascorbic acid unless it is given in a dietary supplement like orange or black-currant juice, and if these are not available they may develop scurvy. Having no teeth the swelling of their gums has a different appearance from that occurring in adults. Painful haemorrhages under the skin of their legs occur, which cause them to cry continuously and scream when they are moved.

17.5   The Ascorbic Acid Requirements of Different Categories of People

It is not easy to assess the ideal daily allowance of ascorbic acid for an individual, and several different factors must be taken into account.

Factors Affecting the Need for Ascorbic Acid

(*a*) **Normal intake.** The recommended daily intake of ascorbic acid for a normal adult is around 30 mg, but this can hardly be claimed to be a scientifically based figure; rather, it represents a reasonable compromise between two points of view. Clearly, an individual showing the symptoms of scurvy is getting too little ascorbic acid in his diet. Not only will 10 mg or so of ascorbic acid a day prevent the symptoms of scurvy; it will, in fact, cure a patient who is already suffering from the disease.

However, if more than 10 mg of ascorbic acid is taken each day, the body goes on absorbing it and the concentration of ascorbic acid in the blood continues to rise until the daily intake reaches about 100 mg. Some workers therefore consider that this level of intake must be best of all. In Great Britain, the recommended daily intake of 30 mg is taken as a reasonable intermediate value, although American authorities recommend double this intake.

(*b*) **Intake following injury.** Injuries such as burns or surgical operations have been found to increase the loss of ascorbic acid from the body in the urine. Healthy, well-nourished people have not been shown to suffer from this depletion of the body's supply of ascorbic acid, but it is sometimes thought prudent to provide supplementary amounts of the vitamin to people convalescing from injury or operations.

(*c*) **Effect on iron absorption.** Ascorbic acid facilitates the absorption of iron (see Section 11.3(*a*)) and supplementary amounts of ascorbic acid can, therefore, be useful in the treatment of iron-deficiency anaemia.

The figures given in Table 17.2 represent a consensus of informed opinion on a desirable ascorbic acid intake under normal circumstances. Other nutritional scientists have come to different conclusions in the past, and the figures given may well change if more information comes to light in the future.

Table 17.2   Recommended daily allowances of ascorbic acid

	mg per day
Boys and girls	
0 up to 1 year	15
1 up to 9 years	20
9 up to 15 years	25
15 up to 18 years	30
Men and women all ages and all degrees of activity	30
Women 3–9 months pregnant and nursing	60

17.6 Losses of Ascorbic Acid in Cooking, Processing and Storage

(a) Potatoes

In those parts of the world where potatoes form a regular article of food, they constitute the biggest single contributor of ascorbic acid to the diet, even though other foods contain higher concentrations of the vitamin, as Table 17.1 shows. This is partly because potatoes can be eaten every day without satiation, partly because the actual weight of potatoes eaten is often greater than that of other ascorbic-acid-containing foods, and partly because the loss of ascorbic acid in cooking potatoes, though considerable, is frequently less than that from other vegetables. Approximate average losses are as follows:

Potatoes boiled in their skins:	15%
Potatoes baked in their skins:	20%
Potatoes fried:	30%
Potatoes boiled:	50%

When boiled potatoes are mashed, so that the area of surface exposed to the air is considerably increased, a further loss of ascorbic acid occurs; the more thoroughly they are mashed, the more ascorbic acid is destroyed.

Almost all the ascorbic acid in fresh potatoes is destroyed during the manufacture of dehydrated potato. It is, therefore, important to make sure when buying dehydrated potato powder that the manufacturer has added ascorbic acid to it. This should be recorded on the packet.

(b) Green Vegetables

Table 17.3 shows how much ascorbic acid can be expected to be lost in the cooking of green vegetables.

Table 17.3 Percentages of ascorbic acid lost in cooking

	per cent
Cabbage	40–65
Cauliflower	25–45
Kale	65–85
Brussels sprouts	25–50
Spinach	25–35
Green peas	45–65
Runner beans	35–55

These considerable losses and the wide fluctuations in them are caused by several factors.

(i) *Losses in cooking-water and those caused by overcooking.* Since ascorbic acid is water-soluble, boiling in large amounts of water increases the loss. Steaming, on the other hand, reduces the loss, unless longer cooking times are allowed. For example, whereas 40 per cent of the ascorbic acid in cabbage is destroyed by 30 minutes' steaming, the loss after 50 minutes rises to 60 per cent. Adding salt to the water in which green vegetables are cooked has little or no effect on its vitamin content. As we have already said, *adding soda greatly increases the destruction of ascorbic acid.*

(*ii*) *Losses due to enzyme action.* The most important factor in preserving the vitamin content of green vegetables is the rapidity with which they are brought to the boil. By putting vegetables in small amounts into briskly boiling water the enzymes which would otherwise destroy ascorbic acid are themselves destroyed before they can have any effect. On the other hand, when green vegetables are put into cold water and slowly brought to the boil, or when a large bulk of vegetables is put into hot water so that its temperature falls to lukewarm, vitamin-destroying enzymes have an opportunity to work while the temperature of the vegetable mass gradually rises. By the time the water is hot enough to destroy the enzymes much of the original ascorbic acid has been lost.

(*c*) Peas

Fresh green peas are a useful source of ascorbic acid, but in western countries most peas are eaten after some form of food processing.

(*i*) **Frozen peas.** About 70 per cent of the ascorbic acid content of the original peas is retained after freezing. Provided a deep-freeze is kept at the proper temperature of −18 °C, frozen peas stored in it lose only about 20 per cent of their ascorbic acid in a year. If the deep-freeze is only kept at −12 °C, however, the peas will lose as much as 80 per cent of their vitamin content in this time.

(*ii*) **Canned ('garden') peas.** About 60 per cent of the vitamin content of the original green peas remains after the canning process; of this, anything up to half may be lost when the peas are heated through for the table. The remainder is much the same proportion as that which is likely to survive the cooking of 'fresh' peas.

(*iii*) **'Processed' peas.** Although these peas, when canned, look like fresh green peas and to some extent taste like them, it is important to remember that they are in fact dried peas which have been soaked in water, cooked, coloured and flavoured. Although they are a useful food, contributing a certain amount of protein to the diet, they contain virtually no ascorbic acid at all.

(*d*) Orange Juice

Canned and bottled orange juice are both useful sources of ascorbic acid, and have the advantage that they can be stored for up to a year with little loss of ascorbic acid, so long as the container is kept closed. Once it has been opened, however, about half of its vitamin content is lost within a week, although the exact amount depends on the conditions of storage.

The considerations we have discussed in this and the preceding sections clearly make it very difficult to assess how much ascorbic acid a person actually receives from any particular diet. As usual, the 'theoretical' amounts listed in Table 17.1 can only be taken as generally representative figures for a particular food: for example, red apples contain more of the vitamin than green ones do. Moreover, the implication of the ascorbic acid losses during cooking and storage is that the vitamin content of a prepared dish—cauliflower cheese or blackcurrant pie, perhaps—is, to say the least, uncertain. However, while the recommended daily allowance of 30 mg may be borne in mind as desirable and prudent, little harm may be expected if the amount actually eaten differs from this from time to time.

17.7 The Effect of Excess Ascorbic Acid

Ascorbic acid is readily and cheaply available as the pure synthetic vitamin. From time to time claims are made that it has some sort of beneficial effect when taken in very large amounts. The most dramatic of these has been that it exerts a protective influence against colds when swallowed at the rate of 5 to 10 *grams* a day. (These doses can be compared with the recommended daily nutritional requirement, which itself may well be generous, of 30 mg, or 0.030 g.) Evidence for this and other similar claims is unconfirmed. At the same time no harm has been recorded from taking these enormous amounts.

Unit Eighteen
Foodstuffs and Nutrition

18.1 Introduction

The preceding units have given some account of the properties of the wide range of nutrients which the body needs, and have discussed proteins, fats, vitamins and so on in some detail. It must always be remembered that people do not eat these nutrients *as such*, but as constituents of foodstuffs, and that whether they are in fact obtained from the diet depends very largely on the type and amount of foodstuffs eaten.

The tables in the Appendix to this book give characteristic nutrient compositions of a variety of foods, but they are meant for reference—not to be memorized in their entirety. Some knowledge of the biology of the plants and animals used for food will enable a nutritionist to make an approximate deduction as to what nutrients are likely to be present in almost any foodstuff, bearing in mind that virtually all material which is eaten is of biological origin. We have already pointed out that man cannot use directly the simple chemical compounds like carbon dioxide, water and nitrates to produce his own more complex nutrients, but depends on the biological functions of plants or of animals that eat them to produce nutrients for his body. Almost every food he eats is obtained by disrupting the life processes of some other organism.

The biological origins of the materials which make up a diet can serve as a very valuable guide to the assessment of its nutrient content. The composition of a food differs according to whether it is derived from a part of an organism which was devoted to, say, structure (like plant stems or bones), or to storage (potatoes, liver), movement (muscle) or photochemical processes (leaves).

18.2 The Structure and Content of Foodstuffs

The basic unit of all organisms is the *cell*. Although the structures of cells vary enormously according to their function, most of them have some general characteristics in common and these can be used to produce a very much simplified picture of a 'typical cell'. However, there are important differences between the cells of animals and plants; we will consider animal cells first.

(a) Animal Cells

The cell can be divided into two clearly defined regions, called the *cytoplasm* (usually making up the largest part of the cell) and the *nucleus*. The whole is surrounded by a cell membrane, which forms a boundary to the cell; it allows soluble nutrients to pass both into and out of the cell, so that an environment is maintained in which the subcellular structures shown in Fig. 18.1 can operate. The membrane itself contains proteins and phospholipids.

The *nucleus* contains the nucleic acids, DNA and RNA (see Section 5.3) which control the growth of the cell and the production and characteristics of new cells. The nucleus is surrounded by a *nuclear membrane* which controls the passage of substances into and out of the nucleus, thus exchanging materials with the cytoplasm.

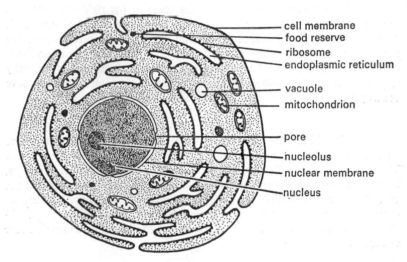

Fig. 18.1 A 'typical' animal cell

The *cytoplasm* is a fluid or semi-solid which fills the cell and which contains the many subcellular particles which contribute to its activities. Both the nucleus and the cytoplasm contain enzymes which virtually control the biochemical processes of the cell.

The minute structures called *mitochondria* play a vital role in the actual process of the production of energy from nutrients; their membranes (phospholipids) and enzymes (proteins) are important in this function.

Ribosomes, usually associated with the folded membranes of the *endoplasmic reticulum*, are concerned with protein synthesis, acting under the control of the nucleic acids of the cell nucleus.

The *lysosomes* contain enzymes which are capable of breaking down most of the cell components. The membrane surrounding the lysosome is normally impermeable to these enzymes, but if they are released, as happens if the cell is damaged, the cell undergoes self-destruction or *autolysis*.

(b) Plant Cells

Some of the differences between plant and animal cells have an important bearing on the dissimilarities between plant and animal foodstuffs. Plant cells have a cell wall external to the cell membrane, which contains the complex carbohydrates like cellulose and pectin, and assists the rigidity of the plant structure. Another difference is that the cytoplasm in a plant cell does not fill the cell completely, but occurs as strands attached to the nucleus, or around the edges of the cell. The remaining spaces are called *vacuoles*; they contain cell-sap, that is, water containing various dissolved substances so that the solution has a high osmotic pressure. This means that the cell tends to absorb water from its surroundings, and the pressure produced by the presence of this absorbed water accounts for some of the rigidity of growing plants; it is known as *turgor pressure*. When plants are picked or harvested, the cell-sap water slowly evaporates, so that the turgor pressure falls and the plants droop and wilt; some autolysis also occurs. This is one reason why fruit and vegetables should always be stored under conditions of humidity and temperature which will minimize evaporation. Lysosomes, however, have not as yet been positively identified in plant cells.

Foodstuffs of biological origin, and that is the vast majority, are either made up of cells or, like sugar, olive oil or lard, are extracted from them. The cells are not normally arranged haphazardly, but usually occur in groups, the members of which resemble each other either in structure or in function, or both. Such a collection of cells, like the heart or the liver, is called an *organ*. Where these organs work in conjunction with other organs, the resulting complex is called a *system*; the digestive system and the skeletal system are examples.

18.3   The Functions of Nutrients in Food Organisms

The nutrients in the biological materials used as foods are present there because of the functions they performed in the original living organisms. We can illustrate this point by reviewing what we know about the nutrients in this context, taking each one in turn.

(a) Carbohydrates

Glucose is the major source of energy for most organisms, although other monosaccharides are sometimes present. Glucose is soluble, and is one form in which energy is transported in living materials. It is stored in the form of larger insoluble molecules, such as some of the polysaccharides mentioned in Section 3.2(e). These stored compounds serve as reserve energy sources, or in plants, as structural components. Alternatively, glucose may be stored as fat.

(b) Proteins

Protein is, of course, necessary for the production of new tissues. While proteins are present to some extent in all cells, they are particularly abundant in cells where rapid growth may be expected, such as eggs or the embryos of seeds. Proteins are also involved in muscle contraction and are therefore plentiful in muscle (meat).

(c) Fats

Fats are used to provide energy and some essential fatty acids. Where fat is stored in animals, it also serves the functions of protection and insulation until it is needed as an energy source. Fat is often stored in seeds and eggs as a reserve food supply; it has an advantage over carbohydrate in this respect because of its higher energy value, which makes it a very concentrated energy source.

(d) Minerals

Some minerals are present in all cells. Phosphorus is necessary for the release and transfer of energy and together with other minerals helps to control the acidity and the osmotic pressure within the cell. Solid structures like bones and teeth contain calcium and magnesium as well as phosphorus. Calcium is present in blood and other body fluids, together with sodium and chloride ions, while magnesium forms part of the chlorophyll molecule and is found in all green plants. Calcium is also found in plants, where it may play a part in maintaining the strength of their tissues. Iron is present in blood as part of the haemoglobin molecule and is also stored in the liver. The large number of blood vessels in the kidney would appear to account for the unexpectedly high concentration of iron in this organ. Iron forms part of the enzymes concerned with the release of energy by oxidation, and hence occurs in both plant and animal cells. The plant organs most concerned with these processes—the leaves—thus contain the most iron.

(e) Vitamins

The roles of the various plant carotenoid pigments, some of which act as precursors of vitamin A, may include the absorption of part of the energy of sunlight, and the protection of chlorophyll from some of the high-energy radiations in sunlight. Although pigments with vitamin A activity are found in carrots and sweet potatoes underground they are also present in green leaves which function in the sun. Vitamin A itself, which is derived solely from animal sources (see Section 13.3), has functions in animals similar to those in man. It is stored in the liver of animals, so that animal and fish livers are rich sources of the vitamin.

Many of the B-group vitamins are concerned with the process of energy release from proteins and carbohydrates, and are therefore found in higher concentrations in all cells where there is vigorous release of energy, such as muscle cells, seeds or rapidly multiplying yeast cells.

Vitamin C and vitamin K occur in plants, and are there involved in the processes of photosynthesis and energy transfer, as well as in some other activities.

Vitamin D is only found in animals, in which its role is similar to that in man. Like vitamin A, it is fat-soluble and is only found in fatty foods; it too is stored in the livers of animals and fish.

18.4   Nutrients in Foodstuffs

Keeping in mind the function of the nutrient in its biological environment, we can now explain and summarize the probable nutrients in foodstuffs under the usual commodity headings.

(a) Animal Foods

(i) **Meat.** Lean meat is the voluntary muscle of animals, that is, the muscle tissue which is under the control of the will. This tissue consists of specialized striped muscle cells which form fibres. The fibres are held together by connective tissue into bundles, which in turn are grouped together by further coverings of tough connective tissue. Meat contains, therefore, two somewhat different types of protein: those proteins which perform the actual contraction, and those of the connective tissue which holds the muscle together.

The contractile proteins are mainly *actin* and *myosin* and those making up

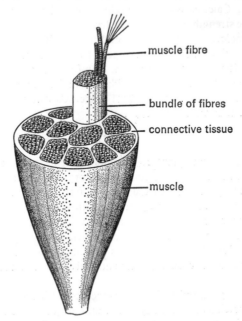

Fig. 18.2 Diagrammatic structure of muscle (meat):
not drawn to scale

the connective tissue are *collagen* and *elastin*. Both collagen and elastin are insoluble, but collagen is gradually converted to gelatin by moist heat. The proportion of collagen increases with the age of the animal.

In addition to these proteins and varying amounts of fat, meat also contains B-group vitamins, because of the continual need of the muscle for energy in its living state. Meat contains very little carbohydrate, since glycogen in the living muscle is broken down on the death of the animal. Iron is present in relatively large amounts, due to its occurrence in blood and muscle pigments. Ascorbic acid only occurs in negligible quantities, and very little, if any, of the fat-soluble vitamins is present (even in the fat).

(*ii*) **Fish.** Although fish flesh, like meat, is voluntary muscle, it differs from meat in one important respect. Because fish live surrounded by water and do not need to support the weight of their bodies physically to the extent that land animals do, their muscles contain a much smaller proportion of connective tissue. The muscles of fish are largely concerned with movement and not, as in animals like sheep or cows, with keeping the creature on its feet. This reduction in the proportion of connective tissue makes fish more easily digestible than meat, especially since the connective tissue largely consists of collagen with little or no elastin. The aquatic environment of sea fish may also be responsible for the presence in it of iodine (see Section 12.1(*a*)).

Oily fish like herring and mackerel have a good deal of fat distributed throughout their muscles, and their flesh is a useful source of the fat-soluble vitamins A and D. The flesh of 'white' fish containing little fat, like cod and plaice, does not contain these vitamins, although their livers, which act as storage organs as in mammals, are extremely rich vitamin sources. Indeed they are so rich that oils like cod-liver oil and halibut-liver oil are recognized as very concentrated dietary supplements; however, it should be emphasized that it is the *liver* only from which these oils are extracted.

(*iii*) **Offal.** This term is generally used to imply any part of an animal or fish which is not voluntary muscle. Its composition depends on its function during the life of the animal. The *liver* in its role of storage organ contains reserves of fat-soluble vitamins and iron. Because of its many functions during life, most of which require energy, the liver also contains an increased concentration of the B-group vitamins required for energy production. It is not a muscular organ and therefore contains little connective tissue; the small amounts present are largely derived from the blood and bile vessels in it.

Tripe, the tissues of the stomach, consists largely of involuntary muscle and connective tissue; it owes its high calcium content entirely to the processing it receives in the factory.

The high iron content of *kidney* has already been mentioned. In life the kidney functions continuously, needing a constant supply of energy to do so; it is therefore not surprising that it is an excellent source of B-group vitamins.

(*iv*) **Eggs.** The familiar hen's egg, like other culinary eggs, illustrates the importance of considering the biological origin of foods.

The function of an egg is to provide food and protection to a developing embryo. It will therefore contain all the nutrients necessary for the early growth of the chick; this does not mean that it is a complete food for people, but it does indicate that the egg contains protein, minerals, vitamins and an energy source. The functions of the shell and white are largely protective, while the yolk is the main source of nutrients for the embryo's growth.

The *white* is composed of several different proteins in water along with some dissolved salts. It acts as a supplier of water and some food to the growing embryo. Although the jelly-like nature of the white provides excellent protection for the chick, the yolk is additionally held in position by two strands of protein called the *chalazae*.

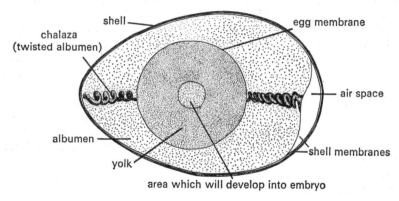

shell

egg membrane

chalaza
(twisted albumen)

air space

albumen

shell membranes

yolk

area which will develop into embryo

Fig. 18.3   Hen's egg with top half of shell removed

The *yolk* contains proteins, minerals and the necessary vitamins for growth and for the production of energy. As an energy source it contains fat in a highly emulsified and readily digestible form.

The twofold value of eggs in cooking, quite apart from their nutritional usefulness, calls for comment. Firstly, the white, being a protein solution which coagulates readily, is ideal for use in aeration and binding; secondly, the yolk is a concentrated emulsion and as such is useful in the preparation of other emulsions like mayonnaise.

(*v*) **Milk.** Milk is a fat-in-water emulsion, and it must be remembered that its constituent nutrients tend to be concentrated in *either* the aqueous *or* the fatty phase, according to their solubility. Fat-soluble vitamins are found in the fatty phase, and lactose, protein, water-soluble vitamins and minerals in the aqueous phase.

The use of milk as a food has been discussed already (see Sections 3.7, 9.3(*d*) and 11.4). When considering manufactured milk products, however, we must take care to ascertain which part of the emulsion goes to make up the final product, before assuming that it will contain any particular nutrient. Butter, for example, is made from cream and contains only 13 per cent of the water-soluble components of the original milk; protein and calcium are virtually absent. Cottage cheese made from skim milk, however, contains both protein and calcium, but little fat; cheese made from whole milk also provides these nutrients, together with fat-soluble vitamins as well.

(b) Plant Foods

(i) **Cereals.** These are the seeds of cultivated grasses and consequently contain the embryo, together with material for its subsequent growth. The greater part of the cereal grain is occupied by the food reserve, the endosperm (see Fig. 16.1). On germination, the material of the endosperm (mainly starch and protein) is broken down by the enzymes in the grain into usable form for embryonic growth. The provision of the energy required for growth necessitates the presence of the B-group vitamins, and the whole, unprocessed cereal grains contain a good deal of these vitamins. The embryo itself is rich in protein, fat and iron.

When wheat is milled, it is largely the endosperm which is used to make white flour, and the valuable nutrient-containing parts like the outer coatings (bran) and the embryo are removed from the grain. To compensate for this, many countries enforce the addition of calcium, iron and some of the B-group vitamins to white flour. The actual regulations vary from one country to another.

(ii) **Fruit and vegetables.** The wide variety of fruit and vegetables are best considered as a single group of foods, since these terms are generally used rather imprecisely. The term *fruit* does not necessarily mean the same to a biologist as to a caterer. Marrows, cucumbers and runner beans are all fruits to a biologist, but rhubarb is not. The term *vegetable* likewise has little meaning in a biological context, although the caterer uses the term for a quite specific group of plant foods. *Root vegetable* is another confusing term, since it is often used indiscriminately for both roots and tubers.

The biological origins of plant foods give a good indication of their likely nutrient content. A few examples will help to establish the point. Green leaves are the centres of photosynthesis and therefore contain the substances needed for this complicated process. Vitamin C, vitamin K, carotene, calcium, iron and magnesium are all involved, and this is why they are found in vegetables like cabbage, lettuce, spinach and watercress. The products of photosynthesis —glucose and the more complex carbohydrates derived from it—are not stored in the leaf, which is only a producing organ; these vegetables therefore contribute little or no carbohydrate to the diet. The storage organ of a plant may be a bulb (onion), a tuber (potato), the stem (sugar cane) or the root (beet). If a particular vegetable normally acts as a food store for the plant, it usually contains a high proportion of carbohydrate in some form.

The parts of the plant concerned with structure and support, for example the stems of celery or rhubarb, contain little food material, nor will most roots, whose function is anchorage and nutrient absorption from the soil. The carbohydrates which make up these structural components are in general indigestible and so contribute little except roughage to the diet.

Vegetables or fruits which are concerned with the reproduction of the species are likely to contain the material needed for the initial growth of the new individual, that is, protein, minerals, vitamins and an energy source (carbohydrate or fat, or possibly both). Such fruit as apples, pears, plums, raspberries and strawberries have evolved into forms which are attractive to birds and animals, so that the seeds within them pass through their consumers and are distributed over a wide area. It follows that, except for the vitamin C and sugar they contain, most fruits are useful primarily for their attractive taste and appearance. Nuts, of course are, or contain, seeds, and are useful sources of proteins, minerals and B-group vitamins; at least part of their food reserve is in the from of fat.

Although in this Unit we have emphasized the nutrient content of foods *in vivo*, we must mention again that all living organisms are individuals and as such will be subject to quite wide variation. The selection and development of strains of plants and animals to enhance their most desirable characteristics has been the basis of animal and crop husbandry for many centuries. The loss of nutrients in the transition from the life-cycle of the plant or animal to our own, however, may be appreciable. It is considerations like these which make nutrition a very inexact science in some of its aspects.

Calculating the Nutritional Adequacy of Diets

19.1 Nutritional Requirements

Perhaps the most important duty of a nutritionist is to ensure that the right amounts of all the nutrients necessary for health are provided in the diet eaten by any particular individual or by a group of people, whether it be a family, the inmates of an institution or an entire community. As we have emphasized in the preceding units, there are several reasons why there are unexpected difficulties in laying down precise standards and asserting unequivocally whether or not a particular diet provides everything that is needed. Firstly, individuals' needs vary from one person to another; secondly, the information determining precisely what a person requires is not always available, because the science of nutrition depends on the gradually increasing acquisition of knowledge, and is still very far from complete. The third difficulty lies in the fact that the definition of the nutritionist's aim of perfect nutrition is itself a matter of opinion to a considerable degree. Some people desire to eat so full a diet that eating more food could not possibly do them any good and might even do them harm. On the other hand, frugally minded people whose purpose in life could be described in the old-fashioned phrase of 'low living and high thinking' would consider a healthy diet as providing subsistence on what physiologists would call 'a lower nutritional plane'.

In spite of these difficulties, several groups of experts working in different countries have drawn up tables of recommended nutritional intake which can help in the design of diets which are adequate in every respect. Table 19.1 lists such recommendations for people with the general outlook on life and on what is regarded as health and good physique in an industrialized country like Great Britain.

19.2 Measuring What People Eat

If we are to assess the nutritional value of any particular diet, we must obviously know, firstly, exactly how much of every item of diet has been eaten or drunk, and what effect processing and cooking have had on it and, secondly, the kind of person who has eaten it, the amount of activity in the kind of life he leads, and whether he is suffering from any disease or condition likely to affect his nutritional needs. None of these essential pieces of information is easy to obtain; in this section, we shall consider only those factors mentioned in the former group.

Table 19.1   Recommended nutritional allowances

age range in years	occupational category	body weight (kg)	energy (Cal)	energy (kJ)	protein (g)	thiamine (mg)
Boys and girls						
0 up to 1		7·3	800	3 300	20	0·3
1 up to 2		11·4	1 200	5 000	20	0·5
2 up to 3		13·5	1 400	5 900	35	0·6
3 up to 5		16·5	1 600	6 700	40	0·6
5 up to 7		20·5	1 800	7 500	45	0·7
7 up to 9		25·1	2 100	8 800	53	0·8
Boys						
9 up to 12		31·9	2 500	10 500	63	1·0
12 up to 15		45·5	2 800	11 700	70	1·1
15 up to 18		61·0	3 000	12 600	75	1·2
Girls						
9 up to 12		33·0	2 300	9 600	58	0·9
12 up to 15		48·6	2 300	9 600	58	0·9
15 up to 18		56·1	2 300	9 600	58	0·9
Men						
18 up to 35	sedentary	65·0	2 700	11 300	68	1·1
	moderately active		3 000	12 600	75	1·2
	very active		3 600	15 100	90	1·4
35 up to 65	sedentary	65·0	2 600	10 900	65	1·0
	moderately active		2 900	12 100	73	1·2
	very active		3 600	15 100	90	1·4
65 up to 75	assuming a	63·0	2 350	9 800	59	0·9
75 and over	sedentary life	63·0	2 100	8 800	55	0·8
Women						
18 up to 55	most occupations	55·0	2 200	9 200	55	0·9
	very active		2 500	10 500	63	1·0
55 up to 75	assuming a	53·0	2 050	8 600	51	0·8
75 and over	sedentary life	53·0	1 900	8 000	48	0·7
pregnancy, 3–9 months			2 400	10 000	60	1·0
lactation			2 700	11 300	68	1·1

[a] 1 nicotinic acid equivalent = 1 mg available nicotinic acid or 60 mg tryptophan

[b] 1 retinol equivalent = 1 μg retinol or 6 μg β-carotene or 12 μg other biologically active carotenoids

[c] No dietary source may be necessary for those adequately exposed to sunlight, but the requirement for the housebound may be greater than that recommended

riboflavine (mg)	nicotinic acid (mg equiv.[a])	ascorbic acid (mg)	vitamin A (µg retinol equiv.[b])	vitamin D[c] (µg chole-calciferol)	calcium (mg)	iron (mg)
0·4	5	15	450	10·0	600[e]	6[e]
0·6	7	20	300	10·0	500	7
0·7	8	20	300	10·0	500	7
0·8	9	20	300	10·0	500	8
0·9	10	20	300	2·5	500	8
1·0	11	20	400	2·5	500	10
1·2	14	25	575	2·5	700	13
1·4	16	25	725	2·5	700	14
1·7	19	30	750	2·5	600	15
1·2	13	25	575	2·5	700	13
1·4	16	25	725	2·5	700	14
1·4	16	30	750	2·5	600	15
1·7	18	30	750	2·5	500	10
1·7	18	30	750	2·5	500	10
1·7	18	30	750	2·5	500	10
1·7	18	30	750	2·5	500	10
1·7	18	30	750	2·5	500	10
1·7	18	30	750	2·5	500	10
1·7	18	30	750	2·5	500	10
1·7	18	30	750	2·5	500	10
1·3	15	30	750	2·5	500	12
1·3	15	30	750	2·5	500	12
1·3	15	30	750	2·5	500	10
1·3	15	30	750	2·5	500	10
1·6	18	60	750	10·0[d]	1 200[f]	15
1·8	21	60	1 200	10·0	1 200	15

[d] Throughout pregnancy
[e] These figures apply to infants who are not breast-fed. Infants who are entirely breast-fed receive smaller quantities; these are adequate since absorption from breast milk is higher
[f] For the last three months of pregnancy

(a) Taking a Dietary History

The most direct way of making a preliminary assessment of the diet eaten by a particular individual is to ask him what he eats. This requires a good deal of skill and persistence if any useful information is to be obtained. People are forgetful, or they may only mention what they consider to be 'meals', omitting the snacks, sweets, ice-cream and pints of beer which may all make a substantial contribution to the total nutritional intake. Moreover, if they know they are being interrogated by a nutritionist they may describe a diet they believe that they *ought* to be eating rather than their actual diet. A further possibility of error arises when the consumer refers to articles known by local names with which the interrogator is not familiar or which bear a specialized connotation in one place different from that which is understood elsewhere. In spite of these difficulties, however, a history in such general terms can prove informative to a nutritionist, while he can give useful suggestions and guidance in equally general terms. For example, people can be advised to make up a diet from a mixture of the following categories of food:

(*i*) *'Body-building' foods* (foods rich in protein)

Meat	Eggs	Cheese
Fish	Milk	Peas and beans
Poultry		

(*ii*) *'Protective' foods* (foods rich in vitamins)
Green vegetables, potatoes, fruit and fruit juices
Butter, vitaminized margarine and liver

(*iii*) *'Fuel' foods* (contributing energy value)

Bread	Cereals
Flour	Fat

(b) Estimating the Quantities of Food Eaten

(*i*) **'24-hour recall'.** A dietary history gives only a general picture of the nutritional quality of the food eaten during the course of a day. However, at the very beginning of this book we emphasized that nutrition is a *quantitative science*, that is to say, it is not only important to know that various nutrients are present but also to discover whether they have been eaten *in appropriate amounts*. Some idea of how much of each different food has been consumed can be obtained by asking people not only what foods they eat, but how much, and requiring them to match what they remember they have had with models, either of actual slices of bread or pieces of potato, for example, or with imitations made of wood or other convenient material. If this method is to produce a realistic assessment, it is best to restrict the questions to the food that *has been eaten on the previous day*.

(*ii*) **Weighing the daily diet.** When it is necessary to measure the dietary intake of a particular person with reasonable precision, this can be done by weighing each article of diet before it is eaten and, if necessary, subtracting the weight of what is left on the plate.

This procedure is useful in designing a nutritionally satisfactory diet for someone suffering from the disease of *diabetes* (see Section 3.4), in which the ability of the body to cope with glucose is lost, either wholly or partly. If a diabetic eats too much sugar or some other carbohydrate, the glucose concentration in his blood may rise so high that it 'poisons' him. On the other hand, if his diet contains too little carbohydrate or if he misses a meal, because he can no longer make the adjustment which occurs naturally in a healthy person, the glucose in his blood may fall to a dangerously low level until he loses consciousness due to lack of sugar.

Diabetes cannot be cured but it can be effectively treated either by insulin injections or by tablets which can be swallowed (*oral hypoglycaemics*). In either case, each patient's dosage must be adjusted very precisely, according to the severity of his disease, the kind of life he leads, his particular physique and the composition of his diet. Since it is not reasonable to expect a diabetic to eat exactly the same food each day, it is essential to ensure that the different amounts of food he does eat should always provide the same total amount of carbohydrate, protein and fat. A dietitian can monitor the diet of a diabetic by weighing every article of food he eats and then, from his knowledge of the composition of each item, calculating the composition of the diet as a whole to see whether it provides the full amount of each nutrient shown in Table 19.1.

A diabetic patient does not need to carry out this calculation himself each day, since he is mainly concerned to maintain a uniform intake of carbohydrate in relation to his intake of protein and fat. He therefore only needs to know to what extent a particular food may be exchanged for a nutritionally equivalent amount of another. Dietitians have compiled lists of foods which contain equivalent amounts of carbohydrate, protein and fat respectively: Table 19.2 shows abbreviated versions of such lists. Using tables like these and substituting one *exchange unit* for another, a diabetic can monitor his own diet and adjust it to suit his individual needs and tastes; for example, he might be told to select a daily breakfast menu that allows him 1 protein exchange and 4 carbohydrate exchanges, plus butter and milk from an appropriate fixed allowance.

(c) A Budgetary Survey

A budgetary survey is a very direct way of discovering the nutritional value of what is eaten by the members of a community, perhaps a family, a residential school, an orphanage, a camp or a prison. This is done by arranging that every item of food and drink bought or otherwise acquired is recorded in a log-book, together with the quantity of each item. In addition, a record must be kept of (*i*) meals, snacks and drinks consumed outside the home or institution, (*ii*) food grown in the garden, produced locally or obtained as gifts, and (*iii*) food withdrawn from a store-cupboard during the week of the survey.

The nutritional value of the total amount of food recorded over, say, a week is calculated; then allowances must be made for waste and loss, by working out (*i*) the proportion of the purchased food which is in fact inedible, (*ii*) the proportion wasted during preparation or left on the plates, and (*iii*) the changes (which may be gains or losses) in the nutritional value of the foods during the cooking process.

Table 19.2   Examples of nutritionally equivalent foods

Each of the following contains about 10 g carbohydrate (1 *carbohydrate exchange*):	15 g jam or honey
	15 g cornflakes
	20 g bread
	30 g chipped potatoes
	30 g boiled rice
	60 g boiled potatoes
	60 g banana (peeled)
	120 g apple
	180 g raspberries
Each of the following contains about 7 g protein (1 *protein exchange*):	30 g lean meat
	30 g cheese
	45 g fish
	60 g egg (1 average)
	140 g milk
Each of the following contains about 12 g fat (1 *fat exchange*):	12 g cooking fat or oil
	15 g butter or margarine
	20 g salad cream
	30 g double cream
	60 g single cream

(*i*) **The inedible proportion of purchased food.** Many foods contain inedible parts in the form in which they come to market and are bought. The outer leaves of cabbages, the skins of root vegetables and the bones in fish and joints of meat are inedible. It is therefore always important to know whether tables of food composition apply to *an entire article* or to *the edible portion only*. Tables referring to food *as purchased* are sometimes called AP tables; those giving the composition of the *edible portion* only are called EP tables. It is equally important to know what proportion of any weight of food purchased can actually be eaten and how much must be accounted inedible wastage. Table 19.3 lists rough estimates of the inedible wastage of several different commodities. The proportion of waste can vary widely depending on the quality of the goods purchased and the skill and care with which the catering is done, so that a nutritionist setting out to assess the value of food received by a particular group must take steps to measure the extent of the actual wastage.

(*ii*) **Preparation and plate waste.** As well as the allowance that must be made for inedible wastage in purchased food, there is inevitably waste in the kitchen while the food is being prepared and cooked, and sometimes this may be considerable. For example, up to 13 per cent of the protein in eggs may be wasted when the eggs are scrambled: this represents the quantity left on the mixing bowl and the spoon and adhering to the shell, before any further allowance

Table 19.3 The average proportions of the purchased weight of foods which are wasted as inedible

	g per 100 g		g per 100 g
Green peas	60	Carrots	20–25
White fish (cod, etc.)	45	Lettuce	20
Melons	45	Beef (good quality)	17
Kippers	40	Mutton	17
Bananas	40	Prunes	17
Turnips	35	Tomatoes	15
Cabbage	30	Watercress	15
Cauliflower	30	Pork	15
Herrings	30	Dates	14
Coconuts	30	Eggs	12 (shell)
Peanuts	30	Bacon	12
Potatoes (old)	25–27	Apricots	8
Spinach	25	Raisins	8
Oranges	25	Plums	6
Stewing beef	25	Onions	5
Pears	25	Cheese	5 (rind)
Apples	20		

is made for what the eater leaves on his plate. Although the extent of such waste can vary enormously, it may not always happen that waste is least among those whose nutrition is least satisfactory, and who are in consequence most in need of food.

The amount of waste recorded by different observers has been found to vary so widely that it is not safe to make a general allowance to be used in assessing the nutritional adequacy of a particular diet. On-the-spot investigation is essential. For example, combined cooking losses and plate waste varying from 25 per cent up to more than 50 per cent have been recorded for meat, while losses ranging from 5 per cent up to at least 50 per cent occur in converting even the 'edible portion' of vegetables into the weight actually swallowed.

The loss of nutrients due to plate waste alone varies quite widely and some effort must therefore be made to evaluate it whenever a nutritional intake is being assessed. For cooked meals it may amount to 4–6 per cent of the original protein, 3–10 per cent of the fat and perhaps 3–10 per cent of the carbohydrate. At the same time, the extent of this waste depends very much on the quality of the cooking and presentation, and the popularity or otherwise of the particular menu served. For example, in one establishment 21 per cent of the weight of the roast beef served was left on the plates as waste, 13 per cent of meat pie but only 7 per cent of corned beef, whereas in another establishment 14 per cent, 9 per cent and 14 per cent of the same dishes was left as waste. Yet where serious efforts were made to improve the catering, total plate waste was kept down to 3 per cent.

(*iii*) **The effect of cooking on the nutritional value of food.** The main effect of cooking on the nutritional value of food is to improve it. For example, a major part of the energy value of the diet is contributed by starch in cereals, which occurs in the form of granules in which its long chains of glucose units are tightly tangled together. These granules are only broken down with difficulty by the digestive enzymes, and this is why uncooked flour and potatoes are not satisfactory nutritional components of the diet. Similarly, dried peas and beans are unsatisfactory as food until they have been cooked, and their hard substance softened and made digestible.

As well as these chemical changes, the components of foods which may be affected by cooking include:

Moisture: after cooking, the water content of foods may be increased (as in boiled rice or pasta) or decreased (as in toasted bread or grilled steak).

Fat: meat which is roasted or grilled loses some of its fat, which separates as dripping during the cooking process. On the other hand, foods increase in nutritional value during frying because they lose water, and at the same time gain fat.

Vitamins: considerable losses of the water-soluble vitamins often occur,

Table 19.4   The differences in composition of certain foods when cooked and raw (per 100 g edible portions)

		energy value (kJ)	protein (g)	fat (g)	calcium (mg)
Beef (ribs)	raw	1 471	16·2	31·4	9
	cooked	1 783	22·4	36·7	10
Lamb (leg)	raw	1 095	16·9	21·0	10
	cooked	1 333	23·9	24·0	10
Pork (loin)	raw	1 350	16·4	28·0	9
	cooked	1 617	23·5	31·8	10
Haddock	raw	330	18·3	0·1	23
	fried	684	19·6	6·4	40
Potatoes	raw	318	2·1	0·1	7
	boiled	271	1·9	0·1	6
	fried	1 119	4·0	14·2	15
Cabbage	raw	100	1·3	0·2	49
	boiled	75	1·0	0·2	42
Haricot beans	raw	1 421	22·3	1·6	144
	cooked	493	7·8	0·6	50

both by solution in the cooking-water and by destruction by heat. The losses of vitamin C during cooking have been discussed in some detail in Section 17.6. The B-group vitamins are susceptible to the heat of cooking in varying degrees. Thiamine is quite easily destroyed and is almost entirely lost at the high temperatures reached in the baking of biscuits. There is a loss of about 8 per cent of thiamine when bread made with yeast is baked, but since thiamine is susceptible to alkali, the loss approaches 100 per cent when baking powder containing soda is employed. When wholemeal bread is baked, although the initial thiamine content is higher the loss may be as much as 35 per cent, even if yeast is used. Still greater losses occur at the very high temperatures used to make toast. Riboflavine and niacin, however, are less susceptible to destruction than thiamine. The fat-soluble vitamins A and D are also comparatively resistant to cooking.

Minerals: Although some of the nutritionally important soluble minerals are certainly lost during cooking, it is not easy to say if the losses are likely to be significant. Some minerals may actually be gained by the food during the cooking process: 'hard' water contributes calcium to food cooked in it, and iron may be derived from the metal of cooking utensils.

Table 19.4 illustrates some of the differences in composition between raw foods and the same foods cooked.

iron (mg)	vitamin A (retinol equivalents) (µg)	thiamine (mg)	riboflavine (mg)	niacin (mg)	ascorbic acid (mg)
2·4	0	0·07	0·14	3·9	0
2·9	0	0·04	0·17	3·5	0
1·3	0	0·15	0·21	4·9	0
1·6	0	0·14	0·25	5·2	0
2·5	0	0·80	0·19	4·2	0
3·1	0	0·88	0·25	5·3	0
0·7	0	0·04	0·07	3·0	0
1·2	0	0·04	0·07	3·2	0
0·6	0	0·10	0·04	1·5	20
0·5	0	0·09	0·04	1·2	16
1·1	0	0·12	0·07	2·8	19
0·4	43	0·05	0·05	0·3	47
0·3	40	0·02	0·02	0·1	24
7·8	0	0·65	0·22	2·4	0
2·7	0	0·14	0·07	0·7	0

(d) National Food Intake

A government responsible for the food supply of an entire nation can obtain a general indication of the extent to which it provides the needs of the population by collecting statistical records of all the imported foods and of all the food produced locally by farmers. The aggregate amounts of units of energy, of protein, fat, minerals and vitamins can be estimated in this way, and the average needs of the population can also be calculated by multiplying the total numbers of each kind of people—the working men and women, the children and the old people—by the recommended allowances given in Table 19.1. This kind of calculation can be useful to administrators by indicating whether what is most urgently needed is energy value, when more cereals or fats are required, or whether the principal requirement is for protein or for one of the vitamins or minerals. Large-scale nutritional calculations of this sort, however, give no idea of whether a particular group of the population is being properly fed. Clearly, therefore, a national assessment of this sort must be reinforced by more detailed investigation of the most vulnerable groups within the community, which are usually infants and children, the old and the poor, and minorities who, because of their colour or religion or for some other reason, are likely to be unfairly treated.

(e) The Precise Assessment of Nutritional Intake

We have mentioned several times in this book how the exact composition of any particular sample of food varies from that of every other sample of the same food. No matter how judiciously materials are selected for analysis, tables of food composition can never do more than list characteristic figures. For example, the percentage weights of protein, fat or calcium in, say, 100 g of food are directly affected by the moisture content of the sample actually analysed, and therefore change as the food dries out. Similarly, the proportion of protein in meat will be affected by the amount of fat it contains. The vitamin A content of carrots is proportional to their degree of yellowness and the vitamin C content of apples to their redness. Because of these natural variations, the nutritional value of a diet calculated from figures given in tables of food composition can at best only provide a general indication of what any particular individual actually receives. For *precise* nutritional studies, it is therefore necessary to weigh exactly every article of food and drink eaten, to collect a representative sample of each item, and to carry out a full analysis of each sample.

Clearly, this procedure is very laborious; it demands considerable skill on the part of the nutritionist, and the availability of a laboratory with full modern analytical equipment.

19.3 Tables of Diet Composition

In spite of the factors described in the last section, which make the most meticulously prepared tables of food composition only a rough-and-ready guide to the nutritional value of a diet, such tables are essential to the practising nutritionist. Furthermore, it is also helpful for any nutritionist to have at his disposal tables relating to the national diets with which he is concerned. For example, the Medical Research Council publishes a table* which is designed for calculating the composition of British diets. American tables are equally useful for natural foods like apples or rabbit, but must be used with care for manufactured commodities; for example, bakers in the USA usually use milk powder, fat and other ingredients not commonly included in British bread, so that American details of bread composition are inapplicable in Britain. Similarly, neither European nor American tables can be used in Asian and African countries, where people regularly eat local foods which are not mentioned in these tables.

* McCance, R. A., and Widdowson, E. M.: Special report series, 297, *Composition of Foods*, HMSO (1974).

Some Socio-economic Aspects of Nutrition

20.1 Introduction

The preceding units of this book have been concerned with the chemical requirements of the living body: its need for material to provide it with energy, and for the various nutrients necessary for its smooth functioning. We have discussed the role of these nutrients, the amount of each which an individual needs under differing circumstances, and in which foods each is likely to be found.

This information constitutes the basis of nutritional science, but, as we mentioned briefly in Section 1.4, there are in real life a number of other considerations which have a direct influence on people's nutritional well-being. In this unit we shall deal with some of these in turn.

20.2 Nutrition and Income

The various ways to assess the nutritional value of the diet being eaten by an individual, a family or a community have been discussed in Unit 19. If the results of such a study, perhaps of families in Africa or Central America, show a diet to be deficient in protein, any recommendation that the people concerned should eat more meat or that children of school age should be given milk to drink will be totally ineffective if the people are too poor to afford milk or meat. In 1936, Sir John Orr (as he was then; he later, as Lord Boyd Orr, became the first Director-General of the Food and Agriculture Organization of the United Nations) carried out a budgetary survey (see Section 19.2 (c)) of the diets of 1 152 families in Great Britain. He found that the poorer the families were, the less nutritionally satisfactory were their diets. The poorest 10 per cent, representing 4.5 million people, were eating diets of a lower energy value and providing less protein, retinol, ascorbic acid, calcium and iron than the allowances recommended at the time for proper nutrition. Some 30 years later, a survey carried out among elderly people in Great Britain showed a surprisingly high percentage of nutritional deficiencies (based on the then current recommendations) in the same nutrients. It is interesting that the deficiencies demonstrated in this latter survey appeared among people who while elderly were not necessarily poor. Clearly, while income has an important contribution to make to nutritional standards, the provision of sufficient financial resources does not guarantee satisfactory nutrition if the individual has to contend with other problems, such as infirmities which make shopping or cooking difficult.

Four possible ways in which the nutrition of people malnourished as a result of low income can be improved are:

(a) *The provision of extra food.* In Britain much has been done in the form of free or cheap school milk, school meals providing a minimum nutritional content enforced by law, and welfare clinics organized at a national level, in addition to the provision in some areas of such voluntary services as 'Meals on Wheels', bringing well-balanced meals to the homes of old or handicapped people unable to cook for themselves.

(b) The legalized *enrichment of some staple foods*, with appropriate vitamins and minerals; white bread and margarine are examples.

(c) The *improvement of the financial status* of some of the poorer sections of a community; this is an enormously complex problem, which is very far from solution.

(d) The *education* of all members of a community in the wise use of whatever income is available: this subject is discussed more fully in Section 20.5.

Although the relationship between income and nutrition holds on a national scale for the developing countries as well as for the poorer sections of industrialized societies like Britain, the United States or the western European countries (see Section 5.5), at a local level the pattern may fluctuate from family to family within a community, due to the unwise or injudicious use of the family finances. Similarly people's unwillingness or inability to participate in provisions aimed at alleviating nutritional shortages may be due to sociological factors other than income.

20.3   Nutrition, Social Class, Height and 'Intelligence'

Social class is probably of little nutritional consequence, at least in an industrialized society, although one might argue that the nutritional excesses of the wealthier classes in some countries are almost as disastrous as the possible dietary deficiencies in the underprivileged. Social factors within each social class are far more important in the question of whether or not people's diets are nutritionally adequate. Some of these factors, like loneliness, apathy or immobility, are of a general nature, cutting across all social classes, while others are more specific and limited to certain localized areas, either geographical, social or age-dependent: rather what could be called a 'nutritional dialect'. These specific factors also include the customs or beliefs of those who for some reason or another do not avail themselves of the whole selection of foodstuffs.

It can be expected that if people eat a diet providing the recommended nutritional allowances given in Table 19.1 from their birth until they are fully grown, their rate of growth will be rapid and they will attain the full adult stature of which their heredity makes them capable. For example, second-generation Japanese who live in California are taller than their grandparents who lived in Japan, mainly because of the ample diet available to them in

America. Although such rapid growth and full stature indicate that an adequate diet gives people who eat it the opportunity to fulfil their physical potentialities, it cannot automatically be assumed that the bigger people who result are *necessarily* happier, more efficient and healthier than they would have been if their food had been less plentiful.

In Table 19.1, recommended protein allowances are listed for different categories of people, although the body can subsist on less than these allowances. Similarly, should substantially less than the recommended energy values be available, the body is capable of reducing its rate of metabolism and maintaining a reduced body weight without ill effects and indeed perhaps with some advantage (see Section 7.1(d)). In the same way, the intake of minerals and of the various vitamins can also be limited to less than the amounts shown in the table.

Yet the argument in favour of a diet providing the full recommended allowances is a powerful one, even if not conclusive. For example, when the heights and weights of boys and girls within a community are studied in detail—even in countries with carefully thought-out nutritional policies, including school meals and milk and a school medical service—the rate of growth and the final stature of the poorest children of casual labourers are both on average less than those of skilled workers. Theirs again is less than those of office and shop workers' children, whose growth and height is, in turn, less than those of the children of the managerial and professional groups who make up the richest section of the community. This observation is perhaps not surprising and can be taken as evidence to support the reasonable assumption that optimum nutrition gives faster growth, even though it leaves unanswered the question whether the bigger children are better and healthier than the smaller ones.

A further observation emphasizes the complexity of the social factors that surround the practice of nutrition. It has been found that *on average* the taller children learn to read at an earlier age and have higher scores in 'intelligence quotient' tests than those who are shorter for their age. This does *not* necessarily mean that the nutritional value of a diet a person eats has any direct effect on his brain, except under the exceptional circumstances referred to in Sections 4.9 and 5.7(b). What it does imply is that children who come from poor homes, where there are few of the facilities for reading, thinking and discussion likely to help them to shine in 'intelligence tests', tend to be given a less satisfactory diet and consequently to be shorter for their age than children brought up in more prosperous homes.

20.4 Nutrition and Food Presentation

In Section 19.2(c), we pointed out that calculations of the nutritional value of food presented in the form of meals must take into account the proportion which is wasted because it is not eaten. It follows that a nutritionist must be aware of the many factors which influence the acceptability of food; variety, colour, form and texture ought to be considered by anyone responsible for the provision and presentation of food, at whatever gastronomic level or to whatever numbers are appropriate to the situation.

In many of the more advanced countries, changes are taking place which may at first sight appear retrograde steps from a nutritional standpoint. However, this need not necessarily be so. Consider the following examples.

(a) Hot Meals or Snacks

People's ideas of the kind of meals they should eat, and of their timing and composition are often remarkably rigid. If circumstances compel a change to be made, such a change may exert an influence on the nutritional value of a diet. In Britain, one such change apparent over the last few decades concerns the fall in popularity of the traditional 'British breakfast'. It is sometimes claimed that a hot breakfast has some peculiar nutritional virtue, but this is not necessarily true. Whereas the milk poured on the breakfast cereal, the bacon and the egg may all make a useful contribution to the protein intake of growing children, the same meal may contribute an undesirable amount of saturated fat and cholesterol to the children's father, who may well be both middle-aged and sedentary. For him, a glass of orange juice and a slice of bread (whether toasted or not is immaterial) may be nutritionally better suited. Similarly, at midday a couple of cheese and salad rolls may compare very favourably, if not advantageously, with a more elaborate hot lunch. The main virtue of a hot meal—often described as a cooked meal—is that it easily provides *variety* and hence contributes a wide range of mineral and vitamin nutrients.

(b) Convenience Foods and the Working Housewife

The way of life accepted by people living in an industrial society depends to some extent on the assumption that a decreasing amount of time will be devoted to cooking and preparing meals. Many housewives are involved in employment outside their homes which prevents them cooking a midday meal and leads them to take advantage increasingly of 'convenience foods'. These may be defined as foods of which at least a part of the work of preparation and cooking has already been done when the food is bought. Commodities like baker's bread and cakes, refined lard and manufactured sausages have of course been available to the housewife for many years, but recently sales of convenience foods have increased enormously, with a vast range of canned, frozen and dehydrated foods appearing on the market, so that complete ready-made meals can now be bought in great variety.

One of the major nutritional advantages in using convenience foods is that they allow a far greater variety (the importance of which cannot be emphasized too strongly) than would otherwise be available, especially due to the seasonally restricted supply of fresh fruit and vegetables and the gradual disappearance of 'home-produced' food. Lawns and flower-beds may be an admirable aesthetic substitute for a vegetable garden, but not a nutritional one!

The influence of processing on the nutritional value of convenience foods. Section 19.2(c) discusses the effect of cooking on foodstuffs, and the principles underlying the loss of nutrients are the same, whether the treatment of the food is for long-term storage, as for most convenience foods, or the short-term preparation, cooking and service of fresh foods.

The losses in each case are controlled by the chemical and physical properties of the nutrient concerned. The loss, for example, of ascorbic acid, which is readily oxidized and easily soluble in water, is far greater in normal cooking and processing conditions than the loss of retinol which is only oxidized with difficulty and which does not dissolve in water to any extent. Moreover, chemical changes like oxidation (whether enzyme-catalysed or not) and physical changes like dissolving are usually accelerated by a rise in temperature, and oxidation may be rapid in the presence of oxygen, either in the air or dissolved in water.

It is for these reasons that the nutritional content of convenience foods, properly used, compares very favourably with many of their freshly cooked counterparts. There are some notable exceptions, but provided that the nutritionist is aware of these, the food can fulfil a very valuable role. The following points should be borne in mind:

(*i*) Because food is carefully selected for canning, dehydrating and freezing by the manufacturers, it is often of higher quality than the produce commonly available on the market.

(*ii*) The contribution of energy value, fat and protein from manufactured convenience foods is very close to that of the same foods unprocessed, and that of most minerals is also the same. In certain circumstances, however, there is an increase in the amount of available calcium, for example, in canned sardines and canned salmon, when the processing of the fish softens the bones so that they can be eaten.

(*iii*) As a general rule, the loss of vitamins from canned, frozen and dehydrated products by the time they reach the consumer's plate is approximately the same as that from the non-processed articles. This is because losses arising during the processing are counterbalanced by the use of fresher foods by the processors, and also by the reduction in the losses occurring during the final stages of cooking and preparation, which are much shorter with convenience foods than with fresh.

Ascorbic acid is the nutrient most easily destroyed during processing; Section 17.6 discusses the degree of its loss in certain manufactured foods.

20.5   Nutrition and Education

In Section 20.2, mention was made of education in nutrition. The detailed study of nutrition is unlikely to be included in the context of general education, nor indeed would it be desirable, but in the same way that sex education has universal application, nutritional education could do much to ameliorate many of the common dietary deficiencies and excesses.

In the industrialized communities with a high standard of living this could well take the form of re-education, requiring its members to assess their requirements less subjectively in terms of their nutritional needs, rather than of personal or social custom. In less fortunate communities, the education could be allied to agricultural and possibly medical training to ensure that the best use is made of the available resources. At a more personal level it could mean explaining why a schoolchild's dinner money should not be spent on potato crisps or sweets, or why an old age pensioner's diet should include more than cups of tea and bread and butter.

Education in nutrition could at least make people more aware of some of the problems, both at a local and a world level; at best it could bring about the final abandonment of many of the superstitions and old wives' tales associated with food.

Unit Twenty-one
Nutrition and Food Hygiene

21.1 Introduction

While nutritional science is primarily concerned with selecting foods which will provide people with the appropriate quantities of the nutrients they need, it is obviously also important to ensure that the diet contains nothing which might be capable either of reducing the nutritional benefit of the food, or of actually harming the people who eat it. Two factors need to be considered in this context: *food spoilage* and *food poisoning*, both of which depend to a large extent on the controllable conditions under which food is stored and prepared.

21.2 Food Spoilage

Generally speaking, food spoilage renders food unacceptable rather than harmful, and it may also reduce the nutritional content by the activities of autolytic enzymes (Section 18.2(*a*)). After the death of an animal or the harvesting of a plant, the natural biological cycle always leads to decay, and it is this natural sequence of events which must be slowed down or halted if food is to remain acceptable until it is eaten.

The term *food spoilage* in its general sense includes damage done by creatures like rats, mice and insects, by micro-organisms, including viruses, bacteria, yeasts and moulds, and by enzymes. Whichever group or combination of groups is responsible for rendering the food less than ideal, much can be done to prevent or retard the processes of food spoilage. Obviously, protection against the larger culprits involves providing storage conditions which will resist their attempts to gain access to the food. But although physical protection may exclude the deleterious activities of these animals, it can do little to combat the activities of those enzymes and micro-organisms which are normally found in or on the food in its natural biological surroundings, or which cannot be excluded from it during its preparation. If these are to be kept to a minimum, conditions have to be created in which the harmful organisms or enzymes are destroyed, or in which their activities are severely inhibited. This is the complex topic of *food preservation*, which ranges from simple cooking processes to the advanced technology involved in the manufacture of some convenience foods, themselves very largely the product of technological advances in food preservation.

21.3 Micro-organisms in Food

The entire environment in which we live is colonized by a huge variety of microscopic organisms; although they are all invisible to the naked eye, they vary in size one from another as widely as gnats and elephants do in the visible world. Those responsible for food spoilage or food poisoning can be classified into the following groups:

(a) Viruses

These are sub-microscopic particles, and not cells in the accepted sense; they are, however, able to use the components of a living cell to produce more of their own kind.

(b) Bacteria

Bacteria are single-celled organisms which can reproduce by division very rapidly when conditions are suitable. Although they are usually classified as plants they contain no chlorophyll, but absorb their nourishment in solution through the cell wall. There are a very large number of different sorts of bacteria, but they can be grouped according to their shape (the round *cocci* and the rod-shaped *bacilli* are the commonest food bacteria), their nutritional requirements and their biochemical behaviour. When conditions are hostile to them some bacteria, mainly the bacilli, are able to form *spores* which are more resistant to the unfriendly environment, and from which they can be regenerated when circumstances improve. When bacteria are actually growing and dividing they are said to be *in the vegetative state.*

(c) Yeasts

These are also single-celled plants, but they are larger than bacteria. They are very widely distributed especially on the skins of fruit and vegetables, and are responsible for much decay. Many of them produce ethanol ('alcohol') and carbon dioxide as the waste products of their metabolism, and are therefore useful in food preparation for fermentation and aeration. They may also add a characteristic flavour to food, and yeast extracts like Marmite are rich in some of the B-group vitamins. Yeasts reproduce by a process of budding, whereby an offshoot becomes detached from its parent cell when it reaches a certain size.

(d) Moulds

Although a single mould cell is invisible to the naked eye, under suitable conditions they form a large complex linkage of cells and develop specialized fruiting bodies, the mass of which becomes visible as a furry structure. The ripe fruiting bodies disseminate spores which can be carried by air or water. They are present in most conditions, which is why many foods go mouldy when left exposed to the air.

21.4 Environmental Considerations which Affect Micro-organisms

While each type of micro-organism has its specific needs for the successful maintenance of its existence, it is possible to make certain generalizations concerning their environmental requirements, especially for those which are involved in causing food spoilage or food poisoning. For simplicity's sake, the material in this section is limited to the consideration of bacteria only, but much of what follows is applicable to other micro-organisms as well, with variations appropriate to their somewhat different modes of life.

(a) Food

Bacteria need food to produce new material and to provide energy in the same way as other organisms. As a group, bacteria can use a wide range of substances as food. Unfortunately the bacteria causing food spoilage or food poisoning have very similar requirements to our own, so that it is quite impossible to eliminate them by denying them suitable food. However, some foods such as meat and milk are much better suited to bacterial metabolism than others like butter or bread. The criterion here is the availability of a source of organic nitrogen in the form of protein. Hence protein foods, so long as they provide the other suitable environmental conditions as well, are likely to be the most suitable medium for the metabolism of these types of bacteria.

(b) Water

Moisture is essential to all living things: virtually all biological mechanisms take place in an aqueous medium and bacterial metabolism is no exception. With simple organisms like bacteria the control of water intake and water loss is much less sophisticated than in the higher animals and plants; bacteria therefore depend on the availability of water in their surroundings, rather than the amount of water. Water which is frozen (ice) is not available to them, and water containing dissolved substances like sugar or salt at a higher concentration than in the bacterial cytoplasm is similarly useless: it may even cause water to flow by osmosis out of the bacteria so that they become dehydrated. This is why freezing, drying and adding salt or sugar may all be used for preserving some foods. The spores of some bacteria can remain dormant under conditions of dehydration and may revert to the vegetative form when conditions are more favourable; foods preserved by these methods which contain bacterial spores may begin to deteriorate when moisture again becomes available.

(c) Temperature

Unlike many higher organisms, bacteria can metabolize over quite a wide temperature range, but within this range, each kind of bacteria has a temperature at which its activity is greatest. This is sometimes called the optimum temperature for the particular bacteria.

(i) *Psychrophilic* bacteria grow at temperatures below about 20 °C. Some are capable of causing food spoilage at temperatures of a domestic refrigerator (4 °C).

(ii) *Mesophilic* bacteria have an optimum temperature range which includes body temperature (37 °C) and are thus responsible for food poisoning and much food spoilage.

(*iii*) *Thermophilic* bacteria can metabolize at temperatures up to 60 °C, but are of little importance in food spoilage or food poisoning.

A temperature below the normal range of a group will not destroy bacteria, but it will slow down to a great extent (depending on the degree of coldness) the rate of metabolism and thus reproduction. Vegetative bacteria are rapidly killed at temperatures approaching boiling point (100 °C), although the spores of some bacteria resist these and even higher temperatures for a considerable time.

Clearly, food kept within the preferred temperature range of food-poisoning bacteria can provide an ideal environment for their rapid multiplication, and thus be a serious potential hazard to the consumer. Legislation in some countries therefore insists that certain protein-containing foods like milk and meat products should be stored either above or below the mesophilic temperature range, that is either above 63 °C or below 10 °C (see Section 22.3).

(*d*) **Gaseous Environment**

Food-spoilage and food-poisoning bacteria can be divided into two main groups with reference to their gas requirements.

(*i*) *Aerobic* bacteria need oxygen for their metabolism.

(*ii*) *Anaerobic* bacteria do not need oxygen; indeed, oxygen is actually poisonous to some anaerobic bacteria.

However, many bacteria can adapt their metabolism to the presence or absence of oxygen and may flourish satisfactorily in food in either aerobic or anaerobic conditions.

(*e*) **Acidity or Alkalinity (pH)**

The metabolic activities of bacteria, like our own, are controlled by enzymes which can only function satisfactorily within a fairly restricted pH range. The food-poisoning bacteria, whose normal habitat may include the human body, prefer the same nearly neutral pH (about 7) that is found in blood and most body fluids. Acid foods like vinegar and many cheeses frequently contain bacteria, but these are unlikely to do any harm because of the low pH of these foods.

These five factors constitute the most important environmental considerations of bacterial metabolism. All except the first are used to some extent to reduce the bacterial content in either the short-term or long-term preparation or storage of food.

21.5 Food Poisoning

Food poisoning can be caused by two different kinds of contamination of food: the presence of *poisonous chemicals* of various sorts, and the presence of *bacteria*.

(a) **Potentially Toxic Chemicals Present in Food**

(i) **Substances deliberately added to food.** Throughout history various chemical compounds have been added to different foods in order to achieve certain desired effects. Sodium chloride (salt) has been used to preserve meat and fish and nitrates have also traditionally been employed in the conversion of pig-meat into bacon. Various pigments of plant or insect origin—annatto, saffron and cochineal, for example—have been used to make cooked food look more appetizing. In modern times synthetic colours, flavours, preservatives and a host of other additives have been developed. Considerable public attention has been focused on these newer additives and elaborate tests imposed to ensure their freedom from toxicity in the concentrations in which they are used. What is disturbing is that there is little international agreement or legislation as to their suitability. An additive permitted in one country may be considered hazardous in another and its use forbidden.

(ii) **Substances accidentally present in food.** This group may not necessarily be regarded as causing food poisoning in the generally accepted sense of an acute attack of illness, in that the effect is often cumulative and chronic. They may be the result of ignorance of a potential hazard or of accidental pollution, or they may be the residues of materials like pesticides and weed-killers used in agriculture. Radioactive materials as well as heavy metals like lead and mercury are attracting increasingly close attention with regard to the levels at which they occur in food. Unfortunately there are still occasional cases of large numbers of people suffering as a result of what can only be called carelessness.

(iii) **Potentially toxic substances naturally present in food.** We have repeatedly emphasized the need for a nutritionist to remember the great variations between biological organisms between members of the same species, which make it difficult to make precise statements about the composition of foods on the one hand and about the dietary requirements of different people on the other. We have also mentioned the incomplete nature of the nutritional knowledge we possess. A really well-varied diet is the simplest way to deal with both these difficulties, since this makes it easy to ensure that all the wide range of nutrients are included in the daily intake. A further advantage of variety is that it offers a means of avoiding an over-dependence on one article of food which might possibly offer some hitherto unrecognized hazard, or contain a toxic substance in very small and otherwise harmless quantities.

The following foods contain natural toxic compounds which are generally quite innocent, but which could possibly become dangerous if eaten in unusually large amounts:

Potatoes which have turned green contain a toxic substance, solanine, which is only dangerous when eaten in excess.

Onions contain an anaemia-producing ingredient which sometimes causes ill effects if they are eaten in too large a quantity.

Cabbage, cauliflower and other plants of the *Brassica* family (especially the seeds) contain goitre-producing compounds which can be harmful under certain circumstances (see Section 12.1(*d*)).

Rhubarb contains oxalic acid throughout the plant. The amounts in the stems which are normally eaten do no harm, but the higher concentrations in the leaves are dangerous.

Cassava, which is the staple food in several developing countries, contains appreciable concentrations of cyanides and can cause poisoning if eaten raw. Even when processed in the conventional way, it may still contain 11 ppm or more of cyanide when eaten.

(*iv*) **Toxins of fungal origin.** It was stated in Section 21.2 that food-spoilage organisms did not necessarily cause the food to become harmful. However, some of the toxins produced by certain moulds (mycotoxins) and other fungi are very serious hazards. *Ergot*, a fungal disease of rye, produces very powerful toxic chemicals in the grain. These have been used in medicine in small controlled doses for many years, but when bread made with diseased rye is eaten regularly, the dangerous condition called ergotism develops. More recently *aflatoxins*, a group of toxins produced by a common mould contaminant of many foods, have been shown to cause illness in animals fed on imported foodstuffs. Although aflatoxins are known to contaminate some human food, more work is still needed to assess with accuracy the effect of these on man.

(*b*) Bacterial Food Poisoning

Although natural toxins and other contaminants are found in foods from time to time, and although the chemical additives used to colour, flavour and preserve foods may, in spite of the most stringent testing, under some circumstances present a possibility of damage to the body, the chances of a person suffering harm from any of these causes is not really very great. On the other hand, in England and Wales alone in 1971 there were more than 8 000 reported cases of food poisoning due to microbiological contamination, and this figure probably does not include considerable numbers of mild attacks. Bacterial food poisoning can be largely prevented by satisfactory standards of food hygiene, and a nutritionist should understand the principles involved so that the people for whom he is responsible may fully benefit from the diets he has planned for them.

Most of the micro-organisms which surround us and which in larger or smaller numbers are found in food are harmless. Some of them indeed are useful, such as those which we deliberately employ in the making of yogurt or cheese. There are, however, several groups of bacteria, any one of which can cause food poisoning, if it gains access to food in conditions in which it is able to multiply. The illness may be caused by the ingestion of living bacteria in the food, which then infect the whole body, or by eating the toxins which the bacteria have produced while in the food. It may be worth pointing out that bacterial toxins are the normal products of their metabolism, and are not produced out of spite!

Of course, standards of hygiene vary from one area to another, depending on the degree of health education and the facilities in the district, so that the advice given by a nutritionist may be considerably affected by the local circumstances. For example, in a western urban community it is sensible to recommend a bachelor girl, whose diet is predominantly made up of sandwiches, cakes and chocolate, to include salads to contribute the ascorbic acid she needs. Similar advice to a family in India, even though their diet is almost exclusively composed of rice, may not be sensible if it is known that uncooked vegetables in the district are often contaminated with food-poisoning microorganisms derived from polluted water used to irrigate the crops.

Similar considerations apply to the use of artificial infant-feeding mixtures. Knowledge of the nutritional requirements of infants has made it possible for women in technologically advanced societies to use these preparations successfully for bottle-feeding their babies. In developing countries where piped water is unavailable, where means of cleaning and sterilizing bottles and teats do not exist, and where dried-milk preparations are comparatively expensive, a nutritionist would be unwise to recommend their use. Far from the babies benefiting, they may fall ill and even die from food poisoning from bacterial contamination, which cannot affect breast milk.

Many different kinds of bacteria have been identified as causative agents of food-poisoning outbreaks; the commonest types belong to the groups called salmonellae, staphylococci and clostridia.

(i) **Salmonellae.** There are several types of salmonellae, not all of which are responsible for food poisoning. Typhoid and paratyphoid, for example, are also caused by salmonellae. The salmonellae which cause food poisoning normally have to be ingested in large numbers before symptoms appear in healthy adults, but in infants, the elderly and the sick, the numbers needed to cause illness may be less.

The characteristic symptoms of salmonella food poisoning usually appear within 12–36 hours of eating the infected food and may last for two or three days, sometimes longer: they include nausea, vomiting, abdominal pain and diarrhoea, and also sometimes headache, chills and faintness.

The main sources of these bacteria are human and animal faeces, duck eggs (and occasionally hen's eggs), poultry and fish. Of these, the commonest source of infection is food animals, such as cows or pigs, which often carry salmonellae in their intestines; consequently it is easy for their meat to become infected at the slaughterhouse. Cross-contamination may then occur in the kitchen, resulting in a 'build-up' of bacteria on surfaces and equipment.

Foods which commonly become infected with salmonellae and are likely to cause food poisoning are cold cooked meats, mayonnaise and other uncooked egg dishes (or dishes cooked only at a low temperature), frozen chicken partially thawed and then inadequately cooked, and water or milk contaminated by sewage.

All salmonellae are destroyed by the heat of ordinary cooking, so that, while it is good hygienic practice to keep raw food clean and free from contamination, danger arises mainly from food eaten cold or consumed without being thoroughly reheated. It is particularly important that cold meats, of all foods, should never be touched with the hands.

(ii) **Staphylococci.** These bacteria, of which *Staphylococcus aureus* is probably the commonest of those causing food poisoning, produce a toxin in any food in which they have an opportunity to grow. If the food is subsequently eaten, the symptoms appear quite quickly, sometimes in as little as half an hour but usually within two or three hours.

The onset of illness is so rapid because the toxin is present in the food before it is eaten. The symptoms include salivation, nausea, vomiting, diarrhoea and abdominal cramp; sweating and prostration may also be evident.

The principal sources of contamination by staphylococci are the human mouth, throat, nose and nasal passages, human skin, especially where there are open abrasions or wounds, or infections like boils, and also clothing and dust. This is why it is so important that food should be protected from being handled and from coughs and sneezes, and why skin wounds have to be covered (see Section 22.2(*c*)).

The foods most often contaminated again include cold meats, meat sauces and gravies, together with dairy products like cream-filled bakery goods and custards, and fish and fish products.

Although staphylococci are themselves readily destroyed by thorough cooking or reheating, the toxin which they produce is often much more heat-resistant and may need higher temperatures or longer cooking times for its complete destruction.

(iii) **Clostridia.** The clostridia which cause food poisoning are different from the salmonellae and the staphylococci in two important respects: they are both spore-formers and are both anaerobic. This means that they are both more likely to be found in food which has only been subjected to moderate cooking and which provides an anaerobic situation.

Clostridium welchii (also known as *Clostridium perfringens*). There are known to be several types of this organism, not all of which produce very clearly defined symptoms.

The illness is due to the presence of large numbers of the bacteria in the food which have produced toxins that cause the symptoms of food poisoning. The bacterium has only been recognized as a food-poisoning organism during the last 20 years.

The symptoms are similar to those produced by staphylococcal food poisoning, but milder; vomiting and sweating are unusual. They usually manifest themselves some 8–15 hours after the affected food has been eaten and may continue for a further 12 hours.

Clostridium welchii is widely distributed, occurring frequently in the intestinal tract of man and animals, sewage and water polluted by it, soil and dust.

Probably the most serious sources of *Clostridium welchii* infection are raw meat, poultry, fish and vegetables. However, because these bacteria are able to form spores, food poisoning can also arise from the following foods: meat or meat dishes prepared on one day and eaten the next (the hazard is exacerbated by the anaerobic conditions inside a large joint of meat or in jellied meat products), cooked vegetables left over from a previous meal, inadequately cooked poultry and fish, and frozen foods.

Contamination of food with this organism is common, but its multiplication is easily prevented by using the correct time–temperature treatment and storage, and meticulous standards of hygienic practice.

Clostridium botulinum. Cases of food poisoning due to this organism are, happily, rare; but it is of great importance to the food industry on account of the very high mortality rate (up to 65 per cent) compared with other kinds of bacterial food poisoning. The most important principle of commercial canning is to ensure that each part of the food in each can is heated to a high enough temperature to ensure the complete destruction of any *Clostridium botulinum* spores which may be present.

Clostridium botulinum food poisoning is caused by the intensely poisonous toxin produced by the bacteria as they grow in food. While both the vegetative and the spore forms of the bacteria can themselves be eaten with impunity, the toxins produced by some strains of *Clostridium botulinum* are among the most dangerous known, and people have died after eating little more than a mouthful of contaminated food.

The symptoms of the illness (known as botulism) usually appear within three days (occasionally very much sooner) and at first resemble those of other forms of food poisoning: nausea, vomiting and headache. These are followed by a gradual paralysis of the autonomic nervous system, shown by difficulties in controlling speech, vision and breathing. Death is due to the paralysis of the muscles of respiration. Even in the minority of cases which recover, the rate of recovery is very slow.

Clostridium botulinum occurs naturally in the soil and in the sediments of lakes, oceans and estuaries, so that it is sometimes found in the alimentary canal of animals and fish. Foods which have been implicated as causing *Clostridium botulinum* food poisoning include canned and potted meat and meat pastes, canned tuna and other fish, and canned and bottled vegetables.

Apart from general hygienic precautions and adequate cooking, it is imperative that any process involving anaerobic conditions of food preservation (like canning or bottling) should include thorough heat treatment to ensure the destruction of any possible spores of *Clostridium botulinum*.

21.6   Other Food-borne Infections

Food may carry other infective bacteria, besides those which cause classical food poisoning; for example, the types of salmonellae which cause typhoid and paratyphoid, and those of tuberculosis and some dysenteries. These diseases are usually considered separately from food poisoning because of the length of their incubation period, their symptoms, or the numbers of bacteria involved; nevertheless, hygienic food handling plays a valuable part in preventing their transmission. Outbreaks of typhoid, paratyphoid, cholera, tuberculosis and bacillary dysenteries have nearly always been encouraged by contaminated water, milk or food, or by a combination of these factors.

Illness may be spread by organisms in food other than bacteria. Amoebic dysentery (caused by a microscopic single-celled animal) may be transmitted by the use of unwashed raw vegetables or salad material. Various parasitic worms use food as their mode of entry into the human body; tapeworm, liver fluke and the minute worm which causes trichinosis all spend at least part of their life-cycle in foods which we eat.

In all these cases good standards of hygiene and thorough cooking should minimize the hazards of food as an agency of infection.

Unit Twenty-two
Prevention of Dietary Infection

22.1 Introduction

The manifold sources of material which we use as food, and the large number of processes much of it undergoes before it is eaten, create a fairly high probability that it might become an infective agent. This risk can be drastically reduced, however, given reasonable standards of hygiene. In many countries there is legislation which aims to establish standards of cleanliness and behaviour in the presence of food such that the likelihood of food poisoning or food-borne infection is reduced to a minimum. The legal enforcement of the ideal in every aspect of food hygiene is, of course, impossible, but much more could be done, and is being done in some countries, by education of the people responsible for the handling of food to lessen the risk of it becoming a source of infection.

In this unit, some of the legislative provisions in Britain will be used as examples of the action taken in many other countries.

From the information in Unit 21, it is clear that the origin of food poisoning normally has three distinct phases:

(*a*) contamination of food;
(*b*) multiplication of the infective agent within the food;
(*c*) ingestion of the large numbers of the micro-organisms (or of their toxins) which has been produced as a result of (*b*).

22.2 Contamination of Food

The infection of food can arise from contaminants either within the food itself, or from the premises or equipment concerned in its handling, or from the people who handle it. More than one of these factors, of course, may be involved. In each case, regulations exist which seek to minimize the particular hazards that can arise.

(*a*) Food as a Reservoir of Infection

Food brought into a kitchen may contain its own contamination due to its method of growth, slaughter, harvesting and so on. In the case of milk, legislation is very strict. Various regulations relate to the health of the cows used for milk production, the conditions existing in the dairy and the efficiency of the pasteurization (heat-treatment) process used to kill some of the more dangerous bacteria. (In passing, it is interesting that milk is one of the few foods for which there is legislation regarding its nutritional composition, as well as for its microbiological safety; there are legal minimum requirements both for its proportion of fat and for its solids-not-fat content.) Slaughter-houses and abattoirs are similarly the subject of regulations which minimize the risk from food-poisoning organisms which may be present either on or within the animal from which the meat is derived.

All meat is inspected to allow a visual examination for the tell-tale signs of some parasites which may be embedded in the meat or offal.

Many foods are, however, subject to no controls other than the buyer's option to refuse the purchase of unsuitable food. Although the presence of bacteria is only evident when the food contains extremely large numbers, the general appearance and presentation of the commodity or product can be a useful guide to its condition. The danger of introducing contaminated food into a kitchen is not only that it may itself cause food poisoning, but (and this can be of greater importance) that it can act as a reservoir of infection for the cross-contamination of other foods by the careless use of unwashed equipment, surfaces and so on.

(b) Premises and Equipment as Reservoirs of Infection

Much emphasis is placed in the British food hygiene regulations on the suitability of the premises in which food is prepared. A great deal can be done in the design and construction of such premises to reduce the risk of contamination of food in this context. Buildings and equipment which are kept in good repair and are easily cleaned are much less likely to harbour the dust and food particles which may act either as breeding grounds for bacteria or as resting places for their spores.

Further regulations control the lighting and ventilation of these premises, and others are concerned with the storage and accumulation of waste food and refuse. The careless disposal of waste food material may facilitate the transfer of any harmful organisms it may contain by insects or vermin.

(c) Food Handlers as Reservoirs of Infection

Unit 21 gave some indication of the common sources of some of the food-poisoning organisms, and it cannot have escaped notice that the human body is prominent among them.

Legislation regarding the personal hygiene of the food handler goes as far as it reasonably can in many respects. Although the prohibition of smoking, spitting and snuff-taking is difficult to enforce, the attempt is at least reasonable, as these activities encourage the transfer of the staphylococci normally to be found in the mouth and nasal passages onto food. It would be completely unreasonable to try to legislate against coughing and sneezing, although some risk of infection is involved. Instead the establishment of acceptable hygienic habits must be attempted by means other than legislation.

The skin is a natural habitat of bacteria, some of which can cause food poisoning given suitable conditions. Compulsory hand-washing is unenforceable, but the requirements for the provision of the means—hot and cold water, nail-brush, soap or detergent and drying facilities—at least encourage good standards to be kept. The onus is placed on the food handler who shall 'keep as clean as may be reasonably practicable all parts of his person which are liable to come into contact with food'. Open wounds must always be covered with a waterproof dressing, in order to minimize the transmission of bacteria.

The other major human reservoir of food-poisoning bacteria is the faeces. The siting, efficiency and cleanliness of lavatories is controlled. They are not allowed to be placed so that they communicate directly with a room in which food is handled. Although, again, mandatory hand-washing cannot be enforced, in this situation it is legally necessary to exhibit a notice requesting users to wash their hands after using the lavatory, as well as providing the necessary facilities for doing so.

Other legislation relates to the wearing of suitable clothing, the provision of storage room for outdoor clothing, the reporting of illness and so on. However, it must be quite apparent that legislation alone cannot eliminate the human body and its clothing as a source of infection or the means of its transmission. Only education in reasonable hygienic practices, allied to legislation, is a satisfactory solution.

22.3   Multiplication of Infective Agents within Food

Many of the bacteria which are responsible for causing food poisoning are constantly present in small numbers and as such do no harm. This is because the body can cope successfully with isolated bacteria. It is when these bacteria multiply and become present in large numbers that they are capable of overcoming temporarily the body's normal defences sufficiently to initiate the symptoms associated with food poisoning.

The prevention of this build-up of large numbers of bacteria is one of the main lines of defence which needs to be used in the preparation of food. The most easily controlled environmental factor for bacterial reproduction in prepared foods is temperature (see Section 21.4(c)). This is why foods like meat and fish dishes, eggs and milk, which are suitable media for bacterial metabolism, are the subject of special legislation which aims at keeping the food outside the temperature range best suited to the metabolism of the mesophilic bacteria. To comply with the regulations, such foods should be brought to a temperature either below 10 °C or above 63 °C as quickly as possible, and kept at these temperatures under hygienic conditions. When cooked food is allowed to cool it may spend some considerable time in the 'forbidden' temperature zone, especially as the cooling rate will depend on the heat conductivity of the food material and the temperature of its surroundings: means to chill it rapidly are therefore important in this context.

22.4   Ingestion of Large Numbers of Bacteria or their Toxins

This is the final stage at which much preventive work can be done. All the food-poisoning bacteria in their vegetative state are destroyed by boiling.

Adequate cooking and reheating will ensure that no vegetative bacteria are eaten in a viable state. Unfortunately the same cannot be said for some of the bacterial toxins. Many of these are broken down into harmless substances at boiling temperatures, but the process usually takes longer than the destruction of the bacteria—up to 30 minutes in the case of staphylococcal toxins. The destruction of all bacterial spores by cooking cannot be assured.

From what has gone before in this Unit, it will be apparent that even if legislation (which is current in most countries) is strictly adhered to, the prevention of bacterial food poisoning cannot be guaranteed, but only assisted. The ultimate responsibility rests firmly with the persons actually preparing and serving the meal. The principles of food safety depend, to a large extent on the following:

(a) choice and purchase of the best available food;
(b) storage of food under hygienic conditions and, where appropriate, at a suitable temperature;
(c) care and cleanliness of premises, equipment and utensils;
(d) personal hygiene and health of the kitchen staff;
(e) adequate cooking and/or reheating of foods.

Appendix

Table of Food Composition

Composition of foods per 100 g (of raw edible portion except where stated)

food	energy value (Cal)	(kJ)	protein (g)	fat (g)	carbo-hydrate (as mono-saccharide) (g)
Milk					
Cream, double	449	1 881	1·8	48·0	2·6
Cream, single	189	792	2·8	18·0	4·2
Milk, liquid, whole	65	272	3·3	3·8	4·8
Milk, condensed, whole, sweetened	322	1 349	8·2	9·2	55·1
Milk, whole, evaporated	166	696	8·5	9·2	12·8
Milk, dried, whole	492	2 061	26·6	27·7	37·6
Milk, dried, half-cream	425	1 781	31·5	15·0	43·8
Milk, dried, skimmed	329	1 379	37·2	0·5	46·9
Yogurt, natural	57	239	3·6	2·6	5·2
Yogurt, fruit	79	331	3·6	1·8	13·0
Cheese					
Cheese, Cheddar	412	1 726	25·4	34·5	0
Cheese, cottage	115	482	15·3	4·0	4·5
Meat					
Bacon, average	476	1 994	11·0	48·0	0
Beef, average	313	1 311	14·8	28·2	0
Beef, corned	224	939	22·3	15·0	0
Beef, stewing steak, raw	212	888	17·0	16·0	0
Beef, stewing steak, cooked	242	1 014	29·0	14·0	0
Chicken, raw	144	603	20·8	6·7	0
Chicken, roast	184	771	29·6	7·3	0
Ham, cooked	422	1 768	16·3	39·6	0
Kidney, average	105	440	16·9	4·2	0
Lamb, average, raw	331	1 387	13·0	31·0	0
Lamb, roast	284	1 190	25·0	20·4	0
Liver, average, raw	139	582	16·5	8·1	0
Liver, fried	276	1 156	29·5	15·9	4·0
Luncheon meat	325	1 362	11·4	29·0	5·0
Pork, average	408	1 710	12·0	40·0	0
Pork chop, grilled	527	2 208	18·6	50·3	0
Sausage, pork	369	1 546	10·4	30·9	13·3
Steak and kidney pie, cooked	304	1 274	13·3	21·1	16·2
Tripe	60	251	11·6	1·0	0
Fish					
Cod, haddock, white fish	69	289	16·0	0·5	0
Cod, fried in batter	199	834	19·6	10·3	7·5

calcium (mg)	iron (mg)	vitamin A (retinol equiva- lents) (μg)	chole- calciferol (μg)	thiamine (mg)	riboflavine (mg)	nicotinic acid (equiva- lents) (mg)	ascorbic acid (mg)
65	0	420	0·28	0·02	0·08	0·4	0
100	0·1	155	0·10	0·03	0·13	0·8	1
120	0·1	44ᵃ	0·05ᵃ	0·04	0·15	0·9	1ᵉ
		37ᵇ	0·01ᵇ				
290	0·2	112	0·12	0·10	0·40	2·0	3
290	0·2	112	0·12	0·06	0·37	2·0	2
813	0·7	246	0·30ᶜ	0·31	1·10	6·9	11
			8·82ᵈ				
940	0·8	143	0·18ᶜ	0·36	1·35	8·2	10
			8·82ᵈ				
1 277	1·1	4	0	0·30	1·73	9·7	10
140	0·1	39	0·02	0·05	0·19	0·9	0
140	0·1	22	0·02	0·05	0·19	0·9	0
810	0·6	420	0·35	0·04	0·50	5·2	0
80	0·4	27	0·02	0·03	0·27	3·2	0
10	1·0	0	0	0·40	0·15	4·0	0
10	4·0	0	0	0·07	0·20	7·8	0
13	9·8	0	0	0	0·20	7·7	0
10	4·0	0	0	0·07	0·20	8·2	0
8	5·0	0	0	0·05	0·22	10·4	0
11	1·5	0	0	0·04	0·17	9·5	0
15	2·6	0	0	0·04	0·14	10·0	0
13	2·5	0	0	0·50	0·20	7·2	0
14	13·4	300	0	0·30	2·00	11·1	12
10	2·0	0	0	0·15	0·25	7·7	0
4	4·3	0	0	0·10	0·25	9·8	0
8	13·9	6 000	0·75	0·30	3·00	17·1	30
9	20·7	6 000	0·75	0·30	3·50	22·4	20
18	1·1	0	0	0·40	0·20	6·1	0
10	1·0	0	0	1·00	0·20	7·7	0
8	2·4	0	0	0·80	0·20	9·2	0
15	2·5	0	0	0·17	0·07	3·9	0
37	5·1	126	0·55	0·11	0·47	6·0	0
70	0·7	10	0	0·18	0·10	5·7	0
25	1·0	0	0	0·06	0·10	6·0	0
80	0·5	0	0	0·04	0·10	6·7	0

ᵃ summer value   ᵇ winter value   ᶜ natural value   ᵈ with fortification   ᵉ less than 1 mg

food	energy value (Cal)	(kJ)	protein (g)	fat (g)	carbo-hydrate (as mono-saccharide) (g)
Fish cont.					
Fish fingers	192	804	13·4	6·8	20·7
Herring	190	796	16·0	14·1	0
Kipper	220	922	19·0	16·0	0
Salmon, canned	133	557	19·7	6·0	0
Sardines, canned in oil	285	1 194	20·4	22·6	0
Eggs					
Eggs, fresh	158	662	11·9	12·3	0
Fats					
Butter	745	3 122	0·5	82·5	0
Lard, cooking fat, dripping	894	3 746	0	99·3	0
Margarine	769	3 222	0·2	85·3	0
Oils, cooking and salad	899	3 767	0	99·9	0
Preserves etc.					
Chocolate, milk	578	2 422	8·7	37·6	54·5
Honey	288	1 207	0·4	0	76·4
Jam	262	1 098	0·5	0	69·2
Ice cream, vanilla	192	805	4·1	11·3	19·8
Marmalade	261	1 094	0·1	0	69·5
Sugar, white	394	1 651	0	0	105·0
Syrup	297	1 244	0·3	0	79·0
Vegetables					
Beans, canned in tomato sauce	92	385	6·0	0·4	17·3
Beans, broad	69	289	7·2	0·5	9·5
Beans, haricot	256	1 073	21·4	0	45·5
Beans, runner	15	63	1·1	0	2·9
Beetroot, boiled	44	184	1·8	0	9·9
Brussels sprouts, raw	32	134	3·6	0	4·6
Brussels sprouts, boiled	16	67	2·4	0	1·7
Cabbage, raw	28	117	1·5	0	5·8
Cabbage, boiled	8	34	0·8	0	1·3
Carrots, old	23	96	0·7	0	5·4
Cauliflower	24	101	3·4	0	2·8
Celery	8	34	0·9	0	1·3
Lentils, dry	295	1 236	23·8	0	53·2
Lettuce	11	46	1·1	0	1·8
Mushrooms	7	29	1·8	0	0
Onions	23	96	0·9	0	5·2
Parsnips	49	205	1·7	0	11·3
Peas, fresh raw or quick frozen	63	264	5·8	0	10·6

calcium (mg)	iron (mg)	vitamin A (retinol equivalents) (μg)	cholecalciferol (μg)	thiamine (mg)	riboflavine (mg)	nicotinic acid (equivalents) (mg)	ascorbic acid (mg)
50	1·4	0	0	0·12	0·16	3·9	0
100	1·5	45	22·25	0·03	0·30	6·4	0
120	2·0	45	22·25	0	0·30	6·9	0
66	1·3	90	12·50	0·03	0·10	10·6	0
409	4·0	30	7·50	0	0·20	8·6	0
56	2·5	300	1·50	0·10	0·35	3·0	0
15	0·2	995	1·25	0	0	0·1	0
0	0	0	0	0	0	0	0
4	0·3	900ᶠ	8·00	0	0	0·1	0
0	0	0	0	0	0	0	0
246	1·7	6.6	0	0·03	0·35	2·5	0
5	0·4	0	0	0	0·05	0·2	0
18	1·2	2	0	0	0	0	10
137	0·3	1	0	0·05	0·20	1·1	1
35	0·6	8	0	0	0	0	10
1	0	0	0	0	0	0	0
26	1·4	0	0	0	0	0	0
62	2·1	50	0	0·06	0·04	1·5	3
30	1·1	22	0	0·28	0·05	5·0	30
180	6·7	0	0	0·45	0·13	6·1	0
33	0·7	50	0	0·05	0·10	1·2	20
30	0·7	0	0	0·02	0·04	0·4	5
29	0·7	67	0	0·10	0·16	1·4	100
27	0·6	67	0	0·06	0·10	0·9	35
65	1·0	50	0	0·06	0·05	0·5	60
58	0·5	50	0	0·03	0·03	0·3	20
48	0·6	2 000	0	0·06	0·05	0·7	6
18	0·6	5	0	0·10	0·10	1·4	70
52	0·6	0	0	0·03	0·03	0·5	7
39	7·6	6	0	0·50	0·25	6·3	0
26	0·7	167	0	0·07	0·08	0·4	15
3	1·0	0	0	0·10	0·40	4·5	3
31	0·3	0	0	0·03	0·05	0·4	10
55	0·6	0	0	0·10	0·09	1·3	15
15	1·9	50	0	0·32	0·15	3·5	25

ᶠ some margarines contain carotene

food	energy value (Cal)	(kJ)	protein (g)	fat (g)	carbo-hydrate (as mono-saccharide) (g)
Vegetables cont.					
Peas, fresh, boiled or quick frozen boiled	49	205	5·0	0	7·7
Peas, canned, processed	96	402	7·2	0	18·0
Peppers, green	21	88	1·2	0·2	3·7
Potatoes, raw	76	318	2·1	0	18·0
Potatoes, boiled	79	331	1·4	0	19·7
Potato chips, fried	236	989	3·8	9·0	37·3
Potatoes, roast	123	515	2·8	1·0	27·3
Spinach	21	88	2·7	0	2·8
Sweet corn, canned	95	398	2·6	0·8	20·5
Tomatoes, fresh	14	59	0·9	0	2·8
Turnips	17	71	0·8	0	3·8
Watercress	14	59	2·9	0	0·7
Fruit					
Apple	46	193	0·3	0	12·0
Apricots, canned	106	444	0·5	0	27·7
Apricots, dried	182	763	4·8	0	43·4
Bananas	76	318	1·1	0	19·2
Blackcurrants	28	117	0·9	0	6·6
Cherries	46	193	0·6	0	11·8
Dates	248	1 039	2·0	0	63·9
Figs, dried	213	892	3·6	0	52·9
Gooseberries	27	113	0·9	0	6·3
Grapefruit	22	92	0·6	0	5·3
Lemons	7	29	0·3	0	1·6
Melon	23	96	0·8	0	5·2
Oranges	35	147	0·8	0	8·5
Orange juice, canned unconcentrated	47	197	0·8	0	11·7
Peaches, fresh	37	155	0·6	0	9·1
Peaches, canned	88	369	0·4	0	22·9
Pears, fresh	41	172	0·3	0	10·6
Pineapple, canned	76	318	0·3	0	20·0
Plums	32	134	0·6	0	7·9
Prunes	161	675	2·4	0	40·3
Raspberries	25	105	0·9	0	5·6
Rhubarb	6	25	0·6	0	1·0
Strawberries	26	109	0·6	0	6·2
Sultanas	249	1 043	1·7	0	64·7
Nuts					
Almonds	580	2 430	20·5	53·5	4·3
Coconut, desiccated	608	2 548	6·6	62·0	6·4
Peanuts, roasted	586	2 455	28·1	49·0	8·6

calcium (mg)	iron (mg)	vitamin A (retinol equivalents) (μg)	chole-calciferol (μg)	thiamine (mg)	ribo-flavine (mg)	nicotinic acid (equivalents) (mg)	ascorbic acid (mg)
13	1·2	50	0	0·25	0·11	2·3	15
29	1·1	67	0	0·06	0·04	1·6	2
9	0·7	42	0	0·08	0·08	0·7	128
8	0·7	0	0	0·11	0·04	1·8	8–30ᵍ
4	0·5	0	0	0.08	0·03	1·2	4–15ᵍ
14	1·4	0	0	0·10	0·04	2·2	6–20ᵍ
10	1·0	0	0	0·10	0·04	2·0	6–23ᵍ
70	3·2	1 000	0	0·12	0·20	1·3	60
5	0·5	35	0	0·03	0·05	0·3	4
13	0·4	117	0	0·06	0·04	0·7	20
59	0·4	0	0	0·04	0·05	0·8	25
222	1·6	500	0	0·10	0·16	2·0	60
4	0·3	5	0	0·04	0·02	0·1	5
12	0·7	166	0	0·02	0·01	0·3	5
92	4·1	600	0	0	0·20	3·4	0
7	0·4	33	0	0·04	0·07	0·8	10
60	1·3	33	0	0·03	0·06	0·3	200
18	0·4	20	0	0·05	0·06	0·4	5
68	1·6	10	0	0·07	0·04	2·3	0
284	4·2	8	0	0·10	0·13	2·2	0
22	0·4	30	0	0·04	0·03	0·4	40
17	0·3	0	0	0·05	0·02	0·3	40
8	0·1	0	0	0·02	0	0·1	50
16	0·4	160	0	0·05	0·03	0·5	25
41	0·3	8	0	0·10	0·03	0·3	50
10	0·4	8	0	0·07	0·02	0·2	40
5	0·4	83	0	0·02	0·05	1·1	8
3·5	1·9	41	0	0·01	0·02	0·6	4
8	0·2	2	0	0·03	0·03	0·3	3
13	1·7	7	0	0·05	0·02	0·3	8
12	0·3	37	0	0·05	0·03	0·6	3
38	2·9	160	0	0·10	0·20	1·7	0
41	1·2	13	0	0·02	0·03	0·5	25
103	0·4	10	0	0·01	0·07	0·3	10
22	0·7	5	0	0·02	0·03	0·5	60
52	1·8	0	0	0·10	0·30	0·6	0
247	4·2	0	0	0·32	0·25	4·9	0
22	3·6	0	0	0·06	0·04	1·8	0
61	2·0	0	0	0·23	0·10	20·8	0

ᵍ vitamin C falls during storage

food	energy value (Cal)	(kJ)	protein (g)	fat (g)	carbo-hydrate (as mono-saccharide) (g)
Cereals					
Barley, pearl, dry	360	1 508	7·7	1·7	83·6
Biscuits, chocolate	497	2 082	7·1	24·9	65·3
Biscuits, plain, semi-sweet	431	1 806	7·4	13·2	75·3
Biscuits, rich, sweet	496	2 078	5·6	22·3	72·7
Bread, brown	237	993	9·2	1·8	49·0
Bread, starch reduced	234	980	10·5	1·5	47·6
Bread, white	253	1 060	8·3	1·7	54·6
Bread, wholemeal	241	1 010	9·6	3·1	46·7
Cornflakes	365	1 529	7·5	0·5	88·0
Custard powder, instant pudding, cornflour	353	1 479	0·5	0·7	92·0
Crispbread, Ryvita	318	1 332	10·0	2·1	69
Flour, white	348	1 458	10·0	0·9	80·0
Oatmeal	400	1 676	12·1	8·7	72·8
Rice	359	1 504	6·2	1·0	86·8
Spaghetti	364	1 525	9·9	1·0	84·0
Beverages					
Blackcurrant juice	229	960	0·2	0	60·9
Chocolate, drinking	410	1 718	5·6	6·8	87·0
Cocoa powder	446	1 869	18·8	22·5	45·0
Coffee, ground	0	0	0	0	0
Coffee, instant	156	654	4·0	0·7	35·5
Tea, dry	0	0	0	0	0
Alcoholic beverages					
Beer, mild, draught	25	105	0·2	0	1·6
Spirits, 70% proof	222	930	0	0	0
Wine, red	67	281	0·2	0	0·3
Puddings and cakes etc.					
Apple pie	294	1 231	3·2	14·4	40·4
Buns, currant	328	1 374	7·8	8·5	58·6
Fruit cake, rich	368	1 542	4·6	15·9	55·0
Jam tarts	391	1 638	3·2	13·8	67·7
Plain cake, Madeira	430	1 802	7·1	24·0	49·7
Rice pudding	142	595	3·6	7·6	15·7
Soup, tomato, canned	67	281	0·9	3·1	9·4
Trifle	162	679	3·1	5·6	26·5

calcium (mg)	iron (mg)	vitamin A (retinol equivalents) (μg)	cholecalciferol (μg)	thiamine (mg)	riboflavine (mg)	nicotinic acid (equivalents) (mg)	ascorbic acid (mg)
10	0·7	0	0	0·12	0·08	2·2	0
131	1·5	0	0	0·11	0·04	2·0	0
126	1·8	0	0	0·17	0·06	2·0	0
92	1·3	0	0	0·12	0·04	1·5	0
92	2·5	0	0	0·28	0·07	2·6	0
100	1·3	79	0	0·18	0·03	2·7	0
100	1·8	0	0	0·18	0·02	2·3	0
28	3·0	0	0	0·24	0·09	1·9	0
5	1·1	0	0	0·60	1·07	6·4	0
15	1·4	0	0	0	0	0·1	0
86	3·3	0	0	0·37	0·24	1·3	0
145	1·9	0	0	0·28	0·04	2·8	0
55	4·1	0	0	0·50	0·10	2·8	0
4	0·4	0	0	0·08	0·03	1·5	0
23	1·2	0	0	0·09	0·06	1·8	0
14	0·5	0	0	0·01	0·02	0·1	206
25	12·0	2	0	0·03	0·09	1·4	0
52	15·0	7	0	0·08	0·30	4·8	0
0	0	0	0	0	0·20[h]	10·0[h]	0
140	4·0	0	0	0	0·10	45·7	0
0	0	0	0	0	0·90[h]	6·0[h]	0
10	0	0	0	0	0·05	0·7	0
0	0	0	0	0	0	0	0
6	0·8	0	0	0·01	0·02	0·2	0
42	0·8	2	0	0·08	0·02	0·9	2
88	1·8	24	0·27	0·14	0·10	2·1	0
71	1·8	56	0·80	0·70	0·70	1·2	0
50	1·3	0	0	0·06	0·01	0·8	0
67	1·4	82	1·20	0·70	0·10	1·8	0
116	0·1	96	0·08	0·05	0·14	1·0	1
18	0·3	46	0	0·03	0·02	0·2	6
75	0·6	73	0·30	0·04	0·10	1·1	2

[h] 90 to 100% is extracted into an infusion

Glossary

absorption: the taking up of fluids or other substances by vessels or tissues of the body

acidosis: a fall in the alkalinity of the blood

amino acid: an organic acid containing an amino (—NH$_2$) group and a carboxyl (—CO$_2$H) group; these acids are the fundamental units of which proteins are composed

anaemia: the condition which exists when the concentration of haemoglobin in the blood falls below a certain level

autolysis: self-digestion: the breakdown of the cell and/or its contents by the action of enzymes produced within it

bacterium (*plural,* **bacteria**): unicellular microscopic organisms, containing no chlorophyll; they can multiply rapidly by simple fission in suitable conditions

basal metabolic rate (BMR): the rate at which energy is used to maintain body processes and body temperature when the subject is completely at rest in a comfortably warm room

biochemistry: the study of the chemical composition and chemical processes of living things

bran: the outer covering of wheat grain, consisting of several distinct layers (the pericarp, testa, aleurone layer and variable amounts of the outer endosperm) and making up about 12 per cent by weight of the whole grain

Calorie (*or* **kilocalorie**): a unit of energy, defined as the amount of heat required to raise the temperature of one kilogram of water by 1 °C: 1 Calorie = 1 000 calories = 4 186 joules

carbohydrate: a compound containing carbon, hydrogen and oxygen, in which the ratio of the numbers of hydrogen and oxygen atoms is 2:1 (although not all such compounds are carbohydrates); the commonly occurring food carbohydrates are sugars, starch and cellulose (*q.v.*)

cell: a discrete mass of protoplasm contained within a membrane, constituting either part or the whole of an organism; in plants only, the term includes the cell wall external to the membrane

cellulose: a long-chain polysaccharide which occurs widely in plants; although it is not susceptible to digestion by human enzymes, it plays a valuable part in food by providing roughage and bulk

co-enzyme: an organic compound with an essential role in an enzyme-catalysed reaction; many co-enzymes are vitamins or substances which are chemically related to them

combustion: the chemical union of oxygen with a fuel, with the production of energy in the form of heat and light

deficiency disease: an illness or condition caused by the lack of sufficient amounts of a particular nutrient; it may be produced either by the absence of the nutrient from the diet, or by the body's inability to absorb it

deoxyribonucleic acid (DNA): *see under* nucleic acid

digestion: the processes of converting the nutrients available in foodstuffs into forms which can be absorbed by the body

disaccharide: a carbohydrate (*q.v.*) which can be considered as being derived from two monosaccharide molecules with the elimination of one molecule of water: for example, sucrose, lactose, maltose

embryo: an organism in the process of development from a fertilized ovum; in man, the term is only used for the first few weeks after fertilization (*see also* foetus)

emulsion: a permanent homogeneous mixture of two immiscible liquids: in foods, these are usually water and an oil or fat, and may consist of oil dispersed in water or of water dispersed in oil

endosperm: the part of the seed containing nutrient materials stored up for the use of the embryo at the beginning of its development

energy value of a food: the amount of energy which can be produced in the body by the metabolism of the food

enzyme: a protein catalyst, that is, a substance which affects the rate of a chemical reaction, but which may itself be recovered unchanged after the reaction is complete; enzymes control nearly all the chemical changes involved in metabolism (*q.v.*)

excretion: the removal of the waste products of metabolism from the body

fats: naturally occurring substances consisting mainly of the glycerides of the higher fatty acids (*q.v.*)

fatty acid: an organic acid, the molecule of which contains the carboxyl ($-CO_2H$) group at one end of a long chain of carbon atoms

foetus: the term used for the embryo (*q.v.*) of a mammal once its characteristic features can be recognized; in man, this is after about eight weeks of pregnancy

food: substances taken into or manufactured by an organism which have a part in maintaining and regulating its life, growth, repair and reproduction

gland: a cell or group of cells specialized for the production and secretion (*q.v.*) of a chemical substance or substances required by the organism

glycerides: the products of reaction of glycerol with fatty acids; *triglycerides* are the products of reaction of three (not necessarily different) fatty acid molecules with each molecule of glycerol

glycogen: a polysaccharide built up entirely from glucose units; the form in which carbohydrate is stored in the muscles and liver of animals and man

hormone: a compound produced by cells in one part of the body which has an effect on the activities of the cells in another part of the organism; in animals, hormones are transported from one part of the body to another in the bloodstream

joule: a unit of energy, defined as the work done by a force of one newton acting through a distance of one metre (*see also* Calorie)

kwashiorkor: a disease appearing in children under five years old whose diet gives them insufficient protein and usually also has an inadequate energy content; it is one of the group of diseases collectively described by the term *protein-energy malnutrition* or *protein-calorie malnutrition*

lean body mass: a measure of body composition which excludes adipose (fatty) tissue, extracellular fluids and the skeleton

lignin: a complex compound found in the cell walls of the woody tissues of plants and trees, which gives them strength and rigidity

lipid: a term used to cover both solid fats and liquid oils

lymph: the colourless fluid found in the lymph vessels, containing the water-soluble components of blood and some cells (lymphocytes); it is produced by the continual filtering of blood through the thin walls of the capillary blood vessels, and is returned to the bloodstream through the lymphatic system

malnutrition: disturbance of form or function of an organism resulting from a deficiency or excess of one or more nutrients in its diet

mastication: the process of chewing

metabolism: the chemical changes taking place in a living organism: they involve both the breakdown of large complex molecules into simpler materials which can provide energy and small building units, and the synthesis of the particular complex substances required by the organism from simple compounds

micro-organism: an animal or plant which is so small that it is only visible with a microscope

minerals: inorganic substances, usually occurring in foods as salts, which are necessary for the body and which must be obtained from foods

monosaccharide: the simplest kind of carbohydrate (*q.v.*), having from three to six carbon atoms in its molecule; for example, glucose, fructose, galactose

nucleic acids: complex organic acids occurring in the nuclei of plant and animal cells; they are important both in the processes involved in the inheritance of the traits typical of the species (deoxyribonucleic acid, DNA), and also in ensuring that the protein synthesized in a cell is of the 'correct' composition characteristic of the particular cell (ribonucleic acid, RNA)

nutrients: components of foodstuffs which can be used by a living organism for the processes of life and growth

obesity: a condition in which an excess amount of fat accumulates in the body; it may be expressed relative to a standard body weight (taking into account variations in height, build and so on), or as the percentage of the total body weight which is made up of fat

organ: a collection of tissues forming a structural unit having a specific function

organism: the material structure of a living animal or plant

osmosis: the movement of water across a semipermeable membrane due to the presence of unequal concentrations of dissolved substances on the two sides of the membrane; the amount of pressure which will just prevent osmosis is called *osmotic pressure*

oxidation: the combination of oxygen with an element or compound resulting in the production of new compounds

peptide: a compound formed when two (or more) amino-acid (*q.v.*) molecules join together by the reaction of the amino group of one molecule with the carboxyl group of the other

peristalsis: waves of muscular contraction which pass along the digestive tract, causing its contents to mix and move along the system

pH: a measure of acidity or alkalinity; the scale goes from 0 to 14, with pH = 7 as the neutral point, so that pH values above 7 indicate alkalinity and those less than 7 acidity

photosynthesis: the process by which green plants build up organic compounds from water and carbon dioxide, using energy absorbed from sunlight by the green pigment chlorophyll which gives them their characteristic colour

physiology: the study of the normal functions and chemical processes which go on within a living organism

polymer: a substance of which the molecules are built up from a large number of small units (*monomers*)

polysaccharide: a carbohydrate polymer of which the monomer may be a monosaccharide or a disaccharide; for example, starch, cellulose, inulin

precursor: a substance found in a living organism which may be converted by a chemical reaction into a biologically active product such as an enzyme (*q.v.*) or a hormone (*q.v.*)

proteins: complex compounds built up from some thousands of amino-acid units, of which up to about 20 different types are common; the properties of a particular protein depend on the number, type and arrangement of amino-acid units within the molecule

reflex action: an involuntary or automatic response by an organism (*q.v.*) to a change in its environment

ribonucleic acid (RNA): *see under* nucleic acids

secretion: the passage of material which has been made within a cell (*q.v.*) to the outside of the cell

soap: a salt of a fatty acid (*q.v.*), usually with an alkali metal; for example, sodium stearate

specific dynamic action: the increase in the production of heat by the body as a result of the intake of food, especially protein

spore: a cell, or group of cells, which become detached from the parent organism and which can eventually develop into a new individual (for example, mould spores); some (for example, bacterial) spores are resting forms of the organism which enable it to survive unfavourable environmental conditions

starch: a polysaccharide which is a mixture of two dissimilar polysaccharides, amylose and amylopectin, both consisting of chains of glucose units; it is the chief food reserve substance of plants

sugar: a simple crystalline carbohydrate which will dissolve in water to give a sweet solution; the commonest sugars in foods are monosaccharides and disaccharides. The term is used colloquially to mean sucrose (cane or beet sugar)

system: a group of organs which function in relation to each other (although they are not necessarily in close proximity)

tissue: a collection of similar cells having the same function

toxin: a poisonous substance produced by the metabolism of a plant or animal, especially certain bacteria

tuber: the part of an underground stem which is swollen with food reserves; it carries buds which can give rise to new plants

vegetable: a plant or part of a plant which is used as a foodstuff; the word is also used as an adjective to indicate plant origins, as in vegetable oil, vegetable protein

vitamin: an organic substance which is essential for the body's metabolism in minute amounts in the diet (*see also* deficiency disease); they frequently act as co-enzymes (*q.v.*)

yeasts: single-celled fungi, many of which produce ethanol and carbon dioxide as the products of their metabolism of carbohydrate foods

Suggested Further Reading

Bender, A. E.: *Dietetic foods*. Leonard Hill (1967).

Cameron, A. G.: *Food: facts and fallacies*. Faber (1971).

Davidson, Sir Stanley: *Human nutrition and dietetics*. Churchill Livingstone (Edinburgh, 1972).

Drummond, J. C. and Wilbraham, A.: *The Englishman's food*. Cape (1958).

Food and Agricultural Organization: *Wheat in human nutrition* (Nutritional Studies No. 23). HMSO (1970).

Fox, B. A. and Cameron, A. G.: *Food science*. University of London Press (1970).

Hutchison, R. and Moncrieff, A.: *Food and the principles of nutrition* (Sinclair, H. E. and Hollingsworth, D., eds.). Edward Arnold (1969).

Jay, J. M.: *Modern food microbiology*. Van Nostrand, Reinhold and Co. (New York, 1970).

Longree, K.: *Quantity food sanitation*. Interscience (Chichester, 1972).

McCance, R. A. and Widdowson, E. M.: *The composition of foods*. HMSO (1970).

Ministry of Agriculture, Fisheries and Food: *Manual of nutrition*. HMSO (1974).

Pyke, M.: *Food and society*. John Murray (1968).

Pyke, M.: *Food science and technology*. John Murray (1970).

Pyke, M.: *Man and food*. World University Library (1970).

Woollen, A. H. (ed.): *Food industries manual*. Leonard Hill (1969).

Index